GORDON PASHA OF THE SUDAN

GENERAL GORDON
IN THE UNIFORM OF
A TURKISH FIELD MARSHAL

(Hulton Library)

GORDON PASHA OF THE SUDAN

THE LIFE STORY OF AN ILL-REQUITED SOLDIER

By

LIEUT. COLONEL
HON. GERALD FRENCH, D.S.O.

WILLIAM MACLELLAN
240 HOPE STREET, GLASGOW, C.2
1958

First Impression . . . 1958

DA
68.32
.G6
F7
1958
Jan.1999

Printed in Scotland by William McLellan & Co., Ltd.
240 Hope Street, Glasgow, C.2

DEDICATED

TO SOLDIERS WHO HAVE SUFFERED

INJUSTICE THROUGH

THE

VINDICTIVENESS

ARROGANCE

NEGLECT

OR

INCOMPETENCE

OF THE

MINIONS OF BUREAUCRACY

CONTENTS

ILLUSTRATIONS

Preface

My reasons for undertaking this task are threefold. To begin with, boundless admiration, shared with millions of others, for General Gordon's unparalleled career. Secondly, my father's participation in the Gordon Relief Expedition as a major in the 19th Hussars—the only cavalry regiment to accompany the Desert Column. And lastly, the impulse to reveal something of the treatment to which soldiers may be subjected through official vindictiveness, or political expediency, or both, with special reference to the deplorable manner in which this most worthy son of a famous Scottish clan was neglected, frustrated, and ill-used by the authorities under whom it was his misfortune to serve.

One might have supposed that, following the tragedy at Khartoum in 1885, lessons would have been learned, mistakes noted for future guidance, and steps taken to guard against the evils resulting from political intrigue. But, like leopards, politicians cannot change their spots, and, as things turned out, they learned precisely nothing from Gordon's noble sacrifice and the mismanagement that led to the disaster; for, no less than thirty years later, my own father—then Field Marshal Sir John French, Commander-in-Chief of the British Army in France and Flanders during the most critical part of the first World War—suffered a grievous wrong through the intrigues of the political authorities of the day.

Apart from the shameful failure to send timely help to General Gordon at Khartoum, the record of *neglect* in our own campaigns during the last hundred years is sufficiently lamentable. There was, for instance, the shocking neglect in the Crimean War (1854-55) to provide our troops with clothing and other necessities, thus adding untold weight to the already heavy burden sustained by the Commander-in-Chief, Lord Raglan. In the Zulu War (1879), operations were impeded by neglect to give adequate support and loyalty to the Commander-in-Chief, Lord Chelmsford. At the outset of the Boer War (1899-1902), Sir Redvers Buller, the Commander-in-Chief, was seriously handicapped by neglect in pre-war preparations. While, in the Great War (1914-18), there was the munitions scandal, exposed by the Commander-in-Chief, Sir John French—a courageous action, for which he paid dearly, but which, nevertheless, saved the day for England and her allies.

As for *interference*, however, perhaps the most glaring example is to be found in the history of the United States. In the Civil War (1861-65), it was President Lincoln's persistent interference with his Commander-in-Chief, General McLellan, that so nearly brought disaster to the northern cause. Not until General Lee's southern army had advanced almost to the gates of Washington, and victory for the Confederates seemed close at hand, did Lincoln turn from his nightly studying of military history and, at last, come to realise the folly of interfering with a professional soldier in the field. Unlike lesser mortals, he was too big a man to shrink from acknowledging his mistake, and his historic words to General Grant, when sending him to repair the desperate situation, might well serve as a model of the proper attitude to be adopted by civil authorities towards commanders in war.

"I neither ask nor desire to know anything of your plans," said the President to his newly appointed Commander-in-Chief. "Take the responsibility and act, and call on me for assistance."

Released from the crippling effect of civil interference, the northern army soon began to gain the upper hand, until, ultimately, on April 9th, 1865, General Lee was forced to capitulate, bringing the long drawn-out conflict to an end.

Though it is probably too much to expect that the weakness, neglect, malice, bureaucratic obstinacy, and obstructiveness set out in this work will be used as a solemn warning against similiar abuses in the future, if these revelations should do anything towards bringing about a better understanding of the relative position of soldier and politician, I should feel my labours had been well worth while.

In conclusion, I would suggest to politicians that they adopt this simple slogan indicating their future attitude towards commanders in the field—"Full support without interference."

CHAPTER I

An Ill-requited Soldier

TO students of military history, neglect to reward the great General Gordon in a manner even moderately commensurate with his prodigious services to the Empire, presents a problem which, at first glance, would appear inexplicable. Yet, close study of his unique career reveals what must surely be the solution, providing, so it seems, the only reasonable answer to the question, doubtless asked of themselves by countless admirers of this outstanding national hero—Why was one of Britain's most illustrious sons denied anything approaching adequate recompense for the successful exercise, in various parts of the world, of his remarkable ability to settle disputes, pacify turbulent peoples, overcome almost insuperable difficulties, alleviate suffering, stamp out abuses, ensure peaceful prosperity to law-abiding persons, while inflicting upon the evil-doer salutary retribution? Is not the answer discernible in General Gordon's inherent aversion to the dilatory, time-wasting methods, commonly called "red tape," so beloved of the bureaucrat; to his straightforward, direct way of dealing with situations, as they occurred, on his own initiative; and, perhaps above all, to the outspoken expression of his opinions, for he always believed in honestly saying what he thought, heedless of whether his views were likely to find favour with his superiors

Had he been a politician, he could hardly have lasted long as a member of any party, because nothing would have induced him to vote as directed by his leaders, if, by so doing, he would have been acting against the dictates of his conscience. Intensely religious, honest as the day, conscientious to a degree, he could never, for one moment, have endured the sordid intrigues, the petty jealousies, the unsavoury methods, that seem to be inseparable from party politics.

But, if politicians, with sufficient strengh of character to "act in accordance with their conscience and defy the consequences,"[1] are unlikely to meet with anything but the strongest disapproval of their party chiefs, soldiers, who follow similar principles, are equally sure of incurring the displeasure of high authority and of suffering accordingly.

When asked by a young Chinese, about to embark on his career, for advice as to how he might gain advancement in the public service, the Grand Secretary of China (Ts'ao Chen Yung) is said ot have uttered the following cynical recommendation—" It is really quite simple; just go on *kotowing*, and never commit yourself to any final opinion on any subject."

Similar admonition came from another Chinese of the same period, who wrote—" If you would be reckoned a hero avoid all reference to vexed questions, be non-committal and invariably humble. The key to success in a high official is to take things easily. In all your duties be plausibly evasive; never criticise adversely and never condemn."

And so it is through life the world over, the frailties of human nature being what they are, the sycophant gaining an advantage over his more honest, and often far more capable, contemporary who, scorning to play the toady, acts and speaks as his conscience dictates, defying the consequences and indifferent to vindictive accusations on the part of those whose dignity has been disturbed by a subordinate venturing to hold opinions of his own differing from theirs, and displaying even more temerity in expressing them.

Now, General Gordon was no sycophant. He would *kotow* to no man. Futhermore, it was his custom to speak his mind freely, to express decided opinions, to take his own line, and to make no secret of his intolerance of incapacity no matter whether it emanated from his subordinates or from those above him. There seems little doubt, moreover, that he would take anything but kindly to interference with his work, on which, it being for the most part of a highly specialised nature, he very properly considered himself the supreme authority.

On account of characteristics such as these, it is more than probable that Gordon was looked upon as something of a rebel by the authorities of his day, who, presumably, were no different from those of any other epoch, jealous of their arbitrary rights, and

---

[1] General Sir Hope Grant's advice to soldiers.

looking askance at anyone showing the smallest inclination to usurp them.

Abundantly provided with strength both mental and physical, Gordon would resist interference, if he believed he was right in doing so, to an extent that seemed suicidal. Here is a case in point, recorded by Demetrius Boulger in his book on General Gordon. Alluding to Gordon's activities in China, he writes—" But as far as the British Government was concerned, its action was limited to giving the Minister, Sir Thomas Wade, instructions to muzzle Gordon and prevent his doing anything that wasn't strictly in accordance with official etiquette and quite safe, or, in a word, to make him do nothing. The late Sir Thomas Wade was a most excellent Chinese scholar and estimable person in every way, but when he tried to do what the British Government and the whole arrayed body of the Horse Guards, from the Commander-in-Chief down to the Deputy-Adjutant General, had failed to do, viz., to keep Gordon in leading strings, he egregiously failed. Sir Thomas Wade went so far as to order Gordon to stay in the British Legation, and to visit no one without his express permission. Gordon's reply was to ignore the British Legation and never to enter its portals during the whole of his stay in China."

But nothing succeeds like success, and, since he was invariably right, and their attempts to intervene were proved, by results, to have been wrong, there remained little that the authorities could do about it. Yet, though obliged to acknowledge the highly satisfactory outcome brought about by Gordon's genius as a soldier, an envoy, and an administrator, and continuing to make use of his indispensable services in matters of acute difficulty and embarrassment, they were obviously unable to forget his direct methods, or the independent attitude he was wont to adopt, and so denied him the just reward of his unremitting devotion.

For services that stand alone in the history of the great British Empire, the man who has been described as second only to Nelson as a national hero, was rewarded by a grateful Government with nothing more than a Companionship of the Order of the Bath, a decoration that is often bestowed on a reasonably capable regimental commanding officer.

Even as a subaltern in the Crimea, where his services were sufficiently conspicuous to gain him the award of the French Legion of Honour, no British decoration came his way. Fortunately, Gordon cared nothing for honours or rewards. He did his duty to the utmost of his ability for duty's sake, without thought or heed of recompense, quite unperturbed by the ingratitude of his own land, which contrasted so sharply with the high honours bestowed on him by foreign countries in acknowledgment of his unparalleled services.

Apart from recognition by France, he was appointed a field marshal in the Turkish army, awarded the Grand Cordon of the Order of the Medjidieh, and granted the title of Pasha; while China also made him a field marshal, besides conferring on him the highest Chinese order ever awarded to a European—the Yellow Jacket. Yet, a decoration that has been considered not unsuitable for rewarding a painstaking Under Secretary, was the only visible sign of acknowledgment by the British Government of Gordon's remarkable achievements in various parts of the globe.

Nowadays, decorations are heaped on fortune's favourites for services quite insignificant compared with those of the great General Gordon. But, after thirty-three years of strenuous, conscientious effort on behalf of his country, often in circumstances involving deadly danger to himself, difficulties, trials, and tribulations that seemed insurmountable, and climatic conditions that few men could have survived, often alone and unaided, culminating in his death at the hands of the Mahdi, the only letters appearing after his name—a name revered and esteemed with devotion amounting to worship by the peoples among whom his work had taken him; a name that, in the course of his wonderful career, had raised British prestige to immense heights in many lands—the only letters attaching to it were the comparatively commonplace C.B.

The fact that his brother Henry, whose career as a soldier, though highly distinguished, could not, of course, bear comparison with his own, received the honour of knighthood in the Order of the Bath, tends to lend weight to the assumption that the great Gordon was deliberately and vindictively denied the just reward so abundantly earned, so richly deserved. That he was well known to be utterly indifferent to titles or other distinctions in no way excuses the authorities of his time for failing to show, in tangible form, proper appreciation of his stupendous work. Such deplorable neglect, which must be assumed to have been deliberate, since neither Gordon nor his activities could possibly have been forgotten or overlooked, will for ever remain an indelible slur on the responsible authorities, just as their failure to send him timely aid, when, at Khartoum, he stood alone, surrounded by the Mahdi's hosts, gained for them the unenviable reproach of posterity.

Gordon's complete disdain of all earthly benefits or profit may be gathered from these words, written by him from the Sudan—" Find me the man, and I will take him as my help, who utterly despises money, name, glory, honours; one who never wishes to see his home again; one who looks to God as the Source of good and Controller of evil; one who has a healthy body and energetic spirit; one who looks on death as a release from misery." Nevertheless, this attitude could in no way justify the shabby treatment meted out to one of the Empire's greatest and most faithful sons, whose entire life was dedicated to its service.

Independence of character such as Gordon possessed would be unlikely to find favour with the autocrats of Whitehall or Pall Mall, military or civil, and it was unquestionably his refusal to be kept in " leading strings " that aroused their antagonism. " General Gordon," we are told, " was a bad listener to advice at any time or from anyone. He acted almost entirely on his own judgment, and still more on his own impulse." But even those whose churlishness withheld from him his rightful meed, could hardly have denied that, but for Gordon's independent methods, his willingness to take sole responsibility, his determination to act as he thought right, without waiting for the dilatory course of cumbersome official machinery, and the belated rulings of far distant authorities who could have no more than the most meagre knowledge of situations with which he, the man on the spot, was thoroughly familiar—but for these qualities, his astonishing achievements would not have been possible.

In many respects, Gordon has been said closely to resemble another great soldier, General Sir Hope Grant, a famous cavalryman who commanded the 9th Lancers, and who served with much distinction in various campaigns, notably the suppression of the Sepoy mutiny in India, when the activities of his cavalry before the walls of Delhi provided a glorious page of British military history. Both were imbued with intense religious fervour; both were the soul of honesty and uprightness; both adhered tenaciously to the spirit of Grant's guiding principle, to act according to his conscience and defy the consequences; both were utterly fearless in taking action they believed to be right; neither could have been surpassed in conscientious devotion to duty; both served the Queen Empress and the Empire to the utmost of their exceptional powers; for doing what they conceived to be their duty, both were accused of insubordination; both — more especially Gordon — received but scanty recognition of their immense services.

No doubt most of us could instance cases, within our own knowledge, where men of outstanding strength of character, men with individuality and of independent mind, in various walks of life, have suffered, on that account, unpopularity with the powers above them, and, in consequence, have been denied the advancement and the rewards merited by their ability and industry; while others, far less capable, who have been prepared to eat out of the hands of their seniors, to " go on *kotowing* and never commit themselves to any final opinion on any subject," have prospered exceedingly and risen to untold heights.

Gordon was certainly something of a law unto himself, and was wont to emulate Nelson's use of the blind eye whenever he considered it right, and in the interests of his mission, so to do. But, just as the great British victory of Copenhagen was only made possible by Lord Nelson's deliberate disregard of the signal to break off the action, so, in the case of General Gordon, had he submitted meekly to attempts by the War Office to prevent his acceptance of an entreaty to go to the help of China in 1880, and, on arrival there, have allowed himself to be " muzzled " and shut up in the British Legation at Pekin in accordance with orders from London, he would not have been in a position to accomplish what was, perhaps, the supreme triumph of his career, namely the prevention of civil war in China, and, simultaneously, of threatened conflict between the Chinese and the Russians.

But, despite the magnitude of this and other achievements, Gordon was, obviously, never forgiven for so often taking the law into his own hands and acting according to his own judgment, even when it was known to differ from that of his masters, whose resentment manifested itself in their lamentable neglect to honour him in anything approaching proportion to the world-wide significance of his great accomplishments. In the official archives, Gordon would probably have been classified as " difficult," a category in which may be found those of independent spirit, with a rooted objection to " leading strings " and unreasonable interference, and a determination to follow the promptings of conscience, defying the consequences.

Some go so far as to use the word " obstructive " to denote those subject to their domination who have the temerity to entertain opinions opposed to their own. But, no matter what the designation may be, the result is invariably the same — the independent-minded are black-marked and need expect neither advancement nor reward. Caring not a jot for honours, Gordon

STATUE OF GENERAL GORDON
AT HEADQUARTERS,
ROYAL ENGINEERS, CHATHAM

(Reproduced by permission of the Commandant, School of Military Engineering, Chatham)

STATUE OF GENERAL GORDON
AS IT STANDS TODAY
AT KHARTOUM

(Reproduced by permission of the Sudan Government Agency in London)

would doubtless have been amused at seeing half the letters of the alphabet appearing after the names of prominent people to-day. Nevertheless, if not for his own sake, in the interests of his family, his corps, the service generally, and, particularly in the interests of justice and fair play, it seems only right and proper to place on record the circumstances in which this remarkable national figure, whose renown extended to the limits of the earth, was allowed to reach the end of his phenomenal career with no more recognition than would, normally, be thought appropriate for a political underling.

Yet, they did not hesitate to call upon him as the one man capable of easing their difficulties in the Sudan, when, in 1884, they sent him alone to Khartoum, and, as things turned out, to his death. Even then, was it too late to make amends for their niggardly treatment of him during his life? Would they not have done something towards erasing the blot on their reputations by conferring on their faithful and gallant servant a substantial posthumous award? Their dismal failure to send him help before it was too late, might, in itself, have urged them to rectify, at any rate to some extent, their past deplorable neglect. But nothing was done, with the result that General Gordon and his life's work passed into history with far more recognition by the rest of the world than that accorded him by the Government of his own country. Posterity will judge between him and the administrations under which he served. But there should be little hesitation in concluding that never before or since has so much been accomplished for so little reward, never before or since has a great man, deserving the highest honours his country could bestow, been so ungenerously treated.

CHAPTER II

Birth, Parentage and Boyhood

ON January 28th, 1833, in a cheerful, if unpretentious, house on the borders of Woolwich Common, there was born a child, whose destiny, could his parents have foreseen it, would have filled them with justifiable pride. For this new addition to the famous Gordon clan, christened Charles George, was, in course of time, to become one of the greatest men ever produced by the mighty British Empire. Had they been able to see into the future, his parents might well have developed swollen heads, and excusably so. But neither of them, so far as we know, being gifted with second sight, there was no reason for any undue elation on their part, or for looking upon the new infant as exceptional, or, in any way, superior to the three sons already born to them.

Charles Gordon's father was a gunner, a fact that accounts for the child's place of birth, Woolwich being then, as it always has been since the earliest days of the Royal Regiment, the headquarters of the artillery branch of the service. When occupied by the Gordon family, the house on Woolwich Common, distinguishable from its neighbours by prominent bow windows on either side of the front entrance, was known as No. 1 Kemp Terrace, a description that has now become No. 29 Woolwich Common. Moreover, the character of Gordon's first home has suffered considerable change in recent years through the modern tendency to convert good sized houses into flats, the residence to-day providing accommodation for three families in three distinct, self-contained homes. Still, the appearance of the exterior has been preserved, and the property seems lucky to have escaped war damage, which, not unnaturally, was extensive in a neighbourhood so close to Woolwich Arsenal.

Like so many branches of their clan, the Gordon family had soldiering in their blood. The great grandfather of Charles George —David Gordon—as a subaltern in the 47th Foot, fought at the battle of Preston Pans (1745), where he was taken prisoner. His son, christened William Augustus after the Duke of Cumberland, Commander-in-Chief of the British Army, served in various regiments, and, in 1759, took part in Wolfe's famous victory at Quebec.

Of his immediate family—four daughters and three sons— William Henry, born in 1786, gained considerable distinction as a soldier, though his chief claim to renown rests on his having begotten the great General Gordon. As an artillery officer, he served in the Napoleonic wars, being present at the successful action of Maida (1806), the first pitched battle ever to be fought by British troops on Italian soil. In the Peninsular War (1807-1814), he saw further service, subsequently holding artillery commands at Corfu and Gibraltar, and, ultimately, attaining the rank of lieutenant general.

He is said to have been " an excellent officer," whose " firm character of noble integrity lived again in his sons." He died in 1865, the year of " Chinese " Gordon's return home, covered with glory, after finally crushing the *Taiping* rebellion. Of William Henry's four other sons, Henry (afterwards Sir Henry), the eldest, and Enderby were the most prominent. Born in 1818, the former served in the 59th Regiment, eventually becoming a commissary-general in the Ordnance Department; while the second son, Enderby, greatly distinguished himself in the Crimea (1854), notably at the battle of the Alma, where his battery played a most conspicuous part in the famous victory, and as a staff officer at Inkerman. He also served against the mutineers in India (1857), finally retiring, as did his father, with the rank of lieutenant general.

It was, however, with his eldest brother that Gordon seems to have been more closely associated throughout his life, just as, in the case of his sisters, it was the eldest, Mary Augusta, who enjoyed the lion's share of his brotherly affection. Those were the days of large families, when a well stocked nursery was looked upon as a blessing, and abundance of children formed the foundation of happy married life. But then a man's income belonged to him. He was not obliged to hand over half of it to the Government. He could afford plenty of children, and the full enjoyment of family life was not denied him.

And so in the family of William Henry Gordon, besides the five sons there were as many as six daughters. Though devoted to them all, Charlie Gordon's attachment to Mary Augusta predominated. Not only was she the recipient of the bulk of his voluminous private correspondence, but to her he bequeathed the whole of his private possessions. A prolific correspondent, who seemed able to find time and amenities for private letter writing, no matter how trying the circumstances surrounding him might be, an intensely interesting collection of his letters, addressed mainly to his family, appeared some seventy years ago under the title of *Colonel Gordon in Central Africa*.[1]

As to the mother of this large and happy brood—Elizabeth Enderby before her marriage—she appears to have possessed, in an exceptional degree, the qualities needed for bringing up a family, her devotion to the children and her strong guiding hand being most marked.

Like many another who became famous in the profession of arms—Lords Clive, Nelson, and Combermere to mention but three notable British examples—Charles Gordon, as a boy, was full of high-spirited mischief, and wont to indulge in devil-may-care escapades. Here is a typical instance of his boyish audacity.

It seems that the Gordon home had become afflicted by a plague of mice, and that young Charles, supported by one of his brothers, determined to adopt a most original plan for getting rid of the nuisance while, at the same time, affording him and his confederate no end of amusement. Having captured a number of these unwelcome invaders, they conveyed them across the road to the house opposite, opened the door, and surreptitiously decanted them into the private residence of the Woolwich garrison commander !

A diversion that helped to relieve the monotony of young Gordon's life on Woolwich Common consisted in taking his younger brother to the house of some stranger. On reaching the front entrance, he would open the door, push the unfortunate Freddy into the hall, and ring the bell, holding the door-handle to prevent his escape before the arrival of an outraged parlourmaid!

But perhaps the exploit he looked back on with most satisfaction was bombarding with shot the windows of a lecture room, where gunners and sappers of the future were being instructed, causing a tremendous commotion, and obliging him and his associ-

---

[1] Edited by George Birkbeck Hill.

ates to take to their heels to avoid retribution at the hands of the infuriated cadets.

Charles Gordon and his brothers would prevail upon the workmen at Woolwich Arsenal to provide them with weapons of the catapult variety, but a good deal more powerful than the ordinary boy's home-made catapult. So formidable, indeed, were these creations of the Arsenal's skilled craftsmen, that the screws they discharged, after drilling clean holes through window panes, would bury themselves to their heads in stout woodwork. Gordon himself, in a letter written many years afterwards to a niece, after chiding her for neglecting to make " proper use of the Arsenal workmen as we did," went on to describe how " one Sunday afternoon twenty-seven panes of glass were broken in the large storehouses," and how a certain Captain Soady narrowly " escaped a premature death; a screw passed his head, and was as if screwed into the wall which it had entered." His concluding words, " those were the days at the Arsenal," showed that, through the years, he had lost none of the dare-devil spirit of his boyhood.

Through these and similar escapades young Charles must have been almost as great a terror in the neighbourhood of his birthplace as he afterwards became to the rebellious Chinese and to the slave traders of Central Africa.

After living for some time with his parents at Corfu, where he came under the notice of the Duke of Cambridge, Gordon was packed off to a school established at the historic west country town of Taunton and enjoying a high reputation as a seat of learning for boys. This was in 1843, when he had reached the age of ten, and there he remained for upwards of five years.

Conceivably, it came as something of a relief to the residents of Woolwich Common when the terror of the neighbourhood eventually departed. At any rate, we may be sure that the tormented parlourmaids of the surrounding houses, wearied and enraged by purposeless ringings of door bells, were thankful for this deliverance. But, as the reader will soon discover, Woolwich had by no means seen the last of master Charles, nor the end of his venturesome exploits.

Known as Fullands School, the establishment where Gordon and his brothers received their early education has long since fallen into disuse, and, quite recently, its buildings were taken over by King's College, a more modern school of the same town. The fact that the then headmaster, Mr. George Rogers, was the brother of a governess in the family, doubtless influenced Gordon's parents in their choice of a suitable place of study for their sons.

Little information is forthcoming about his school days. He seems to have displayed no unusual prowess either at work or at play, but it is probably safe to assume that his penchant for adventurous pranks, indulged so extensively at Woolwich, would be given even freer rein in the midst of so many boys of his own age, and that the notoriety acquired in the neighbourhood of his home would suffer no diminution on the transference of his activities from Woolwich to Taunton. Tending to support these assumptions is an allusion to the Gordon brothers in *Somerset and Dorset Notes and Queries*, quoted in the *Aluredian*—school magazine of King's College, Taunton—that " they are reported to have proved themselves rather difficult young gentlemen "!

Gordon was nearly fifteen when he left Fulland's School to undergo a year's preparation for the army entrance examination, in which he succeeded at the first attempt, passing into the Royal Military Academy (" The Shop ") towards the end of 1848.

It was in 1741 that this famous institution for the training of future gunner and sapper officers came into being, and thereafter it continued to be the main source of supply for commissioned ranks of the artillery and engineer branches of the service, until recently, in accordance with the modern craze for centralisation, it became amalgamated with the Royal Military College at Sandhurst, thus losing its two-hundred-year old identity.

Being still under sixteen years of age when he became a cadet, Charles Gordon's love of practical joking, his boisterous spirits, and his innate predilection for daring escapades, could hardly have been expected to show any signs of relaxing, notwithstanding the military discipline to which he now owed his submission.

A typical instance of his dare-devil pranks has been related by his brother, Sir Henry Gordon, who wrote—" After he had been some time at the Academy and earned many good-conduct badges, an occasion arose when it became necessary to restrain the cadets in leaving the dining hall, the approach to which was by a narrow staircase. At the top of this staircase stood the senior corporal, with outstretched arms, facing the body of cadets. This was too much for Charlie Gordon, who, putting his head down, butted with it, and catching the officer in the pit of the stomach not only sent him down the stairs, but through the glass door beyond. The officer jumped up unhurt, but Gordon was placed in confinement and nearly dismissed."

Ever ready to accept even more than his fair share of responsibility for conceiving these enterprises, and to take, without complaint, such punishment as might be awarded, he steadfastly refused to submit to anything that appeared to him to savour of injustice or abuse of authority. Thus, when told by a superior, whose powers of perception must have been singularly feeble, that he would never make an officer, his high-spirited temperament and Scottish irascibility rose in righteous indignation. Seizing his epaulettes, he tore them from his shoulders and flung them at the feet of his traducer. There, the true Gordon spirit revealed itself.

At that time, the R.M.A. was commanded by a veteran of Waterloo who had lost a leg in the campaign. Referring to this in after life, Gordon is said to have declared — " Never employ anyone minus a limb to be in authority over boys, they are apt to be irritable and unjust."[1] He might well have included those with fat stomachs and bad livers.

But, although he thrived on the hazards inseparable from happy-go-lucky adventures, his indiscretions were not extended to indulgences usually associated with youths of his age. Moreover, despite occasional clashes with the R.M.A. authorities, due to his irrepressible spirit and his unquenchable thirst for adventure, he was, withal, earnest in his endeavours to succeed, and industrious to a degree which, if not outstanding, proved, nevertheless, to be adequate for his purpose.

When approaching the end of his time at " The Shop," however, young Gordon suffered a set-back through treatment that can hardly be said to have erred on the side of leniency. As the result of an inquiry into alleged bullying at the Academy, his commission was put back for six months, his offence amounting to no more than striking a junior cadet with a hair-brush! Furthermore, the informer admitted that the blow was " not severe."

Curiously enough, this trivial happening, followed by retribution consistent with the iron discipline of that era, changed the course of Gordon's career, for, instead of ultimately becoming a gunner as originally intended, he was commissioned at his own request into the Corps of Royal Engineers. Had he, in the normal course of events, been commissioned six months earlier, he would have gone into the artillery, and one cannot help speculating as to the lines on which his career might have developed had he been a gunner rather than a sapper. Would he, for instance, have been able to get out to the Crimea? And, as an artillery officer, would

---

1 From *Charles George Gordon,* by Lt. Gen. Sir William Butler.

he have had opportunities of revealing his exceptional ability such as those avidly seized by him before Sebastopol?

As a gunner, on the other hand, he would have been spared six years of stagnation at Gravesend, constructing useless fortifications on the Thames, and an equally dull spell of duty at Pembroke Dock.

But it may safely be assumed that, no matter which branch of the service he had entered, nor, indeed, what profession he had adopted, his quite extraordinary powers would have brought him to the fore. A man possessing his overwhelming strength of character, his almost superhuman capacity for accomplishing the seemingly impossible, must assuredly have figured as an outstanding personality in any walk of life.

Similarly, in consequence of his independent spirit, his distaste for " leading strings," his tendency to take his own line, his determination to act in accordance with the direction of his conscience, and, above all, his unconcealed contempt for humbugging bureaucrats, he would probably have suffered in any profession, as he did in the army, through jealousies, the disturbed petty dignities of superiors, and their vindictive repercussions.

THE HOUSE ON
WOOLWICH COMMON WHERE
GORDON WAS BOR'N

CHAPTER III

A Subaltern in the Crimea

I T was in June, 1852, that Gordon became a second lieutenant in the Royal Engineers, a corps that in its long and honourable history has enjoyed the services of many distinguished soldiers, though none so remarkable as the subject of this work. The loss of six months seniority got him away to a bad start, but the energy and zeal displayed by him in the execution of his duties at Chatham, together with his pronounced ability as a draughtsman, soon made up for lost time, and, after a period of employment in the construction of fortifications at Pembroke Dock, he was selected to take charge of a large consignment of huts being shipped to the Crimea for the accommodation of our sorely tried troops.

Pembroke Dock appears to have impressed Gordon as a dreary spot, for, in a letter to his favourite sister, Augusta, he expressed sympathy for the officers and men destined to find themselves quartered in those isolated forts. At any rate, he seems to have found ample time for meditation, seeing that, while there, he began to acquire the religious ardour which, thenceforward, was to increase in strength until it became the very essence of his existence.

It was at Pembroke that he first put away childish things, and began to take a more serious view of life. As a cadet at Woolwich he had rejected confirmation, thinking " it was a useless sin, as I did not intend to alter (not that it was in my power to be converted when I chose)." Nevertheless, on Easter Sunday, 1854, he took his first sacrament, and, though still unconfirmed, communed as regularly as possible for the rest of his life.

This rather sudden change from easy going, youthful exuberance to staid, earnest meditation, was due mainly to the influence of his eldest sister and of a certain Captain Drew, a brother-officer imbued with tremendous religious fervour. The effect of his altered outlook is manifested in a letter to his sister, where he wrote—" but thank God, it is different with me now. I feel much happier and more contented than I used to do."

After ten months' service at Pembroke Dock, Gordon, to his immense satisfaction, found himself bound for the Crimea and an infinitely more exciting existence, for which his adventurous, energetic spirit yearned. The war being waged between Russia on the one side, and England, France, and Turkey on the other, had already been in progress for nine months when, in the middle of December, 1854, Gordon set out for Eastern Europe. The great battles of the Alma and Inkerman had been fought and won by the allies, and the world had been roused to ardent enthusiasm by the glorious charges of British cavalry at Balaclava. But Sebastopol continued to hold out and to defy all efforts on the part of the allied besiegers to bring about its fall. Consequently, though much of the campaign had run its course before Gordon's departure for the seat of war, there yet remained time for him to reach the front, gain his first experience of active service, and be " in at the death."

Being an exceedingly poor sailor, he travelled overland to Marseilles, eventually arriving at Balaclava well ahead of the transport vessel conveying the much needed huts. Disembarking on New Year's Day, 1855, at the Crimean port bearing a name that became immortal following the epic charges of Scarlett's Heavy Brigade and Cardigan's Light Brigade of British cavalry, Gordon set about his preparations for the task of erecting some 320 huts—the first step that appears to have been taken towards easing the suffering and hardships so stoically endured by our troops throughout that terrible winter of 1854-55.

Writing home soon after his arrival, he spoke of two officers being frozen to death in the night, and of two others succumbing to the effects of charcoal fumes.

"The tenacity," wrote Major Arthur Griffiths,[1] "with which we held on to the siege not only against enormous odds but in the teeth of the most cruel hardships, prolonged for months and months through sickness, starvation, want, exposure, must command universal admiration. To stand thus firm, a mere remnant, continually harassed and always suffering, implies a higher forti-

---

[1] In *Battles of the Nineteenth Century.*

tude than that of animal courage. It is this which sheds lustre on
that hard-pressed handful for ever on duty, always ill-fed, worse-
clothed, weltering knee-deep in mud, decimated by disease and the
unceasing fire, which was yet never turned from its purpose. In
the glory of this great record we can afford to forget the neglect
and mismanagement that sent the flower of the British army into
an arduous undertaking inadequately prepared for war."

From this is will be clear that Gordon's huts came as a
Godsend, providing as they did some long over-due protection
for the luckless troops who had, hitherto, been exposed to the most
appalling conditions either in the open, or, at best, under canvas.
Three weeks later, Gordon found himself in the trenches before
Sebastopol.

His arrival in the Crimea synchronised with the beginning of
a serious, if belated, attempt to alleviate the sufferings of our troops
and to introduce some order and method in place of the chaos and
mismanagement that had been rife, and that, not unnaturally,
earned for the British Government of the day an indelible
reproach. Chief among the evils resulting from negligence, complacency, and red tape was the deplorable lack of preparation for
the care of the wounded and the sick.

It was about two months prior to Gordon's arrival at the
front that Florence Nightingale, with a few devoted assistants, had
taken up her duties as Lady Superintendent of the British military
hospital at Scutari on the Bosphorus. Only a woman of exceptional qualities and an indomitable spirit could have been anything but overawed by the truly ghastly picture presented by the
Scutari hospital in the early days of November, 1854. Here, the
devastating effects of red tape, rigid adherence to what are commonly called " the usual channels " — to this day responsible for
more delay and inefficiency than almost anything else—shocking
lack of initiative, fear of higher authority, and so on, were revealed
in all their hideous nakedness.

This vast improvised hospital containing four miles of beds,
packed so close together as to be nearly touching, stood over a
sewer, while its atmosphere was polluted by the sickening odour of
adjacent cess-pools. " I have been well acquainted," said Miss
Nightingale, " with the dwellings of the worst parts of most of the
great cities in Europe, but have never been in any atmosphere I
could compare with that of the Barrack Hospital at night."[1]

---

[1] From *Eminent Victorians* by Lytton Strachey.

There appear to have been neither knives nor forks, spoons nor plates, soap nor towels; while as regards medical equipment there was a lamentable shortage of such elementary stores as stretchers, bandages, and ordinary drugs. " The principal doctor," wrote Lytton Strachey, " was lost in the imbecilities of a senile optimism. The wretched official whose business it was to provide for the wants of the hospital was tied fast hand and foot by red tape."

The criminal lunacy to which the evils of red tape were extended may be instanced by the almost unbelievable case of a large consignment of much needed shirts, which, on arrival at Scutari, remained unpacked for three weeks because the hide-bound official concerned declared he was unable to touch them without the authority of a board ! Meanwhile, " the sick and wounded lay half-naked shivering for want of clothing."

But have we yet profited from Florence Nightingale's courageous exposure of the heinous effects that can be produced by rigid adherence to what Lytton Strachey politely alludes to as " official etiquette "? Are not the authorities still, to this day, obsessed with having recourse to the cumbersome, time-wasting procedure of courts martial, courts of inquiry, and boards, when, in a large proportion of cases, the matters concerned could be dealt with by commanding officers?

It would be difficult to imagine anyone more impatient or contemptuous of red tape than General Gordon—a veritable tiger for efficiency, who realised that initiative and direct methods were, more often than not, essential to its maintenance, and who possessed in abundance the force of character and independence requisite for acting on his own responsibility. He hated and despised the toadying sycophant, who, for fear of incurring the displeasure of his seniors and prejudicing his chances of advancement, will shrink from deviating a hair's breadth from the beaten track of red tape, just as he maintained an attitude of complete indifference to reward in any shape or form. What would he have thought of some of our modern trinket collectors, whose services, distinguished though they be, can in no way bear comparison with those of the great Gordon?

Imbued with the Spartan stoicism of the born soldier, Gordon was severely critical of the grumbling he found to be prevalent among British troops serving in the Crimea. In fairness, however, to those outrageously neglected soldiers, it must be remembered that much of their suffering was due, not to the ordinary exigencies inseparable from campaigning, but to the incapacity, apathy, and negligence of the authorities at home, combined with the crippling effects on organisation in the field of that hideous bar to efficiency —*red tape*. Who would know better than the soldiers that " some-one had blundered "? And knowing this, is it surprising that they felt justified in grousing at discomforts which, with the exercise of a little intelligence and forethought, might well have been avoided?

But then Gordon was an exceptional man. Few soldiers can have experienced anything comparable to the privations, hard-ships, sufferings, and dangers, uncomplainingly endured by him for prolonged periods in the heart of Central Africa. He seemed able to withstand the ravages of extreme climatic conditions to which other men succumbed, while his needs were frugal in the extreme. Consequently, it can be readily understood that, being by nature so tough in fibre, so impervious to hardships that affected others, and requiring no more than the barest necessities of life, he could not sympathise with the soldiers' grumbling. He believed it wrong for a soldier to grumble in *any* circumstances; though, doubtless, he would have condemned, with the full force of his dynamic spirit, the deplorable inefficiency that brought about this discontent.

By the time Gordon reached Balaclava, the powerful influence of Florence Nightingale was beginning to bear fruit, and, with the worst of that appalling winter gone by, conditions were gradually becoming more endurable. But, of the 26,000 British troops that had landed in the Crimea four months earlier, considerably less than half that number remained effective, casualties in the costly, if successful, battles of the Alma, Balaclava, and Inkerman, in addi-tion to the ravages of dysentery and other forms of sickness inevi-tably resulting from mismanagement, playing havoc with Britain's contribution to the allied armies in the field.

It is but fair, however, to point out that the conditions would have been less disastrous but for a circumstance over which the authorities had no control. On November 14th, 1854, a terrific hurricane swept across the southern coast of the Crimea, carrying all before it. Tents of the British camps at Balaclava were ripped to fragments and blown into space, leaving their luckless occupants —weak in many cases from lack of food and clothing—exposed to a torrential downpour, soaking their blankets and what little clothing yet remained to them. The camp soon became a morass, the hard ground of winter, in which men had been obliged to dig holes for their hip bones, being converted into deep holding mud

that, if making for softer lying, added immeasurably to the already
heavy toll of sickness.

In mid-February (1855), Gordon received his baptism of fire.
Alluding in a letter to his experiences, he wrote—" The night of
February 14th I was on duty in the trenches. . . . The French
that night determined to join their sentries on their right and our
sentries on our left, in advance of their and our trenches, so as to
prevent the Russians coming up the ravine, and then turning
against our flank. . . . I was told to make communication by
rifle-pits. . . . I got, after some trouble, eight men with picks
and shovels, and asked the captain of the advanced trench to give
me five double sentries to throw out in advance. It was the first
time he had been on duty here; and I never had, although I kept
that to myself. I led forward the sentries, going at the head of
the party, and found the sentries of the advance had not held the
caves, which they ought to have done after dark, so there was just
a chance of the Russians being in them. I went on, however, and,
though I did not like it, explored the caves almost alone. We then
left two sentries on the hill above the caves, and went back to get
round and post two sentries below. However, just as soon is we
showed ourselves outside the caves and below them, bang! bang!
went two rifles, the bullets hitting the ground close to us. . . .
It was not a Russian attack, but the two sentries whom I had
placed above the caves *had fired at us.* . . . The Russians had,
on the report of our shots, sent us a shower of bullets, their picket
not being more than 150 yards away. I set the men to work, and
then went down to the bottom of the ravine, and found the French
in strength hard at work also. Having told them who we were,
I returned to the trench, where I met Colonel —— of the 1st Royals.
I warned him if he went out he would be sure to be hit by our
own sentries or the Russians. He would go, however, and a
moment afterwards was hit in the breast, the ball going through
his coats, slightly grazing his ribs, and passing out again without
hurting him. I stayed with my working party all night, and got
home very tired."

It was in the trenches before Sebastopol that Gordon made
the acquaintance of another fine character, destined, like himself,
to accomplish great things in the profession of arms, and to serve
his country with conspicuous ability; but, unlike him, to be rewarded in accordance with his achievements. This was Garnet
Wolseley, who, in later life, so enjoyed the confidence of his men

that the phrase " all Sir Garnet " became commonly used by British soldiers to denote a satisfactory state of affairs.

There, in the Crimea, under the walls of the great Russian fortress, under the fire of the enemy's batteries, was born a life-long friendship, amounting to deep affection, between these two national heroes in embryo. Although Wolseley reaped a richer harvest, Gordon gained the greater fame. As young soldiers they started on level terms, both being lucky enough to acquire experience of active service early in their careers. Twenty-three years after their first meeting, when both were subalterns, whereas Wolseley had reached the rank of lieutenant general with such illustrious appendages as G.C.M.G. and K.C.B. attaching to his name, the simple, unobtrusive Gordon, who fortunately cared for none of these things, was still a colonel with no British reward for his remarkable services other than a paltry C.B. Prominent among his sensational activities covering that period of his career, that is to say from 1855 to 1878, were his conspicuous part in the China War, his suppression of the *Taiping* Rebellion, and his resolute crushing of the diabolical slave trade in Central Africa.

A pronounced difference in the characters of these two great soldiers revealed itself in the matter of personal ambition. Wolseley cherished ambitions to reach the top of the tree, to gain distinction. And, if no other evidence of this were forthcoming, the truth of it is to be found in his own words when alluding to Gordon's selection for the task of restoring peace in China. " It was a question," he wrote, " whether Colonel Charley Gordon or I should be sent to help China in dealing with the *Taiping* Rebellion. He was most wisely selected. As I have already mentioned, there had grown up between us many bonds of union, for I admired him with a reverence I had never felt for any other man. When he returned from China as the great Christian hero of the *Taiping* war, I said to him laughingly—' How differently events might have turned out had I been sent on that mission instead of you. I should have gone there with the determination of wiping out the rebellion and of becoming myself the Emperor of China! ' How much loftier and nobler were the objects he sought after than the part I aspired to play there? He had no earthly aspirations, for his Master was not of this world, and ambition, as that vice or virtue is commonly understood, had no resting-place in his philosophy."[1]

---

[1] From *The Story of a Soldier's Life* by Field Marshal Viscount Wolseley.

It was in this respect that their characters so noticeably differed, Wolseley, very naturally, being anxious to rise in his profession, to forge ahead of his rivals, to gain the rewards of his success; while Gordon thought only of accomplishing, to the utmost of his ability, the task immediately confronting him, his attitude being almost contemptuous of personal aggrandisement.

Then again, it is improbable that Wolseley would have prospered as he did, had he possessed Gordon's independent spirit; had he habitually stretched initiative to the extent of taking the line be believed to be right irrespective of whether such action coincided with the ideas of higher authority; had he made no secret of an intolerant attitude towards interference; had he displayed contempt for the capacity of superiors; had he attempted to circumvent the evils of red tape—had he offended in any of these, or similar, respects, he would doubtless have been dubbed " difficult," if not " obstructive," and posted to the " black list," where his chances of realising his ambition would have vanished. Years of staff employment, however, had so immersed him in an atmosphere of rigid " military etiquette," militating against divergence, by so much as a hair's breadth, from the cast iron, inflexible usages of army bureaucracy, that he would have avoided being classified as " difficult " and escaped figuring among the " obstructive."

Gordon, on the other hand, must assuredly have appeared promiently on the " black list," for was he not looked upon as a rebel, who cared nothing for the sanctity of " normal channels," and who ruthlessly brushed aside all obstacles from his path, even those specifically prepared by the highest authorities to restrain his activities?

But, apart from this fundamental dissimilarity of character, these two life-long friends had much in common. As subalterns in the Crimea they proved faithful representatives of all that was best in the dashing young British officer of a hundred years ago. In an age of chivalry, when the force of example was considered of paramount importance in leadership, both were pre-eminently conspicuous. Indeed, from the very outset of their careers, it became clear they were cut out for great achievements. In both of them the germs of greatness were plain to be seen during those testing days before Sebastopol, that culminated in the storming of the Redan, the capture of the Malakoff, and the fall of the famous Russian stronghold.

They were alike in the ardour of their conscientious devotion to duty as in other soldierly attributes such as conspicuous gal-

CHARLES GORDON
AS A SUBALTERN SOON AFTER
THE CRIMEA

lantry, supreme contempt for danger, fortitude, dash, and determination. Religion formed another bond of sympathy between them, for, although Wolseley was, perhaps, less ostentatious than Gordon in religious fervour, he, nevertheless, held equally strong views.

Alluding to him as " God's friend " and " in many ways the most remarkable man I ever knew," Wolseley wrote of the other— " We were friends, drawn together by ties never formulated in words. In a conversation I had with him the year he left England, never to return, he told me he prayed daily for two men of whom I was one. In these days of money grubbing, when the teaching of Christianity is little practised and the spirit of chivalry is well-nigh forgotten, I cling tenaciously to every remembrance of our intimacy, because he was one of the very few friends I ever had who came up to my estimate of the Christian hero. He absolutely ignored self in all he did, and only took in hand what he conceived to be God's work. Life was to him but a Pilgrim's Progress between the years of early manhood and the Heaven he now dwells in, the Home he always longed for. History tells of only one faultless Hero, and His story is set forth in the Gospels. The character of Christ as therein depicted was always uppermost in Gordon's mind. When in any difficulty his first thought was, ' What would my Master do were He now in my place? ' It was this constant reliance upon his Maker, this spiritual communing with his Saviour upon every daily occurrence in life, that enabled him absolutely to ignore self and take no heed for what to-morrow might bring forth. It was because of this faith that he cheerfully gave up his life in the endeavour to do what he believed to be his Master's work, the mission he willingly undertook to Khartoum. To understand that Master's will in all the events of his splendid but curiously varied career, he studied the Bible in a way rarely practised since the early days of Christianity. He was mortal, and was not therefore perfect. But the more I study his noble life the more I am dazzled by his untarnished glory, as the eyes are by staring at the midday sun. To those who would belittle his memory I can only say, ' Go and do likewise.' When I first met him in the Crimea, he was a good-looking, curly-headed young man of my own age, both of us being then in our twenty-second year. His full, clear and bright blue eyes seemed to court scrutiny, whilst at the same time they searched into your inner soul. An indifference to danger of all sorts, or, I should rather say, an apparent unconsciousness of it, bespoke a want of the sense which generally warns man of its presence. His absolute single-mindedness of purpose startled me at times, for it made me feel how inferior I was to him in all the higher qualities of character, and how inferior were all my aims in life to his."

Both Gordon and Wolseley regarded the Christian religion as a reality, not as a matter of form or routine, in which the parrot-like repeating of prayers morning and evening, combined with regular appearances in church, figured as the main essentials. No! their attitude towards religion was profoundly sincere, for both were firm believers in God, staunch upholders of the Christian faith, and wholehearted in their acceptance of its teachings. As for Gordon, few of the innumerable letters written by him to his sister, Augusta, were without some reference to the " Power of the Almighty " or the " Will of God."

Little did they know, these two care-free subalterns in the Crimea, whose friendship was but newly born, what fate had in store for them—that thirty years hence one would be in a position of deadly peril, the other hastening to his rescue; that Wolseley's belated expedition for the relief of Khartoum would prove abortive; or that Gordon would die through the apathy of British statesmen.

Gordon was present at the two unsuccessful attacks on the Redan, and, even at this early stage of his career, showed himself impatient of failure. His fiery spirit rebelled against anything in the nature of a set-back, and when, on that memorable 18th of June (1855), the British attack was repulsed, he seems to have allowed his mortified feelings to get the better of him, for of all people to choose as a target for his tempestuous wrath he could not have found anyone less deserving of censure than Gerald Graham (afterwards General Sir Gerald Graham, V.C.), another R.E. subaltern, who had not only been foremost in the attack, but who alone had succeeded in reaching the Redan with a scaling ladder.

I think it was Lord Wolseley who said he considered Graham the bravest man he had ever known. Alluding to their association in the Crimea, he wrote—

" I have more than once walked with him back to camp in the Crimea from some of our advanced parallels upon being relieved after a tour of trench duty, when from sheer laziness—it was a failing of his—he would make straight ' across country,' in the direction of the Middle Ravine picket. He preferred thus to expose himself to the fire of the Russian sharpshooters rather than take the trouble of following our line of trenches where he would have been screened from view. When with him upon such occasions I never relished the manœuvre, but apparently it did not occur to him that there was anything unusual in his proceeding."[1]

This was the man on whose innocent head fell the brunt of Gordon's misdirected outburst. As a possible explanation, it might be suggested that Graham happened to be nearest to Gordon immediately after the retirement from the Redan, and on that account came in for the full blast of Scottish vehemence. Be that as it may, there seems no room for doubt that, in an access of enraged disappointment at the failure of the assault, in preparation for which he had performed conspicuous service—notably in acquiring valuable information as to the Russian positions—Gordon gave way to a storm of uncontrolled anger.

In fairness, it must be stressed that his passionate protest welled up at a moment of excitement, when disappointment and chagrin at the unexpected repulse had, understandably, caused a revulsion of feeling, tempers to rise, and nerves to jangle. But impetuosity when angered or frustrated, thwarted or opposed, was a characteristic that Gordon never succeeded in overcoming, and, at times, this drawback impelled him to say and do things that he must afterwards have regretted. Though severe, he was at heart the kindliest of men, and one can well imagine how bitterly he would have reproached himself for the unjustifiable harangue meted out to his friend and brother-sapper, Gerald Graham.

Gordon was never easy to get on with—those of independent nature, who rail at "leading strings," and possess the strength of character to take their own line, seldom are—and he suffered on this account at the hands of the authorities. But, in the words of Sir Hope Grant's biographer—words that would be equally applicable to Gordon—" It is better to be neglected with men of the type of Hope Grant, than to prosper with the glib- tongued and plausible."[2]

In a letter describing this unsuccessful attempt to take the Redan, Gordon wrote—"At 3 a.m. the French advanced on the Malakoff Tower in three columns, and ten minutes after this, our signal was given. The Russians then opened with a fire of grape, which was terrific. They mowed down our men in dozens, and the trenches, being confined, were crowded with men, who foolishly

---

1 From *The Story of a Soldier's Life* by Field Marshal Viscount Wolseley.
2 From *The Life of Sir Hope Grant*, by Colonel H. Knollys.

kept in them instead of rushing over the parapet of our trenches, and by coming forward in a mass, trusting to some of them at least being able to pass through untouched to the Redan, where of course, once they arrived, the artillery could not reach them, and every yard nearer would have diminished the effect of the grape by giving it less space for spreading. We could then have moved up our supports and carried the place. Unfortunately, however, our men dribbled out at the ends of the trenches, ten and twenty at a time, and as soon as they appeared they were cleared away. . . . The first plan was that we should fire for three hours and go in at six o'clock, but the French changed it, and would not wait until we had silenced the enemy's artillery fire and so we attacked at 3 a.m. My father can tell the effect of grape from twelve 68-pounders and 32-pounders at 200 yards upon a column; but whatever may be the effect, I am confident that if we had left the trenches in a mass, some of us would have survived and reached the Redan."

Of the second abortive attempt, on September 8th, to take this dominating feature of the Russian defences, Gordon was again critical. " Our men," he wrote, " went forward well, losing apparently few, put the ladders in the ditch, and mounted on the salient of the Redan, but though they stayed there five minutes or more, they did not advance, and tremendous reserves coming up drove them out. They retired well and without disorder, losing in all 150 officers, 2400 men killed and wounded. We should have carried everything before us if the men had only advanced."

But the day proved only a partial failure, for the French succeeded in taking, and maintaining their hold on, the Malakoff, thus rendering the Sebastopol defences untenable, and causing the Russians to abandon their positions during the night, after destroying their siege works and setting the town ablaze. Describing his view of the scene, Gordon wrote — " During the night I heard terrible explosions, and going down to the trenches at 4 a.m. I saw a splendid sight—the whole town in flames, and every now and then a terrific explosion. The rising sun shining on the scene of destruction produced a beautiful effect. The last of the Russians were leaving the town over the bridge. All the three-deckers, etc., were sunk, the steamers alone remaining. Tons and tons of powder must have been blown up."

Thus was the Crimean War virtually brought to an end, though Gordon remained for some little time at Sebastopol engaged in demolition work. During the following three years he was employed as Assistant Commissioner on the rather dull duties of boundary commissions for delimitation of the new frontier in Bessarabia and for fixing the Asiatic frontier between Russia and Armenia. On completion of these prolonged operations which, for a man of Gordon's energetic spirit, must have been distinctly irksome, he returned home and, in the Spring of 1859, was promoted to the rank of captain on being appointed second Adjutant of his corps at Chatham, where for just over a year he performed the duties of Field Works Instructor.

CHAPTER IV

China

BEGINNING with the First Opium War in 1839, conflict between Britain and China has been by no means rare, and in almost every instance traffic in opium was the direct or indirect cause of hostilities.   But, contrary to what might well be supposed, it was not a case of the Chinese Government contending for the importation of opium to China and being ready, if need be, to go to war in order to ensure it.   It was quite the reverse, for not only were they opposed to producing the harmful drug in their own country, but they steadfastly refused to allow it to be imported, conscientiously resisting the temptation to avail themselves of the vast revenue that would be derived from legalised traffic in the laudable desire to protect their immense population from the degradation and perils of opium smoking. Britain, to her discredit, defied the Chinese Government's ban, and there began a campaign of wholesale smuggling that brought about the war of 1839 and was the root cause of succeeding conflicts.

It was in the summer of 1860, while Gordon pursued his duties at Chatham, that war in China, which for some time had been following a desultory course, suddenly blazed up with a heavy British defeat before the Taku Forts—strong fortifications on the Peiho River guarding the way to Pekin.   Volunteering at once for active service, Gordon reached Tientsin in September.   But, if just too late to take part in Sir Hope Grant's successful attack on the forts, he arrived in time for the entry into Pekin and the subsequent sacking of the Summer Palace.

Packed with priceless treasures and surrounded by twelve square miles of grounds that would have made Kew Gardens look like the back yard of a railway cottage, this palace of the Emperors of China lay some eight miles to the north-west of the capital. " Here," wrote Sir Wiliam Butler, " all the ingenious diversities and embellishments of Chinese architectural and horticultural art had been exhausted to produce a terrestrial paradise; lakes, rivulets, cascades, pagodas, rocks, open spaces, and woodlands formed the varied setting to the numerous palaces of marble, porcelain, and cedar wood which in turn surrounded the central residence of the Emperor."

Describing, in a letter to his sister, this punishment inflicted on the Chinese, Gordon wrote—" You can scarcely imagine the beauty and magnificence of the palaces we burnt. It made one's heart sore to destroy them. It was wretchedly demoralising work."

The rights or wrongs of the decision arrived at by Queen Victoria's High Commissioner, the eighth Lord Elgin, will always remain a subject of controversy; and, while the severity of the punishment can hardly be denied, nor the seemliness of wantonly destroying property of surpassing beauty and untold value be unequivocally acknowledged, justice cried aloud for the infliction of salutary retribution upon the Chinese for their barbaric treatment of captives. To Lord Elgin, a man of great experience and high attainments, this seemed the most exemplary means of demonstrating to the Emperor of China, and to the nation as a whole, that atrocities would not be tolerated, and that any departure from the accepted rules of civilised warfare would be repaid by punishment of the sternest nature.

To be sure, the British Government, by their immoral insistence on introducing opium into China in violation of the prohibition laws obtaining in the country, could not escape responsibility for wars that were, directly or indirectly, brought about by this illegal traffic. But that was no excuse for the maiming and murdering of prisoners of war. And, if the sacking of the Summer Palace appeared unduly harsh, profoundly shocking the more sensitive of the world in general, the Chinese, by behaving in a manner unbecoming their ancient civilisation, had brought this merciless retribution upon themselves. Through the ages, has it not been proved beyond all question that only by ruthless measures can savagery be overcome? Moreover, if such measures can prevent the recurrence of barbarous atrocities in the future, squeamishness on behalf of sufferers from immediate reprisals must surely be misplaced. The heavier the penalty inflicted, the less likelihood would there be of renewed barbarities.

As the responsible authority, the Emperor, Hsien Feng, was very properly the chief sufferer, and, whether from the shock of this unimaginable disaster, or from other causes, he soon afterwards joined his celestial ancestors. But so venerated was the Manchu throne, and so great the national pride in the glories of the Yuen-Ming-Yuen—" garden of perpetual brightness "—that the destruction of this magnificent home of the Emperor cast a gloom over the entire nation and remained an enduring reminder of the vengeance brought about by the brutality of Chinese troops to helpless prisoners.

The distasteful work of pillage completed, there was a share out of the prize money accompanied by much bartering of loot. A string of pearls, acquired for sixteen shillings, was sold next day for five hundred pounds!

Gordon himself, who cared little for money except in so far as it enabled him to help the needy and relieve suffering, admitted he had done well, his share of the spoil including the Emperor's throne which he afterwards presented to the headquarters of his corps at Chatham.

Imagine the storm that would be raised to-day by the horror-stricken authorities of our time who become almost hysterical if merely a few old blankets taken from prisoners of war are made use of by their captors, and who hastily assemble courts of inquiry, so beloved of the bureaucrat, involving considerable expense and deplorable waste of time, to investigate the iniquity of a British soldier temporarily utilising some well worn article once the property of a Neapolitan thug. Not very consistent, these modern big-wigs of ours, are they? For they will contemplate with satisfied complacency the seizure of towns, villages, homesteads, farms, beasts, and produce belonging to their enemies, while indignantly denouncing the appropriation of a blanket from those same enemies!

In Gordon's time they were more sensible and less inconsistent. The pity of it was that much of the contents of the palace should have been destroyed instead of being seized as a prize of war. But even in those broader-minded days, bureaucrats were jealous of their rights, and, though thousands of miles from the theatre of war, resented the man on the spot using his own initiative and proceeding to act without their approval. Thus it came about that Sir Hope Grant, one of England's greatest soldiers, was hauled over the coals for apportioning the prize money without reference to Whitehall. "Act in accordance with your conscience and defy

Scale: *Approximately* 200 *geographical miles to an inch.*

EASTERN CHINA

the consequences." That was his guiding principle, and in acting as he did he lived up to it. He cared nothing for the approval or disapproval of Whitehall. All that mattered to him was that he had done what he believed to be right. The authorities far away at home, who were not in a position to judge, could take it or leave it.

Fortunately for the British army and for the country, Queen Victoria stepped in, as she so often did in defence of her commanders when unjustly assailed or interfered with by jacks-in-office whose dignity had suffered from someone having the temerity to use his own discretion.

Describing the luxuries of the Summer Palace, Gordon wrote —" The throne room was lined with ebony, carved in a marvellous way. There were huge mirrors of all shapes and kinds, clocks, watches, musical boxes with puppets on them, magnificent china of every description, heaps and heaps of silks of all colours, embroidery, and as much splendour and civilisation as you would see at Windsor; carved ivory screens, coral screens, large amounts of treasure, etc."

In accordance with the peace terms, the Chinese were required to pay ten thousand pounds for each Englishman, and five hundred pounds for each native soldier, who died as a prisoner of war. Soon after the treaty had been ratified, the greater part of Sir Hope Grant's force embarked for home, leaving some three thousand men under Major General (afterwards General Sir Charles) Staveley at Tientsin to enforce payment of the indemnity by instalments.

Gordon remained at Tientsin for eighteen months erecting huts for the accommodation of the troops. These rather dull, though highly important, duties were, however, alleviated from time to time by visits to Pekin and one particularly interesting expedition to the Great Wall, fifteen hundred miles in extent, constructed by the Chinese two thousand years before as a barrier against the incursions of Genghis Khan and his Tartar legions.

Now, the troubles of the Chinese Government were by no means restricted to their disastrous conflict with the European invaders, who included French as well as British troops, since for the past ten years or more the country had been seething with rebellion. In 1837, one Hong Siu Tsuen, schoolmaster of a village near Canton in south China, became afflicted with intense religious mania following his recovery from a serious illness, and, after learning about Christianity from an American missionary, declared himself to be the prophet of God. He even went so far as to assume the title of *Tien Wang*, the Celestial King.

There was no lack of the gullible and curious to listen to his fatuous diatribes, and when, in consequence of a personal grievance against the Government, his religious ravings were extended to rebellious propaganda, urging his hearers to combine and throw off the Manchu yoke, the riff-raff, foreseeing chances of rich plunder, flocked to his standard, so that by the year 1850 he had collected a sufficiently strong force to menace the fertile delta of the Yang Tse Kiang.

Thus began the great rebellion whose avowed object comprised throwing out the Manchus and establishing *Taiping*—" the reign of eternal peace." Led by the fanatical Hong Siu Tsuen, the insurrection ravaged the land for many years: a variety of foreign commanders failed to subdue it: and not until the genius of Gordon had been brought to bear on an intolerable situation was the self-styled *Tien Wang* finally overcome and the prolonged revolt crushed.

In 1853, the *Taipings*, as the rebels were called, captured and occupied the important city of Nankin, ancient capital of the Ming dynasty, where Hong established his headquarters, appropriating a luxurious palace to his own use. There he remained in conditions of splendour somewhat out of keeping with the lowly calling of a village schoolmaster. Nor did he appear to see anything peculiar in the " Celestial King " surrounding himself with innumerable wives and concubines. Operations in the field were left to his lieutenants, while " the prophet of God " retired into the seclusion of his commandeered palace, his time fully occupied with spiritual antics and attendance on the many ladies of his household.

Though hoping to enlist foreign sympathy for the revolt by claiming to be the chosen of God in a mission to uproot the Manchu dynasty and bring to the country the blessings of everlasting peace, the *Taiping* leader, whose followers, if numerous, were composed largely of unscrupulous adventurers, gradually alienated sympathisers with his movement by the savagery and barbarism of his ruthless, undisciplined rabble. To be sure, they often fought with desperate courage, but their valour was stimulated by the greed for plunder, while in the hour of victory such was their lust for blood that they would mercilessly destroy all who fell into their hands, women and children as well as men. In the capture of Nankin, these so-called agents of Christianity reached the peak of infamy, exterminating four thousand families of Manchus. "We killed them all to the infant in arms," they boasted, "we left not a root to sprout from, and the bodies of the slain we cast into the Yangtse."

For years the rebellion dragged on, straining the resources of the Chinese Government to the utmost, until even Pekin, the capital, became menaced by the marauding *Taipings* and the person of the Emperor endangered. But, at last, the tide turned in favour of the Imperial troops, and, by 1859, the rebels seemed to have finally shot their bolt. Short of munitions and supplies of all kinds, the country laid waste by their depredations, they must have been within an ace of throwing up the sponge when much needed aid came to them from an unexpected quarter, for the preoccupation of the Emperor's forces in opposing the foreign invasion so greatly relieved the pressure on *Tien Wang's* ever increasing multitude of buccaneers that they were able to take advantage of this stroke of luck by advancing on the rich international trading port of Shanghai, and, in collusion with the unscrupulous characters who infested the China coast, replenishing their diminished supplies of war material.

The near approach of the *Taipings* caused a certain amount of consternation in Shanghai, whose not inconsiderable foreign community, anticipating little support from the Chinese Government, decided to take their own measures for the safety of the city. Under the leadership of an American named Ward, a mixed force of foreigners and natives was hastily raised, and, after a brief period devoted to organisation and training, this nondescript legion took the field against the rebels. Poor discipline could only be expected in a formation so hurriedly assembled whose ranks contained so high a proportion of adventurers, doubtful characters, self-seekers, and so on. But time allowed of no picking or choosing, every man who offered his services being gladly accepted. Nevertheless, rough as they were, their gallantry could not be denied, and although suffering heavy losses they did succeed in keeping the rebels out of Shanghai, which after all was the original purpose of their existence as a military force. Their ability to check the *Taipings* so pleased the mandarins that the rather theatrical title of "Ever Victorious Army" was bestowed upon this band of volunteers, heedless of the fact that, despite their courageous efforts, the reverses they suffered outnumbered their victories. It was indeed a proud title, but not until Gordon had become its commander, whipped it into shape, and led it to a succession of triumphs in the field could the force be said to have rightly earned so enviable a designation.

Meanwhile, *Tien Wang* continued to be a source of embarrassment to the Government, more and more recruits swelled his ranks, while, owing to his capture of several positions on the coast, he was able to trade with foreign vessels and procure all he needed for the prosecution of his long drawn out revolt.

As to the attitude of the British Government, though at first inclined to sympathise with the *Taipings,* whose intentions they mistakenly believed to be honourable, they eventually tumbled to the truth that *Tien Wang's* movement, far from being instigated by religious fervour, was in reality designed to ravage the country by a campaign of plunder, pillage, and wholesale murder, so as to wipe out the Manchus once and for all and leave the Dragon Throne vacant for his own occupation. In Gordon's view, the *Taipings* were not a people nobly struggling to be free, but a horde of ruthless marauders. It is known that they habitually crucified their prisoners, while as to the suggestion that they were " the agents of Christianity," a missionary who visited *Tien Wang's* headquarters at Nankin in 1860 declared " he could find nothing of Christianity but its name falsely applied to a system of revolting idolatry."

It was consequently decided to move General Staveley's force from Tientsin to Shanghai, and to co-operate with the Chinese Imperial troops against the rebels so long as they threatened the international settlement. In the operations that followed, Gordon played a most conspicuous part, his daring work in sketching the fortifications of Sebastopol, and gaining information as to their construction, being repeated time and time again in preparation for attacks on the walled and moated towns that abounded in the delta of the Yang Tse Kiang. Alluding to Gordon in his despatches, General Staveley wrote—" Captain Gordon was of the greatest use to me when the task of clearing the rebels from out of the country within a radius of thirty miles from Shanghai had to be undertaken. He reconnoitred the enemy's defences, and arranged for the ladder parties to cross the moats, and for the escalading of the works; for we had to attack and carry by storm several towns fortified with high walls and deep wet ditches. He was, however, at the same time a source of much anxiety to me from the daring manner he approached the enemy's works to acquire information."

Now, the rebel leader, *Tien Wang*, had given an undertaking that his followers would not approach within a radius of thirty miles of Shanghai—an undertaking he might have been expected to break, and in fact did break, at the earliest opportunity. To drive the *Taipings* back beyond this thirty mile limit was the purpose behind General Staveley's move from Tientsin to Shanghai, his force being supported by a French contingent under Admiral Protet, and combining with Chinese Imperial troops and with the Ever Victorious Army.

The task of clearing the rebels from this large area of the Kiang Su and Chi Kiang provinces was no light one, for, setting apart the undeniable fighting qualities of the *Taipings*, the intersection of the terrain by innumerable rivers, streams, creeks, and canals could hardly have been less inviting for the conduct of offensive operations. Furthermore, the country was bespattered with fortified, walled cities, each of which had to be carried by assault in the course of an army's advance. Yet, despite stout opposition and heavy losses, including the French commander, killed in the assault on Nanjao, the job was soon done and *Tien Wang's* band of brigands compelled to evacuate the forbidden zone.

This object successfully accomplished, the conflict resumed the character of a purely domestic affair, in which the intervention of foreign troops could no longer be justified. Consequently, both British and French contingents ceased to take part in operations against the rebels.

Of Gordon's services in General Staveley's campaign, Sir William Butler, distinguished as a soldier, a historian, and the husband of a famous painter of military pictures, notably *Scotland For Ever* and *The Roll Call*, wrote—" In all these operations Gordon had taken a prominent part as the senior engineer officer with the English contingent, sometimes pushing on to reconnoitre a city wall to the very edge of the moat which ran in front of it, often placing guns in an advanced position, laying boats to bridge some creek for the storming parties to reach the foot of the breach, and always sketching and surveying the tangled web of canal and water-course, which at first sight seemed to render the theatre of operations a most difficult field of warfare. . . ."

But, although British troops were no longer employed in the field, Gordon at once set about a careful survey of the territory over which they had recently operated. In a letter written when his task had been completed, he said—" I have been now in every town and village in the thirty miles' radius. The country is the same everywhere—a dead flat, with innumerable creeks and bad pathways. The people have now settled down quiet again, and I do not anticipate the rebels will ever come back. They are rapidly on the decline, and two years ought to bring about the utter suppression of the revolt."

In mid-February, 1863, the Ever Victorious Army of some six hundred men with twenty-two guns and mortars, under the command of Captain Holland, a British officer seconded from the Marines, acting in co-operation with an Imperialist force ten thousand strong, suffered a severe defeat at the fortified town of Taitsan, lying about fifty miles north-west of Shanghai. The heavy losses sustained in this major disaster were soon afterwards augmented in an attack on Shaonshing, another city whose defences proved too strong for the ill-disciplined, if valorous, legion. These serious reverses, followed, as might be expected in a motley commando lacking the strict discipline of fully trained troops, by ominous signs of discontent verging on mutiny, led to an urgent request by the Chinese Government for the services of a British officer capable of reorganising the force and converting it from an undisciplined rabble into an efficient body of men, and of undertaking, in conjunction with Chinese Government troops, the task of suppressing the *Taiping* insurrection.

The choice fell on Gordon, who unhesitatingly accepted the appointment. But there followed an unconscionable delay, which must surely have exasperated the Chinese. This was due to a typical instance of the evils of red tape, for not a thing could be done until authority for Gordon's appointment had been given by the great men thousands of miles away in London; and this despite the fact that a seconded British officer, Captain Holland, was even then in command of the Shanghai force. Could anything have been more ludicrous? But there was also a serious aspect to this wholly unnecessary delay, for the longer the rebellion continued the more pronounced became the distress and desolation of the luckless Chinese peasants, who had reached a state bordering on famine owing to the devastation wrought by the *Taipings*.

Referring in a letter to the plight of the people, Gordon wrote—" The people on the confines are suffering greatly and are in fact dying of starvation. It is most sad this state of affairs, and our Government really ought to put the rebellion down. Words could not depict the horrors these people suffer from the rebels, or describe the utter desert they have made of this rich province (presumably the provinces of Kiang Su and Chi Kiang to the westward of Shanghai). It is all very well to talk of non-intervention, and I am not particularly sensitive, nor are our soldiers generally so, but certainly we are all impressed with the utter misery and wretchedness of these poor people. . . . The hardest heart would have been touched at the utter misery of these poor harmless people, for whatever may be said of their rulers, no one can deny but that the Chinese peasantry are the most obedient, quiet, and industrious people in the world."

Yet, because of allegiance to this accursed official etiquette, one British officer could not be replaced by another without approval from the other side of the world, and, in consequence, further steps for suppressing the rebellion and alleviating the terrible sufferings of the Chinese people had to be delayed until the cumbersome, slow-moving machinery of "the normal channels" had wound up a sufficiently satisfying amount of red tape. Thus, it was not until the end of March, 1863, that Gordon received authority to assume command of the Ever Victorious Army, whose headquarters were then at Sung Kiang, some thirty miles inland from Shanghai.

CHAPTER V

Gordon to the Rescue

WHEN called on to undertake one of the toughest jobs of his remarkable career, Gordon had only just passed his thirtieth birthday, and had reached the rank of major by brevet awarded for his services under General Staveley. Thus far, though his work both in peace and war had borne the hall mark of efficiency, the opportunities that came his way had not provided sufficient scope for the full employment of his exceptional gifts. But now, this turn of fortune's wheel afforded him a real chance of revealing his genius for leadership that was destined to lift him out of the ruck, to raise him in public esteem far above his contemporaries, to make his name immortal.

On the day before assuming his command, Gordon wrote to his mother with characteristic feeling—" I am afraid you will be much vexed at my having taken the command of the Sung Kiang force, and that I am now a mandarin. I have taken the step on consideration. I think that anyone who contributes to putting down this rebellion fulfils a humane task, and I also think tends a great deal to open China to civilisation. I will not act rashly, and I trust to be able soon to return to England; at the same time, I will remember your and my father's wishes, and endeavour to remain as short a time as possible. I can say that, if I had not accepted the command, I believe the force would have been broken up and the rebellion gone on in its misery for years. I trust this will not now be the case, and that I may soon be able to comfort you on this subject. You must not fret on this matter. I think I am doing a good service. . . . I keep your likeness before me, and can assure you and my father that I will not be rash, and that as soon as I can conveniently, and with due regard to the object I have in view, I will return home."

48

GENERAL GORDON
DRESSED AS A CHINESE MANDARIN
FROM THE PICTURE IN THE
ROYAL ENGINEERS MESS,
CHATHAM

*(Reproduced by permission of the Commandant, School of Military
Engineering, Chatham, from a print kindly lent by Messrs. Gale
& Polden)*

Besides being endowed with the status of a mandarin — a unique distinction for a foreigner—Gordon was given the rank of general by the Chinese Government. In support therefore of his own strong, vigorous, masterful personality, he was able to bring to his new position high dignity both civil and military that would greatly strengthen his authority over the ill-disciplined, even rebellious, force he was about to command. In thus elevating Gordon to high rank, the Chinese displayed a wisdom for which they have always been celebrated. With the keen, far-seeing perception of their race, they realised that, in undertaking his onerous task, Gordon would benefit from the support and authority afforded him by impressive titles, and that, while as a mandarin he would be respected by his Chinese subordinates, as a general he would be in a better position to control the more unruly elements among the foreigners.

It was at this stage of his career that Gordon came in contact with Li Hung Chang, then a general in the Chinese army, but destined to become famous as a statesman and the strong man of China. Friendly relations which, with one memorable exception, were maintained for many years, became established between them, and when Gordon declared that in eighteen months' time the rebellion would be finally crushed, Li Hung Chang must indeed have felt that something out of the ordinary in western soldiers had been sent to his country's aid. Hitherto, his opinion of foreigners had been formed mainly on his association with soldiers of fortune like the American Burgevine, who had succeeded to the command of the Ever Victorious Army on the death of Ward, and who, after insulting a mandarin and violently assaulting a wealthy Chinese merchant, had been dismissed from the army.

Owing to the illicit trade in opium, the coasts of China in those days were littered with the riff-raff of other countries, who saw in the prohibition of the drug a source of endless easy money; just as in more recent years the liquor prohibition laws in America brought about the bootlegging campaign and attracted to the shores of the United States countless adventurers of the type that will do anything and risk everything for money. Owing to his contact with so many characters such as these, Li Hung Chang had, not unnaturally, become suspicious and sceptical of foreigners in general. But in Gordon, he quickly perceived a very different sample of western humanity—one that had no axe to grind, no thought of self, no aim or desire other than to carry out the duties required of him to the best of his ability.

After their first meeting, Li Hung Chang recorded in his diary —" It is a direct blessing from Heaven the coming of this British Gordon. . . . He is superior in manner and bearing to any of the foreigners whom I have come into contact with, and does not show outwardly that conceit which makes most of them repugnant in my sight."

Now, let us first consider the magnitude of the task that Gordon had promised to accomplish in a year and a half. The territory occupied by the *Taipings,* and populated by twenty million souls, comprised some fourteen thousand square miles of lowland in the once prosperous delta of the Yang Tse Kiang river, intersected by a bewildering network of waterways and characterised by numerous walled cities surrounded by moats. The rebels' centre was at Soo Chow, a large city on the Grand Canal fifty miles to the north-westward of Gordon's headquarters at Sung Kiang. From this central position they were able to control the labyrinth of canals so advantageous for purposes of transport, so beneficial to irrigation, so invaluable as a means of defence. Moreover, the *Taipings* were fortunate in being led by a most able commander who, throughout the greater part of the rebellion, had occupied the position of *Tien Wang's* commander-in-chief. This was Chung Wang, about the only one of the " Celestial King's " followers he could thoroughly rely on. In his conduct of operations he displayed vigour, ingenuity, and resource, enjoying many notable successes, and, year after year, defying all efforts to subdue his host of plundering, murdering ruffians.

This, then, was the problem Gordon had undertaken to solve, and, in order to fulfil his pledge to the letter, he would have to accomplish within the short space of eighteen months, with such material as he could muster, a feat that all the resources of the Emperor had failed to achieve in fourteen years.

It was on March 24th, 1863, that belated approval of Gordon's appointment reached Shanghai, and on the following day he rode over to Sung Kiang, where he assumed command of the ragged, depleted Ever Victorious Army numbering some three thousand of all ranks. He found this strange company of mixed nationality in a state verging on mutiny. There were elements among them clamouring for reinstatement of the discredited Burgevine who, to give him his due, had been noted for his fair distribution of prize money, which was all that mattered to the bulk of this unkempt, dispirited commando.

In less than twenty-four hours from his arrival, however, Gordon had already begun to gain their confidence. Addressing them on parade, he allayed their fears that dismissals would follow his appointment to the command, and assured them he would look after their welfare provided they conducted themselves satisfactorily. Such was the effect of his masterful personality on the wretchedly disreputable, dangerously recalcitrant soldiers of fortune arrayed before him, that almost miraculously they accepted him as their leader without demur.

In the days that followed, Gordon set about the job of converting an undisciplined mob into some semblance of an organised force, fit to start on the immense undertaking that lay before them. But his object was not attained without many an awkward situation. Alone, he would courageously face his mutinous soldiers, in a manner strongly reminiscent of Napoleon on his journey from the south coast of France during the *Hundred Days,* and, like the great little Corsican, would bend them to his will by sheer force of character. Naturally, in dealing with men at once so unreliable and so apt, on the smallest provocation, to kick over the traces, only by enforcing the strictest discipline could he hope to lick them into shape and evolve something like order from the state of chaos that existed. Even the most extreme measures were at times necessary. Gradually, however, his remarkable gifts as a leader of men, an organiser, and a subduer of turbulent people came to his aid and made themselves felt, so much so that in course of time he was able to write to a soldier friend—" I hope you do not think that I have a magnificent army. You never did see such a rabble as it was; and although I think I have improved it, it is still sadly wanting. Now both officers and men, although ragged and perhaps slightly disreputable, are in capital order and well disposed."

But, before reorganisation could be seriously undertaken, a preliminary task demanded Gordon's immediate attention. For some considerable time the *Taiping*s had been laying seige to the town of Chanzu, whose garrison of Imperial Chinese troops was believed to be on the point of surrendering. Accordingly, on March 31st, less than a week after assuming command, Gordon set out by river with a force of twelve hundred men, four 12-pounders, and one 32-pounder for the ruined city of Fushan, about fifty miles to the north of Sung Kiang. On April 4th, after being joined by formations of the Imperial forces, the Ever Victorious Army, in its first action under Gordon's command, drove the rebels from their stockades near Fushan, and, continuing the advance, occupied the besieged Chanzu, ten miles to the north-west, from which the enemy fled.

The Chinese generalissimo, Li Hung Chang, who, as we have seen, had already formed a high opinion of Gordon, was tremendously enthusiastic about this strikingly successful prelude to the campaign, recording in his diary—" If there is anything I admire nearly as much as the superb scholarship of Tseng Kuo Fan it is the military qualities of this fine officer. He is a glorious fellow! "

Supported by the ready help of Li Hung Chang, Gordon, now back at Sung Kiang, busied himself with the reorganisation of his force, whose strength was brought up to four thousand men including the personnel of four siege and two field batteries. Whereas, since the death of Ward, their original commander, the Ever Victorious Army had been obliged to subsist on prize money and loot owing to the Chinese Government declining to supply Burgevine with funds from which to pay his men, a Chinese paymaster was now appointed by Li Hung Chang for the specific purpose of making regular payments to Gordon's command, which, incidentally cost the Chinese Government something like twenty thousand pounds a month. Strong disciplinary measures were introduced, notably the death penalty for looting, while the practice of distributing rewards for successful operations was discontinued. As a recompense for this loss of material benefit, Gordon, exercising a wise discretion, raised the pay of his army.

In preparation for his forthcoming campaign, he displayed the boundless energy for which he had already become celebrated. He drilled and trained his men for the task before them with relentless vigour, and, if at times they showed signs of unrest, Gordon's dynamic personality soon reduced even the most inveterate " barrack room lawyer " to a state of obedient docility. As time went on, he became the idol of his followers and a terror to his enemies, who saw in him something more than human with supernatural powers. If severe in the interests of discipline, Gordon was, above all, just, and it was perhaps this, more than anything else, that enabled him to do what others had signally failed to do, namely to control this band of hot-headed, reckless adventurers.

Realising, as all good soldiers do, that appearance counts for a good deal towards the maintenance of discipline and the training of an army, Gordon provided his troops with uniform in place of the rags they had become accustomed to, thus transforming them from a disreputable rabble into an organised, presentable body of men. He replaced the undesirable type of officer on his staff by others seconded from British regiments in Shanghai: he collected a number of steamboats and Chinese gunboats for use on the many waterways intersecting the country: he instructed and trained his men assiduously in the methods of attacking fortified cities, this being the nature of the task confronting them: and procured pontoons for bridging the countless creeks that formed a positive network over the area of forthcoming operations.

Towards the end of April, Gordon was in a position to take the field, and had made up his miod as to the best way of gaining a strategic advantage. His primary objective was to cut the *Taipings'* communications so as to prevent the flow of supplies both from the coast and from the Yang Tse Kiang, and then to close in on the rebel headquarters at Soo Chow, reducing the walled cities one by one as he advanced. In working out the problem of overcoming these formidable obstacles in his path, Gordon revealed his remarkable ingenuity as a commander in war, for he formulated a plan whereby the labyrinth of streams and canals, that seemed so unmistakably favourable for purposes of defence, could be turned to his own advantage by utilising them for the movement of troops and guns to the rear of positions or to weak points in the defences. The rebels still had access to one or two places on the coast, as well as to the Yang Tse; but, once these sources of supply were denied to them, their position would become precarious.

Gordon's original intention had been first to attack Quinsan, a strongly fortified city on the main canal, about twenty-five miles south-east of Soo Chow; but, on April 27th, news reached him of a serious disaster suffered by Imperial troops at Taitsan, due to a typical instance of *Taiping* treachery, prompting him to turn his attention in that direction as a preliminary measure. According to reports, the rebel commander of the garrison at Taitsan had agreed to surrender the town, and then opened one of the gates so as to admit the Government troops. But, no sooner had some fifteen hundred of them entered the city, all unsuspicious of treachery, than they were fallen upon by the unscrupulous *Taipings* and practically annihilated.

Foreseeing the moral effect of this success on the rebels, following upon the severe defeat inflicted on Captain Holland's force three months earlier by the same garrison, Gordon at once decided that, before pursuing his original plan, the growing confidence of the Taitsan defenders, believed to number ten thousand men, must be destroyed, and their treachery punished, by the immediate elimination of the city as a rebel stronghold. Accordingly, with the

53

least possible delay, he started for Taitsan at the head of three thousand men of all arms, and, after a march of some thirty miles to the north-westward, arrived before the city walls where a force of Imperial soldiers was standing by.

A great believer in the value of personal reconnaissance, Gordon quickly set about finding a favourable point for launching his attack. Rejecting the south gate that had proved so disastrous to Captain Holland, he made his way round to the west side of the town. There, a couple of enemy stockades were taken by assault, and, having selected a likely part of the wall, Gordon brought up his artillery to a position about six hundred yards distant. Meanwhile, part of his flotilla of river boats had arrived on the scene to assist in the operations. Next morning, May 1st, after one regiment had been posted at the north gate to cut off fugitives, the guns opened fire on the city wall, constructed, as in all these Chinese towns, of rubble faced on both sides with brick. The bursting shells, including those fired by the Chinese gunboats on the canal, soon took effect, tons of loose rubble gushing out through holes in the brickwork and cascading down to form a means of ascending to the breach when sufficiently widened by the bombardment. A plentiful supply of ammunition was provided by the river craft, the artillery keeping up a continuous cannonade till the early afternoon, by which time the guns had been advanced to a position no more than a hundred yards from the wall, the gunners being protected by mantlets of wood and iron.

At this point, the river craft moved up forming a bridge over the moat and Gordon ordered the assault, his eager troops swarming across the boats under a murderous fire from the ramparts. Gallantly led by a British officer called Bannon, they reached the pile of rubble that had been blasted from the wall and began to scramble up towards the breach. In the hard fighting that ensued, heavy casualties, including the loss of their leader, eventually compelled the attackers to retire across the moat, giving the rebels an initial success.

Meanwhile, with keen, appraising eye, Gordon had been watching every twist and turn of the fight, and now, undismayed by the repulse of his first attack, he promptly prepared for a second. Fresh troops were assembled and the guns resumed their bombardment. The success of this second attempt was due to Gordon's consummate generalship. As the fight raged fiercely in the breach, the *Taipings* resisting with a tenacity born of success and fortune favouring now one side now the other with victory hanging in the balance, he acted in the manner of a born commander gifted with the power of discerning where and when to strike so as to effectively surprise and disconcert the enemy. Detaching part of his force to a point a little southward of the breach, where he had espied a weakness in the defence, he ordered them to scale the wall. This unexpected diversion, combined with much havoc caused by the howitzers throwing shells *over* the walls among the masses of rebels concentrated immediately behind them, had the effect of breaking down resistance, leaving the way open for Gordon's triumphant entry into the city.

This may be cited as the first revelation of his remarkable flair for leadership. Hitherto, although his services had been highly distinguished both in the Crimea and in China, he had held no independent command, and, consequently, there had been no scope for the display of his exceptional qualities. But now, at the very outset of his experience as a general in the field, he astonished all beholders by an almost uncanny intuition as to the right course to pursue, his superb composure in action, his utter fearlessness, and his unhesitant decisions. It proved, however, but a foretaste of what was to come—a preliminary canter, as it were, before the start of the great event.

Yet, Gordon had not gained his brilliant victory without suffering serious losses. Storming these high-walled, moated cities, defended by a far from insignificant enemy, could not be undertaken without the certainty of heavy casualties, and, while the *Taipings* received salutary punishment in killed and wounded, and in the dispersal of the garrison, the effective strength of the Ever Victorious Army was reduced by not less than two hundred and fifty of all ranks.

Though usually down on the evil-doer like a ton of bricks, Gordon could find it in him to have compassion even for the most barefaced ruffian. Among the rebels in the breach at Taitsan were two deserters from the 31st Regiment of British infantry. One was killed, the other wounded and taken prisoner. On being brought before the commander, the prisoner begged for his life. " Take him down to the river and shoot him," said Gordon, paying no attention to the wretched man's plea. He then gave orders—not in the prisoner's hearing—that he was to be put in a boat, given medical attention, and sent to Shanghai—compassionate treatment that his conduct would hardly seem to have deserved.

Now, it had been Gordon's intention to push straight on to Quinsan, ten miles to the south-west of Taitsan. But his still only partially disciplined army clamoured for a return to Sung Kiang before embarking on further operations. This had been the practice prior to Gordon assuming command, and was popular with the rank and file since it afforded them an opportunity ot disposing of their plunder and spending their prize money after each successful engagement. That such an outrageous situation could have arisen gives some idea of the tough, unruly characters Gordon had to deal with. But, on this occasion, there were other considerations such as the need for reorganising the force, ammunition supply, and so on, that influenced him in arriving at his decision to return to Sung Kiang. Moreover, if Gordon considered it right to let his men have their way in this particular instance, we may take it that it was so, for certain it is that no man on earth has ever been endowed with more conspicuous ability to bring the misguided to their senses, or reduce the turbulent to docility than this master of talents, who relied with implicit faith on the power of the Almighty to guide his actions. Thus it came about that the Ever Victorious Army, exhilarated by their signal defeat of the Taitsan rebels, returned to Sung Kiang where another month went by in reorganisation and training. Casualties were easily replaced by captured *Taipings*, who, once they were taken prisoners, seemed only too ready to fight against their former comrades, and in many cases proved more reliable soldiers than Gordon's own men. It was significant, for instance, that his personal bodyguard numbered in its ranks a preponderance of ex-*Taipings*!

During this month of preparation for the campaign, Gordon had to deal with a case of serious disorder within his own command . Fortunately, his authority was supreme. He was hampered by no war office red tape. He could take such action as he thought right without reference to anyone and without fear of crippling interference. He could even inflict the death penalty if necessary, and had no hesitation in so doing when the need arose. He enjoyed, moreover, the firm support of the Chinese authorities, whose confidence he had gained not only by his initial manifestation of brilliant leadership, but also by the evidence already vouchsafed of his strong character, honesty of purpose, and, in contrast to the great majority of foreigners in China, complete indifference to his own advancement either in position or wealth. And so, when faced with difficult situations as he so often was, he enjoyed the great advantage of absolute freedom to act as he thought best on his own responsibility and initiative.

Thus, on finding himself confronted with insubordinate commanding officers who, as majors, grumbled because the commissariat officer had been given the rank of lieutenant colonel, and demanded that they should be promoted to similar rank, he acted with prompt, energetic, unfettered decisiveness. His emphatic refusal to listen to their submission resulted in the officers' resignation which Gordon promptly accepted, glad no doubt of this opportunity to get rid of some especially undesirable characters. Eventually, two of the commanding officers were reinstated, and, although the affair had some repercussion in the ranks, Gordon's judicious blending of severity with discrimination soon brought both officers and men to heel, so that in the end his army was probably the better for what, at one time, had all the portents of an ugly situation.

CHAPTER VI

The Taking of Quinsan

BY the last week of May, Gordon was ready to move, and, on the 27th, he reached the neighbourhood of Quinsan, a formidable obstacle to his advance, but, once in his possession, a stronghold that would prove of untold value to his subsequent operations, seeing that, from the eminence of a high hill, round which the city walls, five miles in circumference, had been built, close observation could be kept on the surrounding waterways and on the only road between Quinsan and Soo Chow.

Holding stockades before the city's eastern walls were troops of the Chinese Imperial army under the command of General Ching, opposed at a distance of only eight hundred yards by stockades held by *Taipings* drawn from the garrison. In defying all efforts of the enemy to dislodge him from his positions, General Ching had been admirably supported by the armoured steamer *Hyson,* mounting a 32-pounder and commanded by a most capable and gallant officer in Captain Davidson, whose splendid services proved invaluable throughout the campaign.

On the early morning of May 28th, Gordon attacked the rebel position with two regiments of infantry supported by field artillery. Turning the right flank of the enemy's right stockade, the attackers forced them to evacuate their position and retire within the city walls.

Now, Gordon had no illusions as to the difficulties of storming a fortified city standing on the slopes of a hill surrounded by walls from fourteen to twenty feet high and a moat forty yards wide. Furthermore, the garrison of about ten thousand desperate characters was commanded by *Tien Wang's* most able commander, Chung

Wang, of whom Gordon subsequently wrote—" He was the bravest, most talented, and enterprising leader the rebels had. He had been in more engagements than any other rebel leader, and could always be distinguished. His presence with the *Taipings* was equal to a reinforcement of 5000 men, and was always felt by the superior way in which the rebels resisted."

In addition to its other strategical advantages, Quinsan stood amongst an entanglement of waterways including the main canal which afforded direct communication with the *Taipings'* headquarters at Soo Chow, twenty miles to the westward, and provided the city with its chief supply route. All these problems had been carefully considered by Gordon, for no one knew better than he did the need for studying every detail of a position to be attacked, and trying to discern its weakest point where the deadly element of surprise might be introduced. Urged by the impetuous General Ching to follow up his capture of the stockades by an immediate attack on the eastern gate of the city, Gordon felt that such action would be doomed to costly failure, and, to the annoyance of his ally, he decided to make a personal reconnaissance of the south and west sides before finally formulating his plan of attack.

Accordingly, on the following day, he carried out his preconceived idea of turning the numerous canals, creeks, and streams to his own advantage by using them for the purpose of moving round by a circuitous route to the rear of enemy positions. Taking with him the Chinese generalissimo, Li Hung Chang, and the disgruntled General Ching, Gordon set out in the *Hyson* to reconnoitre Quinsan's southern and western approaches, steaming away out of sight of the city before turning down one of the many intersecting creeks towards the south. Making a wide detour, the *Hyson* steamed for three hours, eventually reaching a point on the west side of the city near the main canal and close to the village of Chunye, which lay about eight miles from Quinsan and twelve from Soo Chow.

Having carefully surveyed the western approaches, Gordon had no hesitation in deciding to cut the *Taipings'* main line of communication, that is to say the canal between Quinsan and Soo Chow, and the road running along its northern bank, and attack the city from that side. " General Ching," he wrote, " was as sulky as a bear when he was informed that I thought it advisable to attack on this side of the city." But, despite the attitude of this self-opinionated individual, in whom the qualities of envy and jealousy—marked characteristics of the Chinese race—were conspicuous, Gordon, on returning to his camp, proceeded with his preparations for the morrow.

At daybreak on May 30th, a strange, yet picturesque, flotilla moved silently along the waterways to the east of Quinsan, taking at first an easterly direction so as to avoid observation from the city's high ground, then veering southward, and finally circling the position in a wide sweep to the west. The route was in fact precisely the same as Gordon had followed in his reconnaissance of the previous day. In the centre of this curious fleet steamed the *Hyson,* carrying the originator of this bold, ingenious scheme—a master of the science of strategy. In all there were some eighty vessels, most of them under sail and, after the manner of the Chinese, bedecked with flags of many colours. They certainly presented an imposing spectacle, and had the rebels been able to see them from their citadel, great would have been the consternation and commotion in this city of vital importance to the *Taiping* cause. They had already received more than one taste of Gordon's powers, so that the sight of this mysterious manœuvre would no doubt have filled them wth apprehension. But, as yet, they were spared this discomfort. The shock was to come a little later, for the essence of Gordon's plan was surprise, his aim being to reach the main canal in the rear of Quinsan before the rebels could become aware of his intention.

On this venturesome expedition he took with him one regiment of infantry and one field battery of the Ever Victorious Army, besides a considerable force of Imperial troops. In addition, a number of Chinese gunboats had been sent on ahead to await arrival of the main body. It was midday before Gordon reached the line of stakes guarding the junction with the main canal. These were promptly pulled up by the gunboat crews, and, when the infantry had landed, the whole force advanced towards the intersection which was defended by no more than two weak stockades. Flabbergasted no doubt by this sudden, utterly unexpected appearance of Gordon's expedition, the *Taipings* offered little resistance, taking to their heels and bolting in disorder, some towards Quinsan, others in the direction of Soo Chow. Jostling each other as, panic stricken, they fled by the only available road, many of them fell headlong, either into the canal on one side, or the lakes on the other, and were drowned.

Turning into the main canal, the *Hyson* pursued the rebels towards Soo Chow, her 32-pounder adding to the havoc and indescribable confusion. There was, moreover, a pronounced readiness on the part of the dispirited *Taipings* to surrender, their abject demoralisation being due to the complete surprise sprung on them by Gordon's ingenuity. Hitherto, these same men had fought stubbornly in defence of Quinsan, but then there had been no Gordon to outwit them with the superlative skill of a born commander. Had the fugitives made any attempt to re-form and stand their ground, things might have gone badly with the small steamer, pushing on alone to within half a mile of the main rebel stronghold, for not only were there considerable numbers of the enemy in front, but many more coming along behind who would be met on the return journey. One of these bands did make some show of resistance, peppering the *Hyson* with rifle fire, but a charge of grape soon put an end to this spasm of liveliness.

Nevertheless, the little steamer's return journey proved distinctly hazardous, seeing that in the dusk, and later the darkness, she constantly came upon large bodies of rebels who, but for their precipitate flight, might well have overwhelmed her. Frequently she scared them off with blasts from her siren, this having the additional effect of unnerving the occupants of boats sailing towards Soo Chow, so that they put hurriedly into the banks and abandoned their craft, any number of which were seen drifting about in all directions.

Here is Gordon's written account of what followed as the Hyson approached the village of Chunye—

" It was now 10.30 p.m. and the night was not very clear. At this moment the most tremendous firing and cheering was heard from Chunye, and hurried our progress to that place. Just before we reached it a gunboat disarranged the rudder, and then we were dodging about from side to side for some ten minutes, the firing and cheering going on as before. At last we got up to the junction of the creek, and steaming through the Imperial, and other boats, we came on the scene of action. The gunboats were drawn up in line, and were firing as fast as they could. The stone fort at the village was sparkling with musketry, and at times astounding yells burst forth from it. The *Hyson* blew her whistle, and was received with deafening cheers from the gunboats, which were on the eve of bolting. She steamed up the creek towards Quinsan, and at the distance of 200 yards we saw a confused mass near a high bridge. It was too dark to distinguish very clearly, but on the steamer blowing the whistle the mass wavered, yelled, and turned back. It was the garrison of Quinsan attempting to escape to Soochow, some seven or eight thousand men.

"Matters were in too critical a state to hesitate, as the mass of the rebels, goaded into desperation, would have swept our small force away. We were therefore forced to fire into them, and pursue them towards Quinsan, firing, however, very rarely, and only when the rebels looked as if they would make a stand. The steamer went up to about a mile from Quinsan, and then returned. Several officers landed and took charge of the prisoners who were extended along the bank, and at 4 a.m., 31st May, everything was quiet. The *Hyson* had fired some eighty or ninety rounds during the day and night; and although humanity might have desired a smaller destruction, it was indispensably necessary to inflict such a blow on the garrison of Soochow as would cause them not to risk another such engagement, and thus enable us to live in peace during the summer—which it indeed did, for the rebels never came on this road again. Their loss must have been from three to four thousand killed, drowned, and prisoners. We took 800, most of whom entered our ranks. They lost all their arms and a very large number of boats. At 5 a.m. on 31st May the troops at Chunye and the *Hyson* moved towards Quinsan, and found the remainder of the force, who had been left at the east gate already in the city. The possession of Quinsan was of immense importance in a strategical point of view."

It seems almost inconceivable that this strongly fortified city, so favourably situated from a defensive point of view, should have fallen mainly through the activities of a small river steamer carrying one 32-pounder and no more than forty men. To be sure, it was the sudden appearance of the flotilla as a whole that had started the *Taipings'* panic, and as everyone knows panic once started is apt to spread like a virulent disease. But, for the utter rout of the rebels, Captain Davidson's gallant little vessel could claim chief credit, seeing that, alone and unaided, she had steamed through the midst of the *Taiping* hordes almost to the very gates of Soo Chow, and by the force of her audacity, inspired and directed by Gordon himself, had completed their discomfiture.

"This singular action," wrote Sir William Butler, "an armed steamer with a crew of some forty men all told against many thousand men, was perhaps the most striking representative feat of Gordon's peculiar genius for war."

Thus did the formidable city of Quinsan, key position in the defence of Soo Chow, fall an easy prey to the remarkable powers of the new commander, whose brilliant leadership had now begun to impress itself upon the world. There seems little doubt that by this time the mere presence of Gordon with the Government forces was sufficient to imbue the rebels with alarm, and that they had come to see in him some kind of superhuman being with the power of sweeping away all opposition to his progress with a wave of the small cane he habitually carried as his sole weapon when leading his troops in action. Like Napoleon, Gordon possessed that rare quality of ability to subdue unruly elements by sheer force of character.

Following his great victory, he now determined to transfer his headquarters from Sung Kiang to Quinsan—a far more central position from which to conduct future operations. Moreover, he was anxious to keep his troops away from their undesirable associations, formed when under the command of Ward and Burgevine. Enraged at this decision, the Ever Victorious Army disgraced itself by resorting to mutiny, in which the non-commissioned officers took a leading part. These links between the commissioned ranks and the men, whose duty it was to maintain discipline and to support their commanding officer, set a shameful example to those under them by delivering a written ultimatum to Gordon demanding with threats the return of the army to Sung Kiang.

On receiving this insolent demand, Gordon immediately ordered a parade of the non-commissioned officers, and, appearing with the document in his hand, enquired as to which of them had written it. As no one came forward, he told them that in default of an admission he would shoot one out of every five. At this there arose a murmur in the ranks; whereupon, picking out one whose protest seemed most impassioned, Gordon promptly seized him with his own hands as a ringleader of the mutiny and ordered his bodyguard to shoot him on the spot. When this had been done, he addressed the non-commissioned officers, telling them that unless within an hour they agreed to obey orders, he would carry out his intention of shooting one in every five of their number. That was enough. Brought to their senses by the overwhelming mastery of Gordon's iron will, they submitted without further trouble, and once more a dangerous situation had been overcome by the fearless determination of this great soldier.

Referring in a despatch to the loss of the man's life, he wrote—
" It saved many others which must have been lost if a stop had

not been put to the independent way of the men." Considerable desertions that followed the shooting proved a blessing in disguise, for they were easily replaced by *Taiping* prisoners, who, in Gordon's words, " are much better men than the old ones."

HIS EXCELLENCY
LI HUNG CHANG

(Hulton Library)

CHAPTER VII

Gordon Fulfils His Pledge

GORDON'S energies, always prodigious, were now directed
to organising his force in preparation for attacking the
main obstacle to ultimate success—the *Taipings'* central
position at Soo Chow. Of this once prosperous city, then
falling rapidly into decay owing to the neglect and depredations of
the rebels, Sir William Butler wrote—" It was at this city of Su
Chow that the Emperor Kanghi, second of the Manchu dynasty,
dismounted from his horse and walked on foot through the streets,
in 1689, in order not to injure the magnificent silks and em-
broidered tapestries which the inhabitants had laid profusely on
the ground along the line of his route. The circuit of its massive
walls measured twelve miles: the form of the city was an oblong
square, six large gates opened landwards, as many more gave
entrance towards the lakes: every street had its corresponding
canal, navigable for large-sized craft, while the freshness of the
great body of water that lay adjacent to the place, the richness of
the land between the lakes, the passage through the city of the
Grand Canal, and the presence of a population skilled by the continuous training of countless generations of the best embroiderers
and workers in silk in the world, made Soo Chow in the old days
a rich emporium of trade and a luxurious centre of pleasure."

It had been Gordon's intention to march on Soo Chow at
once while the *Taipings* were still staggering from the blows inflicted on them at Quinsan. But the Chinese authorities would
not support him, with the result that a great chance of ending the
rebellion there and then was allowed to slip by, and many months
of bitter fighting ensued. Here we find the first signs of differences
between Gordon and the Chinese, for, in addition to their refusal
to support him in immediate operations against Soo Chow, he was

subjected to a good deal of annoyance by the temperamental General Ching, who felt aggrieved at gaining no kudos for the capture of Quinsan.

Then, towards the end of July, 1863, failure by the mandarins to maintain the agreed remittance for the pay of his men so angered Gordon that he promptly sent in his resignation. Fortunately, the united conciliatory efforts of General Brown, the British commander in Shanghai, Dr. (afterwards Sir Halliday) Macartney, who later became celebrated for his diplomatic successes in China, and the Chinese generalissimo, Li Hung Chang, succeeded in averting a catastrophe, peace was restored, the arrears of pay to the Ever Victorious Army were made good, and Gordon was induced to reconsider his decision.

But, if an actual rupture had been avoided, there seems no shadow of doubt that relations between Gordon and the Chinese had become permanently strained. Even his most ardent admirer and steadfast supporter, Li Hung Chang, showed signs of resenting Gordon's downright methods of dealing with the Chinese and his tendency to violent outbursts. " General Gordon," he wrote in his diary, " must control his tongue, even if he lets his mind run loose. . . . Why does he not accord me the honours that are due to me, as head of the military and civil authority in these parts? " Two months later, he recorded—" With his many faults, his pride, his temper, and his never-ending demand for money, Gordon is a noble man, and in spite of all I have said to him or about him, I will ever think most highly of him. . . . He is an honest man but difficult to get on with."

Still, although Gordon continued to enjoy Li Hung Chang's support and esteem, in other respects his relations with the Chinese had deteriorated. Thus was he hampered by difficulties he should not have been required to contend with in addition to the heavy weight of responsibility for suppressing the rebellion. In describing him as " difficult to get on with," Li Hung Chang was not very wide of the mark. But, on the other hand, the mandarins, or Chinese authorities of those days, were anything but easy to deal with, and could often be thoroughly exasperating in their dilatoriness and vacillation.

Nor was this all that Gordon found trying on resuming operations against the *Taipings*, for who should reappear and attempt to oust him from his command but the American adventurer, Burgevine, armed with some trumped up authority or other from Pekin. This, however, was ignored by the powers in Shanghai,

who, moreover, refused to offer Burgevine any further employment
in the Government forces. Incensed by their opposition, Burgevine
seized a steamer and, with a certain number of followers, including
no doubt some of those dismissed by Gordon from the Ever Victorious Army, made for Soo Chow to join the rebels. Received in
the *Taiping* camp, he did his utmost to frustrate Gordon's plans
for taking the all important city and finally crushing the rebellion.
But, if troublesome, his efforts proved unavailing.

Gordon did not underestimate the severity of the task before
him. Hemmed in by extensive lakes and surrounded by high
walls twelve miles in circumference, Soo Chow presented a most
intricate problem requiring all his exceptional powers to solve. To
take the city by assault would be both difficult and costly. He
therefore decided to concentrate on cutting off supplies to the
garrison by occupying the nearest towns to the north and south,
and blockading the west side with the *Hyson* supported by Chinese
gunboats. By thus depriving the rebels, many thousands in
number, of necessities from without, coupled with the devastation
wrought by the *Taipings* within, he hoped to starve them into
submission and force them to surrender the town.

With this scheme in mind, he returned to Quinsan from
Shanghai, where he had spent a few days discussing the question
of his resignation and the failure of the Chinese to keep up their
payments to his army. Resuming command, he found that during
his brief absence the *Taipings* had become imbued with renewed
vigour. Such was the dominating influence of his presence that
as soon as his back was turned the rebels took heart and fought as
they had never done before. Indeed, they were within an ace of
retaking certain positions recently ocupied by Gordon, when his
providential return to the field once more cast a spell over their
activities and deprived them of much of their newly awakened
confidence.

Nevertheless, Gordon's sensitive touch on the pulse of their
condition warned him that he might expect tougher opposition
than before, especially now that a number of foreign soldiers of
fortune had followed the renegade Burgevine into their service.
Of the soldierly qualities of this arch traitor, however, Gordon
appears to have formed a poor opinion, for, in a subsequent
despatch, he wrote—"There is no knowing what an immense
amount of damage might have been done if the rebels had had a
more energetic man than Burgevine." These foreigners were employed by the *Taipings* to train their Chinese troops as well as to

lead them in action, and, ruffians though they were, the knowledge and experience gained by them in many a doubtful cause made no inconsiderable contribution to the competence of the rebel forces.

But Gordon's inexorable progress continued with only an occasional check, notably in a night attack on the east gate stockades, which was repulsed with the loss of a hundred and sixty-five officers and men killed, wounded or missing. A serious reverse to be sure, but it was the first Gordon had suffered after a succession of thirteen victories, so that there arose no cause for anxiety or despondency among his troops, who soon afterwards succeeded in taking the stockades, the commander, himself, with only a few men, capturing three of them together with a stone fort.

Wherever danger threatened there was he to be found, cane in hand, a tower of strength and encouragement to those around him. No one knew better than he did the immense value of personal example, especially in times of stress. Consequently, when news reached him of a critical situation, off he would go, himself, at the head of a body of reinforcements and, on arrival at the scene, his mere presence would turn the fortunes of the day in his favour— a presence that inspired his own men to deeds of prodigious valour, while filling the hearts of his enemies with dismay.

Having taken and occupied the stockaded city of Woo Kiang to the south of Soo Chow, thus effectively cutting off supplies from that direction, Gordon worked round to the northward until joining forces with the Imperial troops. This virtually completed the city's investment described by Gordon in these words—" We held the Taiho Lake with the steamers the *Hyson,* the *Tsatlee,* the *Firefly,* and 200 men (Imperialists) which cruised off Moodow, and prevented supplies coming to Soochow up the creek which leads from that village to the small West Gate of Soochow, and where they had many actions with the rebel gunboats. The next great water outlet was closed to the rebels by our possession with 1000 men (Imperialists). Off the South Gate the next main water and road communication to the south was closed to them by our occupation by 1500 men (Imperialists) of the Patachiaou stockades on the Grand Canal, south of the south-east angle of Soo Chow. The next, which led from the east gate of Soochow to Quinsan, was closed by Ching's force of 3000 to 4000 men, nearly two miles from the gate. These men were well posted in strong and well-constructed stockades. The next position held was Lecku, where I had one regiment, and at Wanti there was another regiment."

The fate of Soo Chow, once the most beautiful of Chinese cities, was sealed. In the words of an ancient proverb—" If Paradise is in heaven there is Soo Chow on earth." To give the reader some idea of this city, famed for its gorgeous silks and embroideries, here is the brief description of an eye-witness at the time of the siege:—" Further than the eye could penetrate in the misty morning stretched the grizzled walls of Soo Chow, a city celebrated for ages in the history of China for its size, population, wealth, and luxury, but now stripped of its magnificence and held by an army of *Taiping* banditti against the Imperial forces. To the right and left, mile after mile, rose the line of lofty wall and grey turret, while above all appeared not only the graceful pagodas, which have been for ages the boast of Soo Chow, and the dense foliage of secular trees—the invariable glory of Chinese cities—but also the shimmering roofs of newly decorated palaces confidently occupied by the vain-glorious leaders of the rebellion. The proximity of the rebel line became apparent with surprising suddenness for, following their usual custom, they greeted the rising sun with a simultaneous display of gaudy banners above the line of their entrenchments. The mud walls they had thrown up in advance, scarcely distinguishable before, were now marked out by thousands of flags of every colour from black to crimson, whilst behind them rose the jangling roll of gongs and the murmurs of an invisible multitude."

It was in October, 1863, that Soo Chow's isolation became absolute, and, by the end of that month, like rats leaving a doomed ship, the foreigners had deserted the *Taiping* cause, abandoning their Chinese comrades to their fate. At about the same time, moreover, the rebel leaders, realising the hopelessness of their plight, began to negotiate with Gordon and the Chinese commanders. Finally, in December, they agreed to surrender the city provided they, the leaders, were assured that their lives would be spared.

Guarantees for the safety of the leaders were duly given, supported by Gordon's pledge that his own presence with the Chinese troops could be taken as an earnest of good faith. But there followed a piece of diabolical treachery to which it would be hard to find a parallel, and which must always cast an infamous shadow on the history of the rebellion's suppression.

Now, on the day before Soo Chow was surrendered, the rebel leaders met at a banquet, and there they murdered the only one of their number who refused to capitulate. Next day, with the solemn promise of the Chinese, backed by Gordon, that their lives would be spared, they opened the gates of the city and rode out unarmed to the camp of Li Hung Chang, who had arrived on the scene to witness the surrender. The circumstances of this perfidious deed are far from clear; but the indisputable fact remains that on the river bank, beside the Chinese generalissimo's camp, the rebel leaders of Soo Chow, who had unwisely put their trust in fellow-countrymen, notorious through the ages for treachery, were mercilessly put to death. Gordon, himself, viewed their nine decapitated bodies laid out on the bank, and his fury knew no bounds, for had he not given the *Taiping* leaders his personal guarantee that the promises of the Chinese authorities would be kept?

His predicament was anything but enviable, nor could he help feeling that his honour was involved. Yet, although he had given his word as an assurance of good faith, he could hardly have been held responsible for the deeds of his ruthless associates, committed without his knowledge. Had the *Taiping* chiefs surrendered to him instead of to their own countrymen, whose inherent duplicity they would have been well advised to bear in mind, this disgraceful happening would not have blackened the record of those stirring times, nor would Gordon have found himself in a most invidious position.

Having sent his army back to Quinsan so as to avoid looting, he himself followed in a towering rage that nothing short of warlike reprisals seemed likely to assuage. Indeed, after sending a letter, couched in the strongest terms to Li Hung Chang, complaining bitterly of his treachery, calling upon him to resign from the governorship of Kiang Su Province, and threatening to attack him, Gordon did actually set out in the *Hyson* along the main canal towards Soo Chow with a flotilla carrying troops, intending to punish the Chinese for their shameful conduct. Fortunately, however, wiser counsels prevailed, and, by the time half the distance had been covered, he had thought better of his impulsive design, and had overcome to some extent the initial torrents of his wrath. An unthinkable situation was consequently averted, thanks in no small measure to the sound advice and palliative overtures of Dr. Macartney.

As to the degree of responsibility for putting to death the rebel leaders resting on the shoulders of Li Hung Chang, here are his own words contained in a message to Macartney for conveyance to Gordon:—" Tell Gordon that he is in no way, direct or indirect, responsible in this matter, and that, if he considers his honour involved, I will sign any proclamation he likes to draft, and publish it far and wide that he had no part in or knowledge of it. I accept myself the full and sole responsibility for what has been done. But also tell Gordon that this is China, not Europe. I wished to save the lives of the Wangs, and at first thought that I could do so, but they came with their heads unshaved, they used defiant language, and proposed a deviation from the convention, and I saw that it would not be safe to show mercy to these rebels. Therefore what was done was inevitable. But Gordon had no part in it, and whatever he demands to clear himself shall be done."

In this chivalrous message, Li Hung Chang not only accepted full responsibility for what had happened, but went out of his way to absolve Gordon from so much as a particle of blame for the executions. Nevertheless, the depths of his feelings were profound as instanced by the spectacle presented to Macartney's astonished gaze on visiting him at Quinsan early one morning. Gordon had just got up and was sitting on his bed sobbing. Reaching down beneath the bed, he pulled out something that in the dim light Macartney could not at first identify. "Do you see that?" Gordon exclaimed. "It is the head of the Lar Wang (one of the *Taiping* leaders) foully murdered!"

The treachery of the Chinese, coupled with their refusal to sanction a gratuity of two months' pay to the Ever Victorious Army as a reward for the capture of Soo Chow, resulted in Gordon again resigning his command. But at last he was able to persuade himself that his honour could in no way be affected by the killing of the *Taipings*, and, following strong pressure brought to bear by the British authorities in Shanghai, allied to a general feeling of apprehension that, if deprived of Gordon's restraining power, the Ever Victorious Army would prove troublesome and might even go over to the rebels, he once more consented to resume his command, this decision, arrived at in February, 1864, being influenced by a state of unrest into which the army had declined since his resignation.

Meanwhile, on January 1st, a gratuity of ten thousand *taels*— the equivalent of about three thousand pounds—and other gifts had been conveyed to Quinsan and presented to Gordon by the Emperor's decree in recognition of his immense services to China. Still furious with the Chinese for their betrayal of his pledge, and acting as his sensitive conscience dictated, he flatly refused to accept the presentation. Moreover, in his downright, rather impulsive way, he expressed his feelings by writing on the back of the

Emperor's decree his regrets that "owing to the circumstances which occurred since the capture of Soochow, he was unable to receive any mark of His Majesty the Emperor's recognition."

This was typical of Gordon who, quite apart from his complete indifference to material gain in any shape or form, could not bring himself, even at the risk of offending the Emperor, to accept any reward from those whom he then believed to have let him down. But, as time went on, he began to view the catastrophe with more tolerant eyes and to resign himself to the indisputable truth that duplicity, such as the Chinese had practised on the *Taiping* leaders, had for two thousand years been a traditional characteristic of their race, and that, although their conduct, from a western point of view, had been deplorable, they could not, after centuries of dabbling in treachery, see anything unusual in beheading ruthless enemies who had surrendered on the understanding that their lives would be spared. As Li Hung Chang had pointed out to Gordon in his own defence, " this is China, not Europe." And so it came about that when Gordon withdrew his resignation, he also resumed his former amicable association with the Chinese generalissimo.

By the occupation of Soo Chow he had broken the back of the rebellion, but much yet remained to be done before the ultimate extinction of the "Celestial King" at Nankin. Many fortified cities to the west of Soo Chow and the great Lake of Taiho were still in the hands of the rebels, and it was to reduce these that Gordon set out, towards the end of February, with a more amenable Ever Victorious Army, whose officers and men gladly welcomed back their invincible commander.

Under their valiant leader, Chung Wang, the *Taipings* still fought with stubborn bravery, so that Gordon's relentless advance was not maintained without an occasional check. Indeed, so desperately did they oppose him at a place called Waisso that his forces suffered a serious reverse. When informed that the rebels had doubled back and seized Waisso, though barely recovered from a wound behind the knee received in an assault on Kintang, another of these numerous walled cities, Gordon at once started off with part of his force to this danger spot that threatened his rear. By land and water he covered a hundred and fifty miles in two days, appearing before the walls of Waisso on March 31st. There, the disastrous consequences of over impetuosity were all too clearly demonstrated. Intoxicated by excitement, Gordon's infantry attacked the Waisso stockades without orders and before their astute commander had been given time to carry out his customary personal reconnaissance. Delivered without plan or forethought, the attack was doomed to failure, the disaster being completed by the *Taipings'* cavalry galloping through the panic-stricken fugitives and doing tremendous execution, more especially since each horseman carried a sword in either hand.

This deporable exhibition of indiscipline must surely have been deeply galling to the commander whose victorious progress thus received a serious check. The heavy cost showed what havoc can be wrought by indiscipline in war — seven officers and two hundred and fifty two men killed, one officer and fifty two men wounded. But Gordon knew not what it was to be dismayed, nor did despondency find any place in his make-up. A set-back served merely to spur him on to even more energetic measures than before. And so it was after this unfortunate reverse — a reverse brought about by the undisciplined impetuosity of his headstrong troops.

Drawing off his force, he collected reinforcements and prepared to wipe out this stain on the record of the Ever Victorious Army. In co-operation with a large force of Imperialists, Gordon resumed operations against Waisso on April 6th, employing the element of surprise that so often he had exploited with conspicuous success. Expecting to be attacked from the south, that is to say the direction in which Gordon had retired, the rebels were thrown into a state of confuson by his sudden appearance on the north side of the city, and so complete was their discomfiture that they fled in panic, abandoning the position which fell into his hands with scarcely any show of resistance.

Thus did Gordon provide an object lesson in what can be achieved by an able, resourceful commander, whose plans are carefully thought out and whose arrangements are perfected in every detail before he strikes, in contrast to the impetuous, " bull-at-a-gate " methods, adopted without his authority or knowledge, that had proved so disastrous only a week before.

The *Taipings* retired on Kongyin where, on the following day, they found Gordon at their heels. Giving them no time to reorganise, he pushed relentlessly on, with little opposition, until the rebels became hopelessly demoralised, pursued not only by the troops but by hordes of infuriated local inhabitants who wreaked a savage vengeance on the devastators of their villages and the murderers of their people.

In a letter to his mother, telling her of the dreadful state of the territory occupied by the *Taipings,* Gordon wrote — " The rebels are very much pressed, and three months should finish them. During the pursuit from Kongyin the Imperialists and villagers killed in one village 3,000. I will say this much—the Imperialists did not kill the coolies and boys. The villagers followed up and stripped the fugitives stark naked, so that all over the country there were naked men lying down in the grass. The cruelties these rebels had committeed during their raid were frightful; in every village there were from ten to sixty dead, either women—frightfully mutilated—old men, or small children. I do not regret the fate of these rebels. I have no talent for description, but the scenes I have witnessed of misery are something dreadful, and I must say that your wish for me to return with the work incomplete would not be expressed if you saw the state of these poor people. The horrible furtive looks of the wretched inhabitants hovering around one's boat haunts me, and the knowledge of their want of nourishment would sicken anyone. They are like wolves. The dead lie where they fall, and are in some cases trodden quite flat by the passers-by. I hope to get the Shanghai people to assist, but they do not *see* these things, and to *read* that there are human beings eating human flesh produces less effect than if they saw the corpses from which that flesh is cut. There is one thing I promise you, and that is, that as soon as I can leave this service, I will do so; but I will not be led to do what may cause great disasters for the sake of getting out of the dangers, which, in my opinion, are no greater in action than in barracks. My leg is all right; the eleventh day after I received the wound I was up, and by the fifteenth day I could walk well. The ball went through the thick part of the leg, just below the knee."

At the end of February, 1864, for distinguished service in the field, Gordon received further promotion by brevet, so that, although still a captain of engineers, he now held the rank of lieutenant colonel in the army.

With the fall of Waisso, there remained but two cities to conquer before delivering the *coup de grâce* at Nankin. These were Chang Chu Fu and Tayan, both on the Grand Canal. The former had been strongly fortified with stockades, and it was here that the rebel leader Chang Wang prepared to make a last stand. Impressed by the strength of the position, Gordon assembled a force of four thousand men, augmented by a considerable number of Chinese Government troops who, in their anxiety to gain chief credit for taking the city, carried out several attacks which proved both abortive and costly. But Gordon had, as usual, been right in his opinion of the formidable defences, and, on April 27th, was himself twice repulsed when storming the strong fortifications. A fortnight later, however, despite most stubborn resistance by the fiercely fighting *Taipings,* a carefully prepared attack succeeded in carrying the breach and clearing the way for Gordon's triumphant entry into the city.

This proved to be his last engagement in China, for Tayan was almost immediately surrendered and the rebellion virtually brought to an end. Only the fanatical, luxury-loving *Tien Wang,* in his palace at Nankin, with all that was left of his rebel army, now remained to be rounded up. After consultation between the British and Chinese authorities, it was agreed that this task should be looked upon as essentially a domestic affair to be undertaken by Imperialist troops under a Chinese commander, and that Gordon's services, with those of his own force, would no longer be required. Consequently, the Ever Victorious Army marched back to Quinsan where, in June, 1864, it was disbanded. " Whatever may have been the failings of the force," wrote Sir William Butler, " want of courage was certainly not one of them. Out of one hundred and thirty foreign officers, thirty-five had been killed and seventy-three wounded; and among four thousand Chinese soldiers, five hundred and twenty had been killed and nine hundred and twenty wounded. Few heavier losses, proportionate to strength, can be found recorded in any similar length of war."

No doubt neither the British nor the Chinese authorities, especially the latter, had relished the prospect of four thousand wild legionaries let loose in the great city of Nankin which provided so much scope for the plunderer, and it seems probable that this, more than anything else, influenced their decision. Moreover, it was perhaps only natural that the Chinese should be anxious to finish the job unaided by foreign-led auxiliaries, and thus gain something of the kudos hitherto denied them through the conspicuous work of the Ever Victorious Army and the superb leadership of Gordon.

For his part, Gordon was content to leave the final task to the Chinese. In fourteen months of almost incessant fighting he had crushed the great *Taiping* Rebellion that for years had ravaged the country, terrorised the population, and even imperilled the Manchu dynasty. He had succeeded where all the resources of the great Chinese empire had signally failed, and for his inestimable services he had earned the undying gratitude of China. Fitting it was that, thereafter, he should be known as " Chinese Gordon." Throughout the arduous campaign, he had displayed a genius for leadership that can seldom have been approached in the history of warfare. He revealed a firm belief in the value of personal example, of sharing the dangers with his men, of leading in the true sense of the word. That he habitually carried in his hand nothing but a cane showed how little he cared for his personal safety, and must, in itself, have instilled confidence.

To-day, it is customary for commanders to remain miles away from the scene of action, and to be rarely, if ever, seen by their troops. Gordon would have had none of this, for, to his mind—and who should know better?—the force of personal example is well worth the risk of a commander being incapacitated. No one could have risked more than he did, leading his men in the assault and always to the fore in moments of crisis. Yet, the wound he received at Kintang was the only hurt he suffered during the whole of his adventurous career until his tragic, though glorious, death at the hands of the Mahdi.

Alluding to his decisive victory over the *Taipings,* he wrote— " I have the satisfaction of knowing that the end of this rebellion is at hand, while, had I continued inactive, it might have lingered on for years. I do not care a jot about my promotion or what people may say, I know I shall leave China as poor as I entered it, but with the knowledge that, through my weak instrumentality, upwards of eighty to one hundred thousand lives have been spared. I want no further satisfaction than this."

Gordon, too, returned to Quinsan, and soon afterwards, so as to avoid the fuss of a send-off by his victorious troops, character-istically slipped quietly away to Shanghai, reporting for duty at British headquarters as unostentatiously as though merely return-ing from a spell of normal leave! Such modesty and self-efface-ment contributed no doubt towards the persistent failure of his own country, throughout his career, to reward him in accordance with his deserts; though, as elsewhere suggested, his independence of character would seem to have been the chief cause of this inequi-table treatment.

The Chinese, on the other hand, were by no means lacking in tangible acknowledgment of their indebtedness to Gordon for de-livering their country from its prolonged afflictions, and bringing peace and tranquillity to their people who had become reduced to a state of utter desolation. In recognition of this remarkable achievement, Gordon was invested with the unique order of the

Yellow Jacket, never before bestowed upon a foreigner, besides being raised to the rank of field marshal in the Chinese army.

The origin of the Yellow Jacket is interesting. Dating from the seventeenth century, this singular order was instituted by the Emperor Kanghi after his suppression of a serious rebellion. He decreed that it should be conferred only on general officers commanding in successful operations against rebel forces.

A large gold medal was specially struck in Gordon's honour, and he was also presented with six robes as worn by mandarins who had attained the rank of field marshal. But another attempt to induce him to accept a substantial monetary grant failed to overcome his previously expressed objections. These were probably based on his own personal indifference to money, his reluctance to take from the Chinese Government what he knew they could ill afford, and a feeling that acceptance of the offer would savour of selling his services to a foreign power. Though always willing to go to the aid of other countries in times of adversity—and, as a result of the wide renown following his exploits in China, there was no little clamour for the help of this genius who had suddenly sprung up to astonish the world with his brilliance—he never undertook a task for personal gain, the means of providing himself with the barest necessities being all he asked. Such funds as remained to him after making provision for his meagre needs, were used in benevolent enterprise.

So impressed were the Chinese Government with Gordon's services to their country, that in a document addressed to the British Minister, recounting and praising his work of liberation and pacification, they expressed a hope that the British Government would do as they had done, namely, reward him according to his wonderful achievements. What must they have thought of Britain's reaction to this eulogistic appeal? For, although the fame of Gordon had now reached the uttermost parts of the earth, and he had become idolised the world over, the authorities of his own country considered a comparatively insignificant decoration adequate recompense for what he had done. Even this was not at once awarded, but only after unaccountable delay.

There is an amusing story of a soldier, who afterwards became famous, learning unofficially that it was proposed to give him a C.M.G. He wrote indignantly to his chief, complaining of the insult and declaring that he intended to refuse it. He was given a K.C.M.G. instead! But Gordon never bothered his head about reward. Money, honours, rank, appreciation meant little or nothing to him. As long as he could be satisfied that he had done his duty to the best of his ability, he cared not a rap for what anyone thought.

On his return to Shanghai, he did not resume the ordinary duties of a captain of engineers, but, at the request of the Chinese Government, his services were loaned to them for the purpose of instructing and training their army—employment that engaged his attention for some little time before eventually he was free to go home.

Meanwhile, with a force of eight thousand men, the Chinese laid siege to Nankin, last refuge of the *Taipings,* where the cause of all the trouble—ex-schoolmaster, fanatical evangelist, luxury-loving would-be usurper of the Manchu throne—lay skulking in his palace attended by a host of wives and concubines. Towards the end of June, as the instruments of fate inexorably tightened their grip upon him and all seemed lost, *Tien Wang* abandoned his earthly struggle, and, having consumed a sufficient quantity of poisonous gold leaf, cunningly eluded the vengeance of his pursuers.

In the following month, Nankin fell, the remaining leaders of the rebellion, including *Tien Wang's* son and the insurgent commander, Chung Wang, were duly executed, and peace was at last restored.

Apart from their tremendous admiration for Gordon, the Chinese—a suspicious people not easily reconciled to the ways of foreigners, in whom they would naturally expect to find duplicity similar to their own — trusted him implicitly, though doubtless somewhat puzzled as to the advantages to be derived from such uncompromising honesty, and unable to understand the scrupulous integrity that forbade him to accept payment for his services. " They trust me," he wrote with pardonable pride, " more than any foreigner was ever trusted. I have never cringed or yielded to any of them, and they have respected me all the more."

Though only after his death did Gordon come to be hailed in Britain as a national hero, no sooner had the *Taiping* Rebellion been finally crushed than he became very much a hero in the eyes of all intelligent Chinese. The shameful contrast between his treatment in China and in his own country was concisely recorded by Sir William Butler in these words—" On the strength of his faith in God, his disbelief in Mammon, and his absolute independence of mind and action, the Government and ruling classes of China looked on Gordon as a hero. On the strength of precisely these three things—faith, disregard of money, and straightforward honesty of thought and speech, he was in his lifetime not only without honour in his own country, but was regarded by many of the mandarin and ruling classes of his fellow-countrymen as a madman."

CHAPTER VIII

Six Wasted Years

EARLY in 1865, Gordon returned home after an absence of more than four years. For some few months he spent the leave due to him with his parents at Southampton, where, as he described it, he was " in attendance as A.D.C." on his mother who, like so many women with over-developed maternal instincts, stretched her devotion beyond the bounds of reason. She had been a splendid mother and had good cause to be proud of her children's upbringing, but she displayed to a pronounced degree the quality of possessiveness that is liable to diminish rather than encourage the affection of others. Not that this had any such effect on Charles Gordon, who was a most devoted, faithful son. Nevertheless, to a lover of freedom, fresh from a position of almost unique independence, with the power of life and death and the command of legions, it must have been a trifle irksome, to say the least of it, to find his every movement questioned, his every action the subject of enquiry. His mother could not bear him to be out of her sight. Even when he left the room she would want to know where he was going and what he intended to do. This was not inquisitiveness, nor a desire to pry into his affairs. It was just the result of a doting mother carrying adoration to excess.

Though deeply attached to his family, Gordon found life at Southampton all too dull for a man of his boundless energy and adventurous spirit. Nor could he tolerate the conventionalities of society in England. He detested dinner parties, and felt ill at ease in the presence of women. He hated dressing up, and elaborate meals did not appeal to him. Above all, he abhorred the insincerity so prevalent in what is called society. His many singular characteristics, his unorthodoxy, his independent mind, his hatred of leading strings, his self-abnegation, his tempestuous outbursts, his

THE KINDLY HERMIT
OF GRAVESEND

refusal to be coerced against the prompting of his own conscience —all these, and many other individualities, led to a suggestion that he was mad. But, as Lord Wolseley declared, if Gordon were mad he wished other British commanders had been similarly afflicted.

The inhibitions revealed on his return home were surely not unnatural in a man who had recently spent fourteen months in the devastated regions of China, roughing it in the truest sense of the expression, surrounded almost entirely by foreigners, living on a soldier's rations, clothed perpetually in rough service dress, and completely cut off from the society of white women. After all this, there was surely nothing peculiar in his intolerance of the vapid chatter at dinner parties or other social functions, his prejudice against wearing stiff shirts, his shyness with women, his preference for plain, wholesome food, or his impatience to terminate the dull existence at Southampton and resume his activities as a soldier. To the student of military history, it must come as something of a surprise, if not a shock, to find that the return of this conquering hero received such meagre recognition. Gordon had become a popular, romantic figure throughout the whole world, everywhere greatly admired and esteemed; yet little, if anything, seems to have been done by the authorities to prepare a fitting welcome indicative of public appreciation. Who could be anything but struck by this remarkable lack of official generosity to one whose eminent services had earned the highest mark of his countrymen's regard? For apart, so it seems, from a few references to him in the press, he was allowed to slip into England almost unnoticed. The fact that he disliked anything in the nature of fuss or ostentation, and that he, himself, would infinitely have preferred an unheralded home-coming, in no way excuses the authorities for their remissness.

But an even greater indignity was to follow when, at last, Gordon cut short his leave and returned to duty. On September 1st, 1865, this phenomenal soldier, who should have been held in readiness and made available to proceed to any part of the Empire where danger threatened, so that his exceptional qualities as revealed in China could be utilised to the utmost profit, was given sedentary employment that might well have been undertaken by any reasonably efficient sapper, and condemned to quiescent stagnation for six years!

Could it have been that the War Office authorities were jealous of Gordon's triumph over the *Taipings*, since they could claim no credit for suppressing the rebellion? They had been in the unusual, and, of course, distasteful position of being unable to interfere with a British commander's operations in the field, and it followed that, as Gordon held a supremely independent command, they could have no share in the honours of victory. The War Office has always been jealous of its authority, and, although obliged to accede to the request for Gordon's services, may well have felt none too favourably disposed towards an officer who was prepared to take service outside its jurisdiction in aid of a foreign power engaged in civil war.

Such a theory, unwelcome though it must be, combined with other reasons already suggested, may help to throw light on the mysterious failure to utilise Gordon's remarkable talents to the best advantage, or to reward one of Britain's greatest men for his phenominal contribution to the welfare of mankind. Moreover, this neglect on the part of the British authorities to employ him in positions requiring the exercise of energy and spirit for which he had become famous, may conceivably have accounted for his own inclination eagerly to undertake missions or tasks outside the ordinary run of a professional soldier's career.

Is it not surprising that, up to now, historians seem to have made little effort to unravel the mystery of Gordon's lamentable neglect by the authorities of his time? Indeed, this almost casual passing over of Gordon's niggardly treatment fills one with aston-ishment, for surely no national hero of any epoch, or any nation, has ever received less appreciation from the Government of his own country—and let it be repeated that Gordon has been said to occupy a place in British history second only to Nelson as a national hero. That, after his death, they tried to repair the wrong by erect-ing a statue in Gordon's memory, tends but to emphasise their churlish attitude during his lifetime. Furthermore, the statue in Trafalgar Square[1] became a monument to their neglect, since every sightseer, every tourist, on reading the inscription, would naturally wonder why a soldier, whose services to his country were deemed worthy of perpetuation in a statue, had not been rewarded with anything more fitting than a Companionship of the Order of the Bath.

The task now allotted to this adventurous, highly talented conqueror of the *Taipings* was nothing more exacting than the construction of a few forts at the mouth of the Thames. Following an attempt on the life of Napoleon III by means of lethal material alleged to have been procured in England, apprehension became rife as to possible reprisals by France. Consequently, it was decided to strengthen England's southern defences, the scheme allowing for

---

[1] Since removed, for reasons best known to the authorities, to Whitehall Gardens.

five new forts in the neighbourhood of Gravesend, where Gordon assumed command of the engineers employed on the work. In his thirty-third year, fit and vigorous as a man could be, his bodily health unimpaired by excess of any kind, his energies renewed by well earned rest following his arduous experiences, was he not suited to something more commensurate with his great capacity than a position analogous to that of a foreman of works? Was it not a shocking waste of talent so to isolate a man of Gordon's proved worth, and to keep him in seclusion for six long years?

For his part, with his innate modesty and readiness to accept without complaint whatever came his way, in the firm belief that it was the will of God, he threw himself into his new duties with energy and thoroughness. So thorough, indeed, was his supervision that before very long he discovered the proposed siting of the forts to be wrong and the plans for their construction faulty. His representations meeting with traditional rebuff, he was compelled to continue the work on lines that he knew to be wrong. Some years later, the useless forts were demolished and replaced by others of proper construction! Thus were six years of Gordon's comparatively short life thrown away to no purpose other than a vast expenditure of public money on worthless enterprise.

At Gravesend, Gordon lived a solitary life in a fairly spacious house with a nice garden. He wore clothes that were almost trampish and subsisted on the meanest diet, always bearing in mind that the less he spent on himself the more would remain for the furtherance of his many charitable projects. But his personal needs were remarkably few, and, since he seldom entered into the amusements normally indulged in by people of his age, only on rare occasions straying far from his own house, the proportion of his income devoted to himself was extraordinarily small. Nevertheless, having nothing but his pay, and the demands on his benevolence being considerable, he was often hard put to it to make ends meet, his self-denial for the good of others vying in heroism with his more spectacular activities. Not wishing to attract sympathy, or make a martyr of himself, he was wont to eat his food at a table with a convenient drawer in front of him, so that, should a visitor chance to appear, he could quickly scramble his frugal meal out of sight. He would not have liked anyone to think he half starved himself so as to be able to help the needy.

The interesting side of Gordon's life at Gravesend had nothing to do with his official duties, which must have been dull enough in all conscience, especially as he knew the work was being carried out on wrong lines. Fully aware that no good could come of the fort construction, he made up for the futility of his daily occupation by devoting his evenings to humane activities; and, by the people of Gravesend, he was afterwards remembered not as a colonel of engineers, but as the good Samaritan who turned no one from his door, whose house was as open to the passer-by as any place of public worship, who tended the sick, helped the decrepit, pulled youngsters out of the gutter and set them on their feet. What a transformation from the great deliverer of China, field marshal, mandarin, holder of the Yellow Jacket, to the ill-clad, poorly fed hermit of Gravesend!

But Gordon made these years of stagnation worthwhile by the cheer and encouragement he voluntarily and readily brought to the lives of those who, from one cause or another, were in dire need. Imagine the astonishment of his recent associate, Li Hung Chang, had he been able to see the pacifier of his country sitting up far into the night mending the ragged garments of the boys he had rescued, or kneeling at the grate of an old bedridden woman's garret lighting her fire. Such acts of mercy came natural to Gordon, whose saintly life pulsated with zeal to succour the poor and the afflicted.

His chief concern at Gravesend was for the rough youths who hung about the streets, got into bad company, and were headed for a life that, more likely than not, would lead them to crime and prison. Collecting as many of these waifs and strays as he could find room for, he housed, fed, and clothed them, schooled them till they became decent lads, and, finally, helped them to secure employment. Many of them went to sea and to jobs abroad, but wherever they went Gordon kept track of them by means of a large map on which flagged pins marked the whereabouts of his boys.

Apart from his protégés, he made few acquaintances in the neighbourhood. In the year 1867, however, he met a married couple who, in their modesty, have preferred to conceal their identity under the designation of Mr. and Mrs. F., and with them and their three children he formed a firm friendship that endured to the end of his life. Gordon constantly visited their home, and, after leaving Gravesend, kept up a correspondence with Mrs. F. until shortly before his death at Khartoum in 1885. In her book " More About Gordon " by " One who knew him well," published about sixty years ago, she wrote—" The last of the eighty-six letters I received from him was written to me from Khartoum on the day after his arrival. I do not doubt that he wrote after that, but that his messengers did not succeed in getting safely away with the letters. I have a facsimile of one letter he sent to the Governor of Darfur, which the messenger concealed under his thumb nail, and so carried out his mission successfully. But no doubt other messengers did not succeed so well."

Though impressed by Gordon's looks and personality from the day they first set eyes on him, these new friends never for one moment dreamt of connecting him with the celebrated "Chinese Gordon," until, one evening at tea, their visitor happened to speak of China. "Oh, were you ever in China?" asked his hostess. "Do tell us something about life there." To which her husband added—"Did you see anything of the *Taiping* Rebellion when you were there?" "I should think I did," replied Gordon. "Why, it was I who put an end to it."

So astounded were his hearers that they could scarcely believe it; but, after questioning him closely, they realised that during the past few weeks they had, all unknowingly, been associated with a most remarkable man. Mrs. F., with a woman's keen perception, had, from the first, discerned something in Gordon that singled him out from his fellows. She had felt there was something distinctive about him, but had been unable to find a solution of the problem until the chance mention of China, as they sat at tea, overwhelmingly settled the question.

At the age of thirty-four, this is the picture he presented to the eyes of Mrs. F.—" He was of medium height, and had a thin yet well-knit figure; his movements were very rapid; his articulation not very clear, and at times he talked extremely fast; he had a well-shaped head covered with short dark curly hair, and a well-developed forehead; a nose rather short and broad in the bridge; a mouth, not sweet in expression, but firm, and a square strong jaw; he wore a slight moustache and whiskers, but no beard; and then the eyes—I have left them to the last—in colour they were a very light grey and fine in shape, and were intensely penetrating and clear. I always declared he could see through a millstone, and I certainly think he saw through everybody in a most wonderful way."

The chief bond of sympathy between Gordon and his new friends was probably the religious fervour that animated them. Faith and trust in the Almighty being the keynote of Gordon's life, he would naturally be strongly attracted to devout Christians like Mrs. F. and her husband; so that it was not surprising he should make special friends of them and become a regular visitor at their home, where he would expound his beliefs, astonishing his listeners with the depths of his ardour. Gordon gave them a key to his garden, inviting them to make use of it whenever they liked. Letting themselves in one day, they were surprised to find a number of other visitors, mostly old and infirm, sitting or strolling about the grounds. These were Gordon's protégés, found by him in straitened circumstances. He gave them all keys so that they could enjoy the quiet and peacefulness of his secluded garden.

From Gordon's housekeeper Mrs. F. learned that he would never touch the fruit or vegetables grown in his garden, every part of which was laid out in allotments for the poor and needy, who were at liberty to take the produce for their own use. Visiting Fort House[1] one evening when Gordon's tea was on the table, Mrs. F. expressed astonishment at the unappetising appearance of his meal. Whereupon, he picked up a hard loaf of bread, stuffed it into the slop-basin, and emptied the tea-pot upon it, explaining that "in a few minutes it would be ready to eat, and in half an hour after it would not in the least matter what he had eaten."

He was in the habit of eating only when he felt hungry, and, after passing the day with little or no nourishment, he would often raid the larder during the night and satisfy his hunger by sucking raw eggs. Perhaps the quite remarkable good health that all his life he enjoyed and that enabled him to endure, almost without a day's illness, the pestilential climate of Central Africa, where his subordinates died like flies—perhaps this can be accounted for, at any rate to some extent, by his practice of consuming food only when he felt the need of it. Unorthodox and unconventional, especially when orthodoxy and conventionality seemed to him opposed to the tenets of common sense or the laws of nature, he could see no point in sitting down to a meal without any desire to eat simply because the clock had struck one heralding the conventional hour of luncheon, or eight when everyone must necessarily appear for dinner. Civilised society insists that one must eat at certain stipulated hours, and, like sheep, most people follow one another in obedience to the custom without a thought as to whether it is wise or not to eat when feeling disinclined for food. But Gordon was no sheep, very much the reverse, for he went his own way rather than blindly following the path of conventionality. In China, those around him marvelled how he managed to keep body and soul together, so little did he appear to eat. Yet,

---

[1] Gordon's residence at Gravesend.

throughout the rigours of the *Taiping* campaign, indeed during the whole of his service in China, except for a mild attack of smallpox, he was never laid low by illness.

It is probable that few succeeded in taking a mean advantage of Gordon's benevolence, for his powers of discernment were every bit as penetrating as his steely grey eyes, and he could usually sum up the true character of a man in no time. Nevertheless, at Gravesend, he was once deceived by a family who, after accepting his generous help, turned out to be a good deal better off than they had led him to believe. Their duplicity unmasked, they soon found that the colonel could be as severe as he was kindly, for that proved to be the end of his liberality so far as they were concerned. Deceit or dishonesty brought down upon the culprit the full force of his wrath, which, when directed against wrong-doers, could be devastating in its violence.

Sir William Butler has this to say of Gordon's character—" Wherever I have been able to watch and weigh the life and acts of Charles Gordon, I find him always even, practical, earnest, unemotional in his charity, full of sound common sense, hitting hard and straight at poverty and vice, even as he hit hard and straight at Chinese city or stockade, no cheerier companion, no one with keener sense of humour or quicker power to catch the light and shade of life. It is perhaps inevitable that around such a man the extremist of every class and creed should endeavour to raise his own particular glasshouse of ethics or religion, and to make Gordon austere, enthusiastic, ascetic, fanatical, or peculiar; but the real Gordon was absolutely unlike such a creation; nay, in manner, mode of action, and method of life there was almost the opposite of these attributes. His life at Gravesend was that of a sound commonsense Christian man, intent upon doing the best he could to better the misery that lay around him."

As an instance of Gordon's conscientiousness and the severity of his self-discipline, it is said that, for fear of occupying time which might be spent more profitably on behalf of others, he gave up the pleasure of dabbling in photography and got rid of his camera. Again, when asked for a contribution towards the fund in aid of famine-stricken Lancashire, and having no ready money at the moment, he promptly sold the gold medal presented to him by the Emperor of China, forwarding the proceeds (£15) to the organisers of the charity.

Among his more prominent characteristics, his tireless energy was conspicuous. He never moved slowly, more often than not hurrying along at a kind of half run half walk, or what in a horse would be called a triple. Laziness or idleness he abominated, and was at pains to avoid the smallest waste of time. He would have liked to break himself of smoking—his solitary luxury—because, as he said, it took up so much of his time; but, despite his great strength of character and phenomenal will power, he could not find it in him to renounce his only love.

In 1867, when it became necessary to send an expeditionary force to Abyssinia to release the British prisoners at Magdala and to punish the King Theodore for his misdeeds, Gordon eagerly volunteered for service under Lord Napier, who had been appointed to command the expedition. So bitter was his disappointment at the refusal of his application that he is said to have shut himself up in his room for a whole day and declined to see anyone. As an explanation of this curious attitude on the part of the authorities, it has been suggested that since the force under Lord Napier was formed from the Bombay army, the application of an officer serving at home could not be considered. That may have been the reason given; but if so, in the case of an officer of Gordon's exceptional qualities, it was an exceeding poor one, for it mattered not an iota where, or from what sources, the force was to be formed. The plain fact cried aloud that, in the crisis confronting the British Government, and in the interests of forthcoming operations, the services of the most brilliant soldier of the day should be utilised no matter how much red tape intervened to prevent it. But, as usual, red tape won, and so " the best soldier in England was left in inglorious and uncongenial inactivity." To what extent antagonism, engendered by Gordon's independent character, prejudiced the authorities in arriving at their decision will never be known. It is not, however, altogether unreasonable to suppose that the fatal word " difficult " had not been without its effect on the minds of those who denied Lord Napier the services of a genius, employed at that time on the construction of useless fortifications in the obscurity of Gravesend.

The wasted years dragged on—wasted that is from the viewpoint of his profession and the value of his talent to the empire— until, at last, the denizens of the " rabbit-warren,"[1] whether from shame at the scandal of a man of Gordon's calibre being shelved for six years, or because the usefulness of his knowledge, gained when employed on the boundary commission in Bessarabia, could

---

[1]Nickname of the old War Office in Pall Mall.

not be denied, released him from worthless fort-building and sent him to Galatz to join the international commission on the Danube navigation problems. Still, this did little more than give him a change of air, and employment only slightly less dreary than before. The authorities seemed bent on denying him the smallest opportunity of giving free rein to that independent spirit, that intolerance of the " usual channels," that determination to take his own line, that impatience of dilatory bureaucracy. They appeared to be nervous of letting him loose, for, like Nelson, he would use the " blind eye " when he conscientiously believed it to be in the interests of his country. Is it not significant that these two famous men, rated numbers one and two among Britain's national heroes, should both have been conspicuous for this independence of character, this distaste for leading strings, this superb reliance on their own powers of initiative?

It was seldom that Gordon complained of anything, but he did tell his friend Mrs. F. that he thought he had been shelved at Galatz, and wondered why. " I told him," she wrote, " I believed he was like Moses, who had eighty years in the desert in which to be prepared for his great work, and that like him he (Gordon) was being prepared in solitude and loneliness for some great work that he was yet to do, and this prophecy was justified by after events."

Gordon was undoubtedly right. He had merely been transported from one back-water to another. Of his new surroundings, he wrote—"As for the place, I cannot say much for it; it is semi-civilized, and therefore worse than if thoroughly barbarian. The people are most uninteresting, and I do not much care for the few English: there is no bond of union between me and them; but I am quite happy and comfortable, have read up a mass of work, and shall soon finish it." There followed a typical protest at being badgered by people with suggestions as to what he would like or what he must do. But Gordon was not a good subject to advise even on trivial matters, for to suggest he might like this or that would be the surest way to make him hate it, or to advise him to go here or there would in all probability drive him in the opposite direction. He would most certainly have subscribed to the dictum of Jack Mytton when offered advice by his agent—" What the devil is the use of my having a head on my own shoulders," he exclaimed, " if I am obliged to make use of yours? "

During his sojourn on the Danube covering a period of two years, the War Office had another opportunity of utilising Gordon's genius for leadership. This was on the west coast of Africa where rebellion in Ashanti necessitated the dispatch of a punitive expedition. But his old friend of the Crimea, Sir Garnet (afterwards Viscount) Wolseley was appointed to command the force, and poor Gordon was again denied the chance of active service. Many a man would have chucked his hand in and refused to submit any longer to such studied neglect. Gordon, however, cared as little for personal advancement as he did for honours or rewards, and, although a man of his daring, intrepid spirit would naturally be disappointed—as he had been in the case of Abyssinia—at missing the excitement and the chance of serving his country, no thought of adding to his laurels would ever have entered his head. And so, with his inherent modesty, he was content to slog along, firm in his conviction that all things come about through the will of God, though at the same time, as we have seen, a trifle mystified as to *why* he had been shelved.

In 1872, from Galatz, he paid a visit to the Crimea, going over the famous battlefields of Inkerman, the Alma, and Balaclava. In the course of a letter to Mrs. F., written after his return, he recorded — " The Russians were very much surprised at our coming, and did not like it much; they were polite, and that is all. Our cemeteries are in a very bad state, through neglect, and through the Tartars digging up the bodies for rings, buttons, etc. The body of Sir R. Newman has been out of the grave more than once. The town (Sebastopol) is still in a state of ruin; very little has been done to repair it. We saw the troops, which did not look much improved; they were—with their officers—very grubby. . . . We went to Kertch, and passed the fortifications so much talked about. They might have secured the passage of the straits of the Sea of Azov for a much less sum than that expended. The Russians themselves think it a great mistake. The Russians have built a magnificent chapel in one of the cemeteries, where 40,000 of the dead are buried. I send you a photograph of Gortschakoff's monument, which was put up by his widow, and cost £2,000. He was brought from Warsaw and buried there. The French dug up all their dead and collected the bones and buried them in seventeen large mausoleums. They found some of the bodies not decomposed, and they had to take the flesh off! I send Eddie [Mrs. F.'s son] some flowers from the Malakoff and Redan."

As it happened, Gordon's banishment to the dreary delta of the Danube proved a blessing in disguise, not merely to him, but also to multitudes of oppressed people who might otherwise have

remained indefinitely in bondage; for his residence at Galatz facili-
tated his visit to the Crimea—a journey that took him to Constantinople, where a chance meeting altered the whole course of his
career, rescued him from the stagnation he had suffered since returning from his triumphs in China, and set him off on a mission
of mercy and liberation.

CHAPTER IX

A Momentous Mission

IT was at the British Embassy in Constantinople that Gordon chanced to meet the distinguished Egyptian minister, Nubar Pasha. Now, this astute statesman, said to have once declared that "England owes little to her officials; she owes her greatness to men of a different stamp," soon discerned in Gordon qualities that, in his view, raised him high above the heads of his contemporaries. Indeed, so deep an impression did the shelved colonel of Gravesend and Galatz make on Nubar Pasha, that the latter, displaying a good deal more wisdom than the authorities of Pall Mall, approached Gordon with the object of inducing him to undertake a mission in the service of the Khedive. Why, he must have asked himself, should Egypt not take advantage of Britain's neglect to employ this remarkable man in a manner befitting his ability and attainments? Why should his country hesitate to profit from this neglect? For, in the unassuming, yet impressive, colonel of engineers the sagacious Nubar instinctively perceived the germs of greatness, and sensed that they had found the man they needed. Moreover, the Khedive was anxious to show deference towards England by entrusting the great task he had in mind to a British officer.

Now, the Khedive Ismail, or ruler of Egypt, had been greatly troubled by the ever growing scandal of the slave trade in the southern Sudan, or Equatorial Provinces as they were called. This nefarious traffic in human beings had its origin in the early part of the nineteenth century, when numerous European fortune hunters, frequenting the southern provinces in quest of ivory, foresaw more lucrative results from human cargoes, and transferred their activities to dealing in native slaves. From slave dealing they took to slave hunting, until this immense tract of equatorial territory lying between Khartoum and the great Victoria Nyanza lake had become reduced to the pitiable state described, in 1872, by Sir Samuel Baker, Gordon's predecessor in the Sudan, in these words—"It is impossible to describe the change that has taken place since I last visited this country. It was then a perfect garden, thickly populated, and producing all that man could desire. The villages were numerous, groves of plantations fringed the steep cliffs on the river's bank, and the natives were neatly dressed in the bark cloth of the country. The scene has changed! All is wilderness. The population has fled! Not a village is to be seen! This is the certain result of the settlement of Khartoum traders. They kidnap the women and children for slaves, and plunder and destroy wherever they set their foot."

But, by this time, the pace had become too hot for the white men who, probably more from fear of the consequences than prickings of conscience, abandoned the shameful trade, leaving their even more ruthless Arab assistants to carry on without them. After an unsuccessful attempt to punish the slave traders and put an end to their savage depredations, his force being cut to pieces, the Khedive felt himself powerless to take further action unaided. In response, therefore, to the reproaches and representations of scandalised foreign powers, he sought their help in his conscientious desire to rid his country of the stigma attaching to it.

Of England he asked the services of Gordon, reported by his minister, Nubar Pasha, to be the very man for the job. But, although Gordon at once agreed to undertake the task, provided the British Government had no objection (quite a concession on his part!), a whole year went by before anything was settled—a year in which, but for the dilatoriness of officialdom, he might have been devoting his great gifts to alleviating the misery of the wretched people of Central Africa, who, with unbelievable brutality, were being driven from their homes and forced into slavery.

Will the official mind never profit from experience, never learn its lessons? Will it never come to realise the human suffering that could so often be minimised, if not actually prevented, by prompt action and a little less rigid adherence to such brakes on efficiency as those soul destroying "usual channels?" Gordon's career provides three conspicuous instances of the evils resulting from official lassitude. First, there was the unconscionable delay in his appointment to command the Ever Victorious Army in China, affording the *Taiping* rebels an unnecessarily prolonged lease of life, while, at the same time, keeping the luckless peasantry waiting with oriental patience and stoicism for deliverance from their appalling destitution. Then, we have this long hold up in releasing him for the greatest work of his life, with the consequent needless postponement of energetic measures against the iniquitous slave traders, though how much of the delay could be attributed to the Egyptians is not by any means clear. Finally, and worst of all, there was the criminal apathy on the part of the British Government that Queen Victoria, herself, did her utmost to dispel, but which brought about the fall of Khartoum, the death of Gordon, and the over-running of the Sudan by the Mahdi's hosts during the ensuing thirteen years. Evils such as these are liable to follow in the wake of official listlessness or blind insistence on everything passing through the cumbersome, time wasting machinery known as the " usual channels."

It was not until February, 1874, that Gordon reached Cairo. Alluding to this new venture in a letter to his family, he wrote— " For some wise design, God turns events one way or another, whether man likes it or not, as a man driving a horse turns it to right or left without consideration as to whether the horse likes that way or not. To be happy, a man must be like a well-broken, willing horse, ready for anything. Events will go as God likes."

Gordon stayed in Cairo for a fortnight. There he had several talks with the Khedive who appointed him Governor of the Equatorial Provinces with a salary of ten thousand pounds a year. With characteristic independence, however, he declined to accept more than two thousand, feeling no doubt that the larger the sum the greater would be the hold exercised over him by the Egyptian Government. Moreover, he would be anxious, as in China, that there should be no question of his undertaking the task for personal gain. After visiting one of the ministers in Cairo, he wrote to his sister Augusta—" I let him understand that your brother was not an hireling."

How strongly he felt on the matter of his remuneration may be judged from this explanation in his own words—" My object is to show the Khedive and his people that gold and silver idols are not worshipped by all the world. They are very powerful gods, but not so powerful as *our* God. From whom does all this money come? From poor miserable creatures who are ground to produce it."

The magnitude of Gordon's mission is revealed in the following abstract of the Khedive's instructions, handed to him on February 16th, 1874—" The province which Colonel Gordon has

94

undertaken to organise and to govern is but little known. Up to the last few years it had been in the hands of adventurers who had thought of nothing but their own lawless gains, and who had traded in ivory and slaves. They established factories and governed them with armed men. The neighbouring tribes were forced to traffic with them whether they liked it or not. The Egyptian Government, in the hope of putting an end to this inhuman trade, had taken the factories into their own hands, paying the owners an indemnification. Some of these men, nevertheless, had been still allowed to carry on trade in the district, under a promise that they would not deal in slaves. They had been placed under the control of the Governor of the Sudan. His authority, however, had scarcely been able to make itself felt in these remote countries. The Khedive, therefore, had resolved to form them into a separate government, and to claim as a monopoly of the state the whole of the trade with the outside world. There was no other way of putting an end to the slave-trade, which at present was carried on by force of arms in defiance of law. When once brigandage had become a thing of the past, and when once a breach had been made in the lawless customs of long ages, then trade might be made free to all.

"If the men who had been in the pay of these adventurers were willing to enter the service of the Government, Colonel Gordon was to make all the use of them that he could. If, on the other hand, they attempted to follow their old course of life, whether openly or secretly, he was to put in force against them the utmost severity of martial law. Such men as these must find in the new Governor neither indulgence nor mercy. The lesson must be made clear, even in those remote parts, that a mere difference of colour does not turn man into wares, and that life and liberty are sacred things.

"One great error must be avoided into which others had fallen. The armament must be so well supplied with provisions that there shall be no need, as heretofore, to take from the tribes their stores of corn. By doing such as this distrust had been sown, where the Khedive had hoped to establish a feeling of confidence. The lands must be tilled by the troops, and crops raised. If, as seemed to be the case, Gondokoro was an ill-chosen position, situated as it was on a thankless soil, the seat of Government must be moved to a more favoured spot. Among the natives who should be rescued from the slave-dealers many would be found who had been carried away from countries so far off that it would be impossible to restore them to their homes. They could be employed about the stations in tilling the ground.

"Another object of the new Governor should be to establish a line of posts through all his provinces, so that from one end to the other they might be brought into direct communication with Khartoum. These posts should follow, as far as was possible, the line of the Nile; but for a distance of seventy miles the navigation of that river was hindered by rapids. He was to search out the best way of overcoming this hindrance, and to make a report thereon to the Khedive.

"In dealing with the chieftains of the tribes which dwell on the shores of the lakes, the Governor was above all to try to win their confidence. He must respect their territory, and conciliate them by presents. Whatever influence he gains over them, he must use in the endeavour to persuade them to put an end to the wars which they so often make on each other in the hope of carrying off slaves. Much tact will be needed, for should he succeed in stopping the slave-trade, while wars were still waged among the chiefs, it might well come to pass that, for want of a market, the prisoners would in such a case be slaughtered. Should he find it needful to exercise a real control over any of these tribes, it will be better to leave to the chieftains the direct government. Their obedience must be secured by making them dread his power."

Gordon, as might be expected, held his own with the Egyptian ministers, refusing to alter his opinions to suit them, or to agree to anything not strictly in accordance with the promptings of his conscience. In effect, the line he seems to have taken in the discussions amounted to this—"You have invited me to undertake this work. I have agreed to do it. Now you must give me a free hand to act as I think best." That would be the Gordon attitude. No leading strings. No advice. No interference. Just show him what was wanted, and leave him to do the job in his own way. If they didn't like his direct, outspoken methods, let them find some one else.

He appears to have formed an unfavourable opinion of the Cairo authorities, except Khedive Ismail, whom he liked. Nubar Pasha's manner had changed since their meetings in Constantinople, rousing Gordon's quick, fiery temper. In a letter to his sister from Cairo dated February 18th, he wrote—"Nubar and your brother do not hit it off, and the other evening —— said foolishly, 'Do not make an enemy of Nubar: he will or may do you a mischief.' It was too much, and your brother replied in the midst of

HIS HIGHNESS ISMAIL PASHA
KHEDIVE OF EGYPT,
WITH HIS SON TEWFIK
WHO SUCCEEDED HIM

(Hulton Library)

a circle of guests, that there was no one living who could do him the slightest injury which he could feel, and that he would not shape his face to suit anyone, beyond acting loyally. . . . I think that they think me very queer, and I am, I dare say. When I get away I shall be better with them all. Your brother has been so dosed with advice, and is so indignant, but he does not in reality care a bit. . . . You have no idea of the intrigues here; it is a regular hot-bed, and things cannot last long like this. They are paying thirty-six per cent. for money."

Gordon was no doubt glad to get away from Cairo with its intrigues and all the fuss he abominated. Travelling by special train to Suez, he embarked for Suakin on the Red Sea, where, with an escort of two hundred Egyptian soldiers, he arrived on February 25th. In a letter from there, he revealed the impression already gained as to " the rottenness of Egypt." Neither in Cairo, nor during this first stage of his long journey to the heart of Central Africa, had he found much to applaud, and, in his customary out-spoken way, he doubtless made no secret of his contempt. " I think the Khedive likes me," he wrote, " but no one else does; and I do not like them—I mean the swells, whose corns I tread on in all manner of ways." But, with supreme confidence in the power of God to help him in the great task that lay ahead, he concluded— " If He wills, I will shake all this in some way not clear to me now."

From Suakin, Gordon and his escort proceeded across the desert by camel to Berber on the Nile. Though as yet a stranger to the " ship of the desert," he accomplished the long ride of over two hundred miles without difficulty. Leaving Berber by river steamer on March 9th, he set off up the Nile, and reached Khartoum exactly a calendar month after starting from London. He made an impressive entry into the Sudanese capital, being received by the Governor-General, Ismail Yakoob, with a salute of guns, a parade of troops, and blaring bands. " The day before," he wrote humorously to his sister, Augusta, " your brother had his trousers off, and was pulling the boat in the Nile." How quick he was to see the funny side of life, and how amusingly he worded these frequent witticisms in his correspondence. Midst all the pomp and ceremony attending his arrival, he could not help drawing a comparison between the new Governor's stately entry into Khartoum and the spectacle of his bare-legged figure helping to pull the boat off a sandbank. Here again, we find evidence of Gordon's firm belief in the value of personal example. The Egyptians were often thunderstruck at seeing him taking a hand in quite menial tasks alongside his men, just as they gazed open mouthed, with bulging eyes, at this Englishman of high rank cooking his own breakfast. But, as he said, " Self is the best officer to do anything for you."

Awaiting him at Khartoum was a piece of most encouraging information that would shorten very considerably his journey into the wilds. This concerned the breaking up of the " sudd " or massed aquatic vegetation, that had blocked the passage of the White Nile between Khartoum and Gondokoro, where he intended establishing his headquarters. " You can scarcely imagine," he wrote, " the advantage of this opening to me. It took people eighteen months and two years to go to Gondokoro from here (Khartoum), and now it is only twenty-one days in the steamer."

Gordon stayed for a week at Khartoum, with its flat-roofed houses of mud, busying himself collecting all possible information that might prove useful in setting about the gigantic task entrusted to him. He reviewed troops, and inspected hospitals and schools. The little blacks, he said, were glad to see him, but he wished " that flies would not dine on the corners of their eyes! "

After a banquet given in his honour by the Governor-General, Gordon was entertained with a ballet, in which a number of quite nude women took part. Ignorant of his guest's strict adherence to the rules of propriety, or of his ardent piety, Ismail Yakoob, in countenancing the performance, made a serious mistake, for Gordon rose from his seat in disgust and left the room.

His departure from Khartoum was attended by another flourish of trumpets as he embarked on the thousand mile journey up the Nile to Gondokoro without waiting for his supplies from Cairo. Some two hundred miles up river, he passed the island of Abba, where at that time there lived, in the seclusion of a cave, a comparatively obscure Dervish named Mohammed Ahmed, who, ten years later had styled himself the Mahdi and, at the head of an enormous army of rebellious fanatics, was laying siege to Khartoum. If Ahmed had been peering from the mouth of his cave watching the passing steamer, how little could he have forseen that one day the severed, dripping head of that lonely figure, pensively pacing the deck, would be brought triumphantly into his camp.

Steaming slowly up the river against the current, Gordon found much to interest him on either bank. Every day, as the vessel pushed on, the country became more and more wild and uncivilised. Hippopotamuses, showing only their snouts above the surface of the water during the heat of the day, revealed their huge proportions at night, their hides glistening in the brilliant tropical moonlight. Crocodiles drowsed lazily on the banks, their open jaws displaying formidable teeth. Giraffes stretched their long necks to the tree tops in quest of forage beyond the reach of less elongated creatures. Flocks of wild geese were to be seen, besides pelicans and thousands of storks varying in size from the small egret to a large bird with an immense beak. The phenomenon of a laughing stork brought forth from Gordon a typically humorous comment. "All of a sudden," he wrote, " from a large bush came peals of laughter. I felt put out; but it turned out to be birds who laughed at us for some time in a very rude way. They are a species of stork, and seemed in capital spirits and highly amused at anybody thinking of going up to Gondokoro with the hope of doing anything."

Troops of monkeys came down to the river to drink, their quaint antics providing the lonely crusader with plenty of amusement. In using the word "lonely," it is not intended to imply that, at this stage of his mission, Gordon was entirely without the support of white men, for accompanying him in the steamer were Colonel Long of the American army and one or two junior members of his staff. But Gordon was certainly lonely in the sense that on him alone rested the onus of evolving a scheme whereby the unhappy people of this vast wilderness, into which he was now deeply penetrating, might be delivered from their misery and the abominable slave trade effectively crushed. On his shoulders alone crouched the heavy burden of responsibility for the success of this great endeavour. On him alone depended the future security and welfare of every native, every woman and child, in the southern Sudan.

Herds of elephants were often seen, but the most ferocious beasts encountered during the journey were coal black buffaloes, described by Gordon as " by far the most dangerous to shoot of any wild animals."

As to the natives, they seemed shy, for, as soon as field glasses or telescopes were levelled in their direction, they hurriedly disappeared. Their timidity was perhaps not unnatural, bearing in mind the sufferings they had endured at the hands of the brutal slave hunters; and no doubt they wondered apprehensively what new horror the passing steamer portended. Some of them wore gourds on their heads, others nothing at all.

Soon after passing Fashoda—notable as the scene of an international squabble that nearly brought about conflict between

Britain and France—the steamer stopped for a time and pulled into the side. Whereupon, a large crowd of timorous looking natives called Dinkas, curiosity getting the better of their fears, emerged from a clump of trees. Clothed in nothing but a neck-lace, the chief was, with difficulty, persuaded to go aboard accompanied by one or two of his followers. " He came up to me," wrote Gordon, " took up each hand, and gave a good soft lick to the backs of them; then he held my face, and made the motion of spitting in it. He was very greedy; and when we gave him something to eat, he did not hesitate to take his neighbour's portion."

From his observation during this journey up the Nile, Gordon was horrified at the ill-fed, pitiable condition of the people generally; but, in the depths of his brave heart, he believed he could do much to alleviate their suffering. Before leaving Khartoum, he had issued his first decree as Governor of the Equatorial Provinces of the Sudan. This declared a Government monopoly of the ivory trade, and prohibited the import of arms and powder, the levying of armed bands by private persons, and the entry of anyone without a passport.

On April 11th, the steamer reached Bohr, five days from Gondokoro. Bohr was notorious as a slave trading centre, and Gordon could not fail to discern the resentment of these scoundrels on learning the details of his decree. Always so energetic and quick off the mark in his actions, he had lost no time in striking at them and striking hard, even before he had reached his headquarters.

At Gondokoro, he found more evidence of Egyptian dilatoriness, for he was not expected, nor had anything been heard of his appointment! Realising, after a few days, that little could be done without his stores, he decided to return to Khartoum with the object of rousing the lethargic authorities and expediting the transport of his baggage. Six days had sufficed to make it clear to this far-seeing soldier that he would have to start from scratch, and that the task confronting him was even more formidable than he had anticipated. Egyptian authority appeared to be practically non-existent apart from a couple of forts, one at Gondokoro (300 men), and the other at a place called Fatiko (200 men). These soldiers, whose duty it was to maintain law and order, were, however, thoroughly corrupt, spending much of their time cattle stealing and in all manner of reprehensible practices. This, very naturally, enraged the natives, who in turn became so hostile to all representatives of the Government that, in Gordon's words,

" you cannot go out in any safety half a mile—all because they have been fighting the poor natives and taking their cattle."

Gordon's position could hardly have been more difficult, seeing that he had to deal with a discontented native population, while the only instrument at his hand for the enforcement of his orders and the preservation of peace was undisciplined, avaricious, and disloyal. With his quick insight he realised almost at once that, before his campaign against the slave traders could be effectively pursued, he must gain the confidence of the natives and put an end to the monstrous conduct of the Egyptian soldiers. The marshy, fever stricken country was laid waste by the depredations of the Arab slave dealers, whose activities were winked at by the Egyptian officials in return for bribes. The climate was pestilential, the heat intense, and the mosquitoes, of a singularly virulent kind, seldom relaxed their unwelcome attentions.

Through all these fires Gordon passed with the calm imperturbability of a man whose trust in the unfailing help of God never for an instant wavered. From the midst of seemingly unsurpassable difficulties he wrote home assuring his family that he was well and happy, and that he confidently believed he would be able to devise means of bringing succour to the unfortunate people around him.

Leaving Colonel Long at Gondokoro to establish his head-quarters, Gordon hurried back to Khartoum, accomplishing the journey down river in eleven days. The Egyptian Governor-General was anything but pleased at the unexpected return of this straight-laced Englishman, whose energy astonished him and whose predilection for prying into everything caused him uneasiness. Nor was he without reason in his concern, since more than once Gordon found it necessary to speak to him severely. " I have had some sharp skirmishing with the Governor-General of Khartoum," he wrote to his sister. " I think I have crushed him. . . . It was undiplomatic of me, but it did the Governor-General good."

With his usual energy Gordon pushed on to Berber, where at last he found his long delayed stores and the remaining members of his staff. Sending them on ahead up river, he himself followed next day, resolved to put into force a plan for the discomfiture of the slave trader very similar to the blockhouse system employed in the South African war twenty-seven years later. By constructing a line of forts across the country, he hoped to check the activities of these pests and gradually bring them to book. The first of these blockhouses was built on the Saubat River (about sixty miles due south of Fashoda) where Gordon was held up for some weeks await-ing the rest of his steamers, which had been delayed, one of them suffering serious damage through colliding with a hippopotamus.

But the time was not wasted, seeing that, in addition to form-ing what he described as " a nice station," he established the most friendly relations with the local tribe, known as Shillooks, thus making a promising start in his efforts to gain the confidence of the natives, and to show them that he came, not as a hard task master or a bullying dictator, but as a deliverer, whose chief aim was to free them from the tyranny of the slave trade, and restore them to a life of peace and happiness. " They are poorly off," wrote Gordon of the Shillooks, " and I have given them some grain; very little contents them. I have employed a few of them to plant maize, and they do it very fairly. The reason they do not do it for themselves is, that if they did plant any quantity they would run the chance of losing it, by its being taken by force from them; so they plant only enough to keep body and soul together, and even that is sown in small out-of-the-way patches. . . . I hope to get their confidence, and really do something at each of my stations."

He would probably have curtailed his stay on the Saubat River and continued his journey to Gondokoro ahead of the other boats, but for a feeling of disquiet among the soldiers detailed to occupy the new fort, who were much alarmed at the unhealthiness of the climate in those parts. True to his belief in the benefit of personal example, Gordon decided to remain with them for a time, so that, by his presence, he might inspire them with confidence and restore their morale.

It was during his prolonged halt at the Saubat station that Gordon gained his first personal experience of the pernicious trade which for years had been ravaging the southern Sudan. By a piece of great good luck, he intercepted some letters, being conveyed from a leading trader called Nassar to the *Mudir*, or Governor, of the district of Fashoda, informing this official that the writer was bringing him two thousand cows (stolen from neighbouring tribes), and " all to satisfy your wants " (meaning slaves). As a result of Gordon's prompt and skilful action, the cows were confiscated, the slaves, numbering about three hundred, were liberated, and Nassar fell into the hands of the avenger come to put a spoke in the wheel of these scoundrelly traders. In this, his first operation against them, Gordon achieved a most encouraging triumph that was bound to have far-reaching effect. It demonstrated to all concerned in the illicit trade what they might expect if they continued to defy the Khedive's authority now that a man of exceptional capacity had arrived in their midst with full powers to enforce the law.

A Dinka chief, who had been put in irons by Nassar and afterwards released by Gordon, could not conceal his joy at seeing the cruel slave hunter under arrest. Certainly, there was no love lost between the natives and the ruthless interlopers, who, by means of enslaved soldiers, made war on the native tribes, seizing their people and their cattle.

Before resuming his journey to Gondokoro, Gordon enjoyed another success in his war against slavery. Hearing that some boats had arrived with slaves on board, he promptly liberated them to the number of a hundred and twenty, besides confiscating two thousand pounds' worth of ivory from the traders. " Of course," he wrote, " all this business is not conducted without many hard words and actions on my part; and at night I think sometimes that perhaps a quiet life in a civilised land would be preferable, but in the morning one is all on fire again, and goes on with the same zest."

Back at his headquarters after an absence of about three and a half months, he plunged into the work with redoubled vigour, fully conscious, as he had become, that he must depend almost entirely on himself and could expect little support from the Egyptian Government which was lethargic and half-hearted in its attitude towards the project. But Gordon felt convinced he could do much good by his own unaided efforts, and resolved steadfastly to pursue his plan despite the many obstacles that hindered his progress. His difficulties were made no easier by torrential rain which flooded the country, and, since the water could not run away into the rivers, whose banks were higher than the land, it gradually soaked into the ground, forming unhealthy swamps.

As one of his staff, he had taken into his employ an Arab named Abou Saoud. Now, this man had been a slave trader, and the authorities both in Cairo and Khartoum had done their utmost to dissuade Gordon from taking so unreliable a character on the expedition. Had they but realised it, that was the surest way to drive him in the opposite direction, for Gordon would accept gratuitous advice from no man, preferring to be guided by his own judgment. Any attempt to turn him from a decision made him all the more determined to carry it out.

In the case of Abou Saoud, he appears to have felt that, if he could secure the man's loyalty, his experience and knowledge of the inner workings of the slave trade would be invaluable to him in conducting his campaign against it. At first, his confidence seemed justified, the Arab, a man of strong character, proving of great assistance. But, as time went on and Abou Saoud gained more and more power, it went to his head, until, at last, his conceit and effrontery became so intolerable that Gordon was obliged to get rid of him. Nevertheless, he had served his purpose, for, through him, valuable information had been gained as to the activities and scheming of the traders.

Gordon's own views on the ethics of slave dealing are particularly interesting. "In spite of what Livingstone says," he wrote in a letter to Mrs. F., "I do not myself find about here that any affection exists between the parents and children; there is a mutual pleasure in parting with one another. I think the slavers' wars—made for the purpose of taking slaves—detestable, but if a father or mother of their own free will, and with the will of the child, sells that child, I do not see the objection to it. It was and is the wholesale depopulation of districts which makes slavery such a curse, and also the numbers killed, or who perish in the collection of slaves. A fair and properly conducted emigration would be the best thing for these parts, and I think the blacks would respond gladly to such a scheme. It will be a very, very long time before much can be done to civilize them; the climate is against it, and there can be no trade, for they have nothing to exchange for goods. Poor creatures, they would like to be left alone. . . . The blacks are glad of a little handful of maize, and live in the greatest discomfort; they have not a strip to cover them, but you do not see them grunting and groaning all day long, as you do scores and scores in England, with their wretched dinner-parties and attempts at gaiety when all is hollow and miserable."

It was on September 3rd that Gordon arrived at Gondokoro, to be greeted with the satisfying news that, in consequence of the despised Abou Saoud's influence, all the native chiefs of that area had formally pledged their submission to the Khedive's authority. Anticipating friction between Abou and one Raouf Bey, who had been Governor of Gondokoro for six years, and "had done absolutely nothing," he packed off the latter to Cairo, soothing his ruffled feelings with an ostentatious display that delighted Raouf but annoyed Abou! Such were the jealousies, envies, and intrigues inherent in these people, that Gordon's difficulties were considerably enhanced, and much solving of problems that should not have arisen fell to his lot.

He considered the climate of Gondokoro " much better " than
at Saubat. Yet, by the middle of September, two of his staff had
died, and nearly all the others were down with fever. He, himself,
whose constitution must have been remarkable, remained well,
" but a shadow." The position of Gondokoro being only five
degrees north of the equator, the heat was, of course, intense, while
the extensive marsh land produced myriads of mosquitoes. " The
mosquitoes in these parts," wrote Gordon, " are very bad, worse
than I have ever met with either in China, Batoum, or the Danube,
and that for two reasons—first their bite is very venomous, sharp,
and burning; and second, they do not hesitate to bite you. The
moment they arrive their gimlet is in you, and it is too late to
brush them off."

As much time as he could spare from his innumerable tasks
was now devoted to care of the sick, and if there has ever been
anything approaching a modern equivalent of the trials and tribulations of Job, these seemingly endless troubles and adversities, that
continued to beset the gallant crusader of the Sudan, must surely
have been well in the running for close comparison. " However,"
he wrote to his sister, " I am quite well, but my temper is very,
very short, and it is a bad time for those who come across me the
wrong way."

One day, leaving the sick in the care of a most able Italian on
his staff named Gessi, he set off up river in quest of a more suitable
spot for his headquarters, on higher ground that would be less
flooded than Gondokoro. Eventually, he found just what he
wanted at a place called Rageef, about sixteen miles due south of
Gondokoro. Before he got back, another of his staff had died; yet,
in his letters, he courageously made light of the incredible difficulties that daily confronted him and that would have discouraged
anyone less gifted with the qualities of determination, resourceful-
ness, and steadfast faith. " I am quite well, and things go on
smoothly," he wrote in another brave letter, " and I have a conviction that God willing, I shall do much in this country. The
main point is to be just and straightforward, to fear no one . . .
and to be hard to all if they do not obey you. All this is not easy
to do, but it must be my aim to accomplish it."

The strictest of disciplinarians, he would come down heavily
on the transgressor—indeed his vengeance could be terrible. But
no one could have been more compassionate when his sympathies
were aroused. His fierce wrath would soon subside, and often he
would repent him of severe penalties which, in his infinite mercy,

he would reconsider. No doubt many of Gordon's unorthodox methods of dealing with indiscipline would have horrified the rigid adherents to the letter rather than the spirit. But these unimaginative creatures would be incapable of understanding that forbearance may, in certain circumstances, be more beneficial to the interests of discipline than severity. Gordon was, of course, well aware of this, and, caring nothing for etiquette or orthodoxy, acted according to his own judgment and conscience. Nor was there any narrow-minded superior to interfere with him.

When asked why he had gone to the heart of the dark continent, he replied—" I felt too independent to serve, with my views, at Malta or in the corps, and perhaps I felt I had in me something that, if God willed, might benefit those lands, for He has given me great energy and health, and some little common sense." He most certainly did benefit those lands to an extent that probably no other man could have done. This, however, would not have been possible had he been entangled in the coils of red tape, and subjected to interference by incompetent superiors. Mercifully, he was in the enviable position of complete freedom from official shackles, leaving him unrestricted for the exercise of his exceptional powers.

Whereas, previously, the Egypt an officials had compelled the natives to do anything required of them without payment, and thus incurred their bitter hatred, Gordon soon put a stop to all this, insisting that fair payment should be made for whatever service they performed. He, moreover, supplied the natives with the means of cultivating the land, formerly shockingly neglected, and purchased their ivory. The result was that, in no time, they threw off their fear of the Government, and unhesitatingly brought in their produce. Gordon, for his part, strengthened this new-born confidence by fearlessly going out alone among them—an example no Egyptian official would have dared to emulate.

It must not be supposed that all his innovations were put into force without grumblings and growlings on the part of officials of the old régime. Far from it, for Gordon constantly found himself confronted with opposition to his decrees. But, for all jibbers and objectors he had one remedy, and one only. He gave them the option of obeying his orders without question, or instant dismissal. Now, dismissal would have entailed finding their own way back through hundreds of miles of devastated country inhabited by natives whose hatred they had invited, and who would certainly have killed them. By this ingenious method, Gordon held them in the hollow of his hand, their fear of reprisals at the hands of those they had so cruelly oppressed compelling them to accept the first alternative and to promise obedience.

Meanwhile, work was progressing on the construction of the line of forts extending far up the Nile towards the great lakes bordering Uganda. This blockhouse system would prove an effective barrier for thwarting the slave dealers, whose boats on their way to Khartoum would be obliged to run the gauntlet of the forts constructed at intervals along the river. For navigation of the lakes, a large steamer was being conveyed up the Nile in sections, to be put together on reaching its destination.

Now almost bereft of his staff, most of whom had either succumbed to the climate or been invalided back to Khartoum, Gordon was indeed bringing something of civilisation to this wild, desolate country, and doing it practically single-handed. Prodigious as his energies continued to be despite the enervating climate, it must have been an immense relief to him when his chief of staff, Colonel Long, at last returned, after an absence of about six months, from a mission to Mtesa, the King of Uganda. Though Long's embassy doubtless broke the ice and paved the way for establishing friendly relations, Gordon was to find the Uganda tribes troublesome, and their king untrustworthy. But there will be more of this to record at the appropriate stage.

It was at Rageef that Gordon finally got rid of the intolerably conceited Abou Saoud. In his letter of dismissal, his sense of fairness in giving the culprit detailed reasons for his action, as well as his relentless severity to a man who had received nothing but compassionate treatment at his hands, and who had wickedly abused the kindness extended to him—these were notable features of the document which ran as follows:—

"Abou, when I took you up at Cairo, there was not an Arab or a foreigner who would have thought of employing you, but I trusted to your protestation and did so. When I got to Gondokoro, you were behaving properly, and I congratulated myself on your appointment to the high post I gave you. Soon, however, I came little by little to repent my action, and to find out my fair treatment was thrown away. You tried to deceive me . . . you misstated . . . you told me falsely . . . etc. etc. To come to more personal matters, you strangely forgot our relative positions; you have forced your way into my private apartments at all times, have disputed my orders in my presence, and treated all my other officers with arrogance, showing me that you are an ambitious, grasping man, and unworthy of the authority I gave you. If you do this under my eyes and at the beginning of your work, what will you do when away from me? Now hear my decision. Your appointment is cancelled, and you will return to Gondokoro and wait my orders. Remember, though I remove you from your office, you are still a government officer, subject to its laws, which I shall not hesitate to put in force against you if I find you intriguing."

Gordon's remarkable power over savage, rebellious peoples was constantly demonstrated during his unrivalled career. His independent character, his impatience of delay, his outspokenness, his intolerance of interference, his fiery temper, his reluctance to accept advice, his determination to go his own way, his distaste for routine—all these qualities combined to produce in him a longing to get away on his own, free from the hindrance of red tape, the rigid inflexibility of cast iron regulations, the bondage of conventionality, free from what he called " leading strings." No one knew better than Gordon, himself, how unsuited he was to the ordinary course of a soldier's life. He could not have tolerated for long the constant irritations and annoyances suffered through undue interference, while his plain speaking and undisguised contempt for incompetence in his seniors must inevitably, sooner or later, have involved him in serious trouble. Consequently, it seems providential, from every point of view, that time after time opportunities should have arisen giving scope for the exercise of his phenomenal gifts, unhampered by the meddling of superior authority.

He firmly believed that in the Sudan he was acting as the instrument of God, and there can be no shadow of doubt that the steadfastness of his faith enabled him to overcome the incredible difficulties of his mission, and to pass unscathed through dangers and adversities that decimated his followers, leaving him almost alone to carry on his great work.

His power over the natives was not the result of harsh methods. On the contrary, compassion and sympathy were conspicuous features of his administration. He detested brutality, and would deal severely with anyone found guilty of resorting to it. Where others would have condemned and punished, he would often adopt a diametrically opposite line of action, foreseeing, with his penetrating insight, advantages that never would have occurred to those who see no farther than the tips of their noses, who know not what it is to depart however slightly from a line of strict orthodoxy, and in whom initiative is unknown.

Gordon gained the confidence of the wild tribes around him by methods utterly different from those of the old régime, his first concern being to get rid of the fear instilled in the unfortunate natives by the cruelty of Egyptian officials and soldiers before his arrival on the scene. By means of kindly treatment and fair dealing, he gradually induced them to cast off their suspicions and approach him without fear, realising, as they came to do, that he was a friend, not an enemy, that he was there to help, not to oppress them, to deal with them honestly and straightforwardly, not to rob and defraud them.

Simple inoffensive people for the most part, they had become soured by years of ill-treatment, and their bitterness, not unnaturally, engendered hostility towards the Government and its corrupt, tyrannical officials. This hostile attitude gradually became transformed into one of respect and devotion as a result of Gordon's sympathetic methods; though there were, of course, exceptions, when his striking personality, his indomitable courage, his superb calm, would convert an ugly, threatening situation into one of submissive quiescence.

On one notable occasion, learning that a revolt was imminent in a district some eighty miles from his headquarters, Gordon promptly mounted his camel and, alone except for one or two attendants, rode off across the desert to the scene of the trouble. On his arrival, so amazed were the rebellious chiefs at the audacity of this lone Englishman riding into their midst with complete unconcern, and so subdued by his overpowering demeanour, that he had little difficulty in bending them to his will and persuading them to obey his orders.

Again, on the road between Gondokoro and Rageef, he chanced to meet a hostile sheikh who, after a friendly talk with him, went away only to return with a number of armed men, who began to surround his tent. For a time, Gordon calmly watched their movements; then, getting up, he quietly placed his two guns in a position of readiness and ordered the sheikh to go. The man instantly obeyed. " I feel sure," wrote Gordon, " he meditated hitting me on the head with one of his knob sticks."

It is given to few men, this remarkable ability to overcome seemingly overwhelming opposition, to reduce to docility the inflamed passions of revolutionaries, by sheer strength of character. But Gordon was the happy possessor of this power to an incomparable degree. Just as in China the rebel *Taipings* had come to look upon him as some kind of supernatural being, against whom nothing could avail, so in the Sudan the uncanny effect of his dominating personality was very much the same. He was, undoubtedly, cut out for this kind of work, and it is questionable whether any other man could have accomplished a shadow of Gordon's extraordinary achievements. There exists a common theory that no man is indispensable. To such a rule Gordon might be said to provide the exception that proves it. One can well believe his eye of steely grey, that even those of his own station in life found disconcertingly penetrating, would have been devastating when directed in disapproval on men of coloured races, who, by reason of their creation as a lower order of humanity, are inherently imbued with a sense of inferiority to the white man.

In the rare instances where hostile tribes were not so amenable to his rule, Gordon would punish them severely, adhering closely to his dictum that to succeed he must strike hard at any who disobeyed his commands.

Pursuing his policy, Gordon started to teach the natives the use of money. " I began," he wrote, " by paying each man who worked some beads. Next day I gave each man who worked half a piastre (one penny) in copper, and offered to sell him beads to that amount. They soon saw it, and would not buy; they said, ' We will keep the money till we get more, and can buy more expensive things.' I have fixed certain prices for certain things, and made out little lots of beads and wire to sell for certain prices—in fact made a regular shop, much to the discontent of all the old hands, who are dead against these new-fangled ideas, though I say they will eventually gain, for they will be able to keep shops."

Towards the end of 1874, he gave up the station at Gondokoro on account of its pestiferous climate and moved its personnel and equipment twelve miles down river to a far healthier place called Lardo. There he set up workshops for the advancement of his plans, and arranged for the establishment of a hospital where all his sick could be concentrated.

CHAPTER X

An Inhospitable Region

WITH the coming of the new year, Gordon had every reason to be satisfied with the progress of his mission. Already he had imposed an effective check on the slave traders: established friendly relations with most of the tribes: opened up a number of new stations on his proposed blockhouse line: rigorously condemned the corrupt and evil practices of the former régime: and made considerable headway in opening the communication route between Khartoum and the great lakes.

For his part, the Khedive was more concerned with the success of the last named project than with Gordon's progress towards the abolition of slavery, for would it not greatly extend the limits of his already vast dominions? But before reaching their ultimate objective and enlarging the Khedive's realm as far as the Victoria Nyanza, the expedition would have to pass through the territories of Mtesa, the savage, unreliable King of Uganda, and his even more intractable satellite, Kaba Rega, who ruled over the province of Unyoro. It would, consequently, become part of Gordon's task either to induce these two inhospitable potentates to be friendly, or, failing that, leave them in no doubt that hostility would be met by the sternest measures.

From the very start of the expedition, his methods in dealing with the wild tribes had been conciliatory. He gave them presents, encouraged them to cultivate the land, entertained them with a magic lantern, impressed on them that he came as their friend and their protector against the tyranny they had hitherto endured, striving to imbue them with confidence and banish their fears. But, to those who kicked over the traces, as for example the savage, troublesome Baris, Gordon revealed the opposite extreme of his nature, for, while no one could have shown more kindliness and

compassion so long as he considered them deserved, when impeded
in the work of his great crusade by open hostility the weight of
his avenging hand would come down with shattering force, and the
offenders could expect little mercy.

During the first half of his six year sojourn in the Sudan,
the opposition he encountered did not seriously delay his progress,
but, even so, it could more easily have been swept aside but for
the poor quality of the Egyptian troops at his disposal. Besides
being indifferent shots, their hearts were not in the business, their
discipline was almost non-existent, and they had little thought for
anything but their own welfare. It must be remembered, however,
that for years they had practically run loose, thriving on plunder,
oppressing the natives, and doing just as they liked. Moreover,
since they were split up into small garrisons of forts many miles
apart, Gordon could not keep them all under his own eye, and
had to rely on subordinates whose presence could not be expected
to have the same electrifying, invigorating effect as that of the great
man himself who, as we saw in China, possessed the remarkable
power of galvanising men to superlative efforts by his presence
alone.

After a time, he enrolled Sudanese natives in his service. These
proved far superior to the Egyptians as soldiers, especially those of
the Niam Niam tribe, described by him as presenting a most fear
some appearance. " The ladies," added Gordon in his humorous
way, " wear a bunch of leaves as full dress! "

It was early n 1875 that his advance up the Nile was harassed
by the warlike Baris, whose venerable chief, Bedden, had resisted
all Gordon's efforts to establish a friendly understanding. True to
his fine principles and kindly instincts, he would not punish offend
ing tribes by force of arms unless they were guilty of actual
aggression. But disobedience of his orders and lawlessness could
not be overlooked, so, upon those who refused to toe the line, he
inflicted the effective penalty of cattle confiscation, raiding their
kraals by night and seizing a considerable number of their beasts.
" I do most cordially hate this work," he wrote, " but the question
is what are you to do? You must protect your own people, and
also the friendly sheiks; and you cannot make them give in except
by the capture of their cattle."

Yet, so anxious was he to be scrupulously fair to the natives
that even this method of punishment was abandoned after an un
fortunate episode in which cattle belonging to a friendly chief were
mistaken for those of a transgressor. Though he promptly re

turned them to their owner, Gordon declared—" I have done with raids after my misfortune with my friendly sheikh, and only if attacked will I sanction reprisals, and I will also see whether I have not given cause for attack." It was this almost fastidious attention to fair treatment, and his obvious desire to avoid harsh measures, that appealed so strongly to the natives, making them, for the most part, docile and easy to handle.

Some may have thought him over lenient in his dealings with the native chiefs. But let it be remembered that, combined with the quality of mercy, was that uncanny insight into character. Perhaps, indeed, by means of his penetrating eye that seemed to bore clean through you, he was able to look into a man's very soul and discover his potentialities for good or evil. On the whole, it is probable that few attempts were made to take advantage of Gordon's kindness, and that far more good came of his sympathetic methods than could ever have resulted from harsh treatment. Like the Chinese, the natives of the Sudan gradually came to look upon him as a superior being endowed with mystical power to overcome all obstacles in his path, and to do whatsoever he wished. Nor could they forget that he was their deliverer from the oppression of the Egyptians.

He became thoroughly disgusted with the generally accepted methods applied by white men to black, which he summed up in these words—" These are their maxims. If the natives don't act after the most civilised manner, then punish them for not so acting, but if it comes to a question of our action, then follow the customs of the natives—viz., recognise plunder as no offence whatever. They weigh the actions of ignorant natives after one and their own code; they act towards the natives after the native code, which recognises the right of the stronger to pillage his neighbour. Oh! I am sick of these people. It is they, and not the blacks, who need civilisation."

Gordon, who always called a spade a spade and said precisely what he thought, often meditated, during his loneliness in the wild regions of equatorial Africa, as to how soon the Khedive would become weary of his outspokenness, his criticisms, and his demands, and would repent of having engaged the services of so candid, so independent a man. "Some might care if they were dismissed," he wrote to his sister, "as the world would talk. Thank God, I am screened from that fear. I know that I have done my very best, as far as my intellect has allowed me, for the Khedive and I have tried to be just to all; so if I go, do not expect to see your brother broken-hearted. . . . I acknowledge to feeling a sort of regret if I have to leave before opening the river to the lakes, but it would soon pass off, and I should think it God's will that I should not do it."

He quite expected to receive notification of his dismissal almost any day. But, far from contemplating for one moment the termination of Gordon's services in the Sudan, the Khedive knew he had found a treasure, a man possessing an astonishing array of truly remarkable qualities unlikely to be concentrated in any other individual. Realising this, Khedive Ismail was concerned only to keep Gordon as long as possible, and would have been ready and willing to grant almost any concession to avoid losing him.

Bearing in mind Gordon's variety of innovations, foremost among which were his measures for the suppression of the slave trade, and the abolition of malpractices by Government servants, especially in so far as they affected the natives, it was not surprising that he became surrounded by enemies, who made it their business to seize every opportunity of attempting to discredit him at Khartoum and Cairo. But, whatever the effect of these vindictive grumblings on the Egyptian Government as a whole, the Khedive remained loyal and friendly to the great Englishman who had come forward so gallantly to help his country at a time of crisis, and had already worked wonders in conditions of unbelievable difficulty and hardship.

Chief of Gordon's nuisances was the Governor-General at Khartoum, Ismail Yakoob, whose resentment at the disturbance of his indolent existence by the Englishman's whirlwind energy goaded him to assert himself, thereby afflicting Gordon with much unnecessary annoyance. It may be taken for granted that in the end Yakoob came off second best, though, to be sure, Gordon had enough trouble to bear without the unwelcome attempts of this inept official to interfere with him.

Of the innumerable trials and perplexities encountered in putting down slavery, subduing unruly tribes, struggling against the ravages of the unhealthy climate, contending with opposition to his new régime and with intrigue, and opening communication to the great lakes, perhaps nothing gave rise to more anxiety, nor entailed more arduous labour, than the Nile's uncompromising obstructions represented by waterfalls, cataracts, and rapids. The terrific labour of dragging *nuggars*[1] up the rapids, with the current

---

[1] Boats specially constructed for use on the upper waters of the Nile.

running strong and the river rising, was alluded to by Gordon in a letter to his sister, Augusta. "A day of agony to me," he wrote. " I am really quite exhausted—more mentally than physically. It has indeed been a fearful day; one *nuggar* nearly sunk. It is the violent eddies that are so terrible. The slightest faltering in the haulers would be fatal. Your brother prays the *nuggars* up as he used to do the troops when they wavered in the breaches in China, but often and often the ropes break and it has all to be done over again. However, I feel sure that we shall have fully made known to us the mystery of these matters. Sometimes I think I am punished for some arbitrary act I have been guilty of, for the soldiers have tried me sorely. I do not feel that I ever could do any more work after this command. It certainly takes the edge off one, and adds to one's age."

The trend of these last three sentences suggests the baneful effect, even on so strong a constitution as Gordon's, of the poisonous climate, the endless labour, the constant anxieties, the solitude, the almost insuperable difficulties. It seems, moreover, to indicate some little disorder of his normally impervious nerves. Of the climate, he wrote—" The moment the sun goes down, a cold damp arises, which enters one's very bones. There is not an interval of five minutes between the setting of the sun and the rising of the dreadful damp, and you feel the danger, as it were, at once." On the Arabs, especially, the climate had a devastating effect, their resistance to its ravages being conspicuously ineffectual. Out of a reinforcement of a hundred and fifty, considerably more than half of them were on the sick list the day after their arrival. Of fifteen sick sent down by Gordon, only two survived to reach Khartoum.

Though usually so cheerful and sanguine, the lone crusader would occasionally be what he called " down," or in the grip of the " doles." When afflicted by these bouts he would sometimes shut himself up in his tent, refusing to see anyone. But they would soon pass and he would once more be himself, brimming over with zeal and energy, warm heartedness and humour. Perhaps the most noticeable feature of his reaction to the exacting conditions in which he lived was the effect on his temper, frankly admitted by him to have become unreliable. Yet, after subjecting offenders to the rough of his tongue, and even, on occasion, to the weight of his hand, he would, as a rule, be sorry for his outburst and feel pity for the chastened.

Progressing higher and higher up the river and approaching nearer and nearer to the equator, Gordon found the natives increasingly difficult to deal with. A party of about forty men under a French member of his staff called Linant, sent out to punish a hostile tribe by burning their huts, was ambushed by the natives and almost entirely destroyed. Linant had himself suggested the expedition, and it was with some diffidence that Gordon had given his consent. The result could hardly have been more unfortunate, for apart from the losses suffered, the prestige of the Egyptian soldiers would not be improved, nor would the natives' fear of fire-arms be anything but diminished. But Gordon persevered with his settled policy of propitiation, presenting the natives with gifts of beads and grain, repairing their watches and musical boxes, and, on one occasion when a chief's daughter had fallen into the hands of his troops, he returned her to her father after decking her out in the most sumptuous costume the local stores could provide.

For weeks at a time, he uttered no word of his own language, being entirely alone except for Arabs and natives. When his German servant fell a victim to the decimating fever, Gordon had to rely for personal attention chiefly on two nine year old Shillook boys, who vied with one another in their eagerness to carry out his orders. "Two mosquito-like scraps of Shillooks," wrote Gordon, " who stagger under a few pounds' weight; they are amusing little creatures about nine years of age, hate one another, and run like mad to fulfil your wishes if they know them by signs; they have now learned to do a good deal for me."

And so the eternal toil went on, day after day battling against the great heat, the deadly plague of malaria, the incredible difficulties of negotiating the Nile's endless obstructions. Of the great undertaking, Gordon was the mainspring, hurrying from one point of perplexity or trouble to another with a spirited energy that nothing seemed able to subdue, and stimulating those around him wherever he went. Even the debilitating ague of malaria failed to curb his tireless activity for any length of time, for no sooner had the shivering and shaking abated than he would be up and off again as though anxious to make up for wasted hours.

Writing from Rageef in April (1875), he said—" The great difficulty I have to contend with is how to get the heavy portions of the steamer to the point where the Nile is navigable above the generally accepted cataracts—a distance of a hundred miles from

Gondokoro." One reason for his rather tedious progress is to be found in his reluctance to act on information until he had confirmed it by his own personal observation. He could never entirely rely on what he was told, owing to the intrigue and duplicity that hampered his operations; consequently, he felt obliged to see things for himself despite the additional time occupied in this way.

At a chance meeting with the hostile chief, Bedden, an old man partially blind, Gordon treated him kindly, gave him some tobacco, and persuaded him to visit his camp at Rageef. Two days later, the chief arrived, when, to the consternation of the Arab interpreter who would have skinned the old ruffian alive, Gordon made much of him, presenting him with twenty confiscated cows, a roll of copper wire, and a pair of scissors, thus making him his friend for ever. Of his interpreter, he wrote—" The more I see of my Levantine the more I feel evil towards him, for he has not my thoughts, and is, to my mind, short-sighted. He does not see that my (to the blacks) extraordinary conduct towards Bedden will spread through all the tribes, and make them see that I act justly and generously towards them."

By June, Gordon had reached Kerri with a hundred men, there to establish a new station and to construct yet another of his forts. Between Rageef and Kerri, some seventy-five miles apart, the Nile passes through a narrow gorge, where the current raced at such speed that it was only with the utmost difficulty that the *nuggars* could be pulled through. " It was terrible work," wrote Gordon, " and I was fearful of a shipwreck. However, thank God! we got through safely, and now are making a *seriba*[1] on the hill."

A good deal of trouble and danger seems to have been experienced from hippopotamuses, which were sometimes encountered in considerable numbers. Though normally comparatively docile, these huge beasts were capable of crushing a boat in their enormous jaws, or of overturning almost any river craft with the tremendous weight of their bodies.

By this time, the northern part of the Equatorial Provinces had become unbelievably transformed by Gordon's masterly hand. Evils that formerly beset these regions, now being left behind him, had largely been eradicated, lawlessness and strife giving way to more peaceful, orderly conditions. Whereas, before Gordon's

---

[1] Alternative spelling zariba—a Sudanese thorn fence used for purposes of defence.

arrival on the scene, the roads or tracks were unsafe for parties of less than about twenty men, now the natives had become so friendly that individuals could move about in comparative security. Instead of taking the law into their own hands as had been their wont, they now brought their complaints to Gordon or his representatives, confident that justice would be done. Altogether, thanks to his wise administration, far better understanding had been reached between the Egyptian officials and the natives, fear and mistrust of one another being noticeably overcome. Twelve months earlier, all steamers and *nuggars* on the river were escorted by five or six soldiers. Now, they travelled up and down stream entirely without protection. That this almost miraculous change could have been brought about in so short a space of time by the wisdom and exertions of one man, poorly supported alike by the Egyptian authorities and the material provided for his assistance, seems quite phenomenal, and must surely have been highly gratifying to Gordon, himself, as well as to the Khedive.

But there was much arduous work ahead in continuing the crusade through the southern regions, not only in battling against river obstructions, but also in establishing amicable relations with the tribes, whose attitude, as the expedition advanced, tended to deteriorate. Drums were to be heard at night, while in daytime natives armed to the teeth could be seen on the hilltops sullenly watching this incursion into their territory. Nevertheless, at this stage of the journey, the tribesmen gave far less trouble than the river, whose redoubtable barriers were a source of constant anxiety. Moreover, the Nile rose higher than ever before in the memory of the natives, thus adding appreciably to the difficulties and dangers of the boats.

Gordon seemed mystically impervious to afflictions from which others would suffer serious, or even fatal, consequences. One night, a scorpion succeeded in finding its way inside his mosquito net, stabbing him several times with its poisonous tail. Yet, after calmly drowning the deadly creature in a glass of water, he returned to bed apparently none the worse; nor does he appear to have suffered any serious after effects from this exceedingly unpleasant experience.

At Kerri, he was relieved to find no mosquitoes. "You can have little idea," he wrote, "what an intense comfort this is. At Gondokoro they swarmed, and bit you under the table and wherever any skin was tight—trousers, shirt, or coat was to them no obstacle. They liked a cane-bottomed chair best for you to sit on." His description of the ant-lion is particularly interesting. "They are small insects, with a flexible leg," he explained. "They make a crater and rest in the apex of it, throwing up, with the flexible leg, now and then, a shower of sand. Ants walk on the edge, and slip down. As they are getting up the slippery bank, the flexible leg throws up a shower of sand, and then another and another; till at last, as if in the cinders of Vesuvius, the ant gets smothered, and falls to the bottom, where a pair of nippers takes him into an inner chamber, and dinner is ready!"

He found that the Sudanese soldiers, when transferred from one station to another, were in the habit of leaving their wives behind so as to retain possession of the huts they had occupied. This irregular practice, which tended to swell unnecessarily the size of the stations, rendering them more vulnerable to attack, was soon put a stop to by Gordon, who was reminded, so he said, of the theory expounded to the young cadets at Woolwich by their French instructor. "Von vife at Paris, von vife in London," he would declare, "dat is de vay to enjoy life!"

On learning that he would be honoured by the Royal Geographical Society as soon as he reached the lakes, Gordon, with his inherent modesty and distaste for ostentation, decided he would not go on the lakes himself, but would delegate their navigation to one of his subordinates. In this way, he hoped to avoid any recognition by the society of his own achievements. But, apart from his desire for self-effacement, he considered that "they (the society) have no more business to be giving medals to the people than the people have to give medals to them. Sovereigns and representative assemblies of nations, and old corporations that date from centuries, can confer honours; not any society which may spring up."

For long periods he heard no word from the Khedive, who, at least, left him to run his own show; though, to be sure, some more tangible support would not have come amiss. But, as Gordon said—"Thank God, He prevents me caring for any man's favour or disfavour."

When thinking of his ultimate departure from the country, he would wonder whether he was really justified in bringing the people to a state of docility that might render them easy prey to his Egyptian and Turkish successors. "If I stay," he wrote, "I trust to the Higher than the Highest to look to the welfare of these heathen (His inheritance) after I go."

Few men could have endured Gordon's life in this uninviting country half as long as he did. Except when some delay or other held up operations, his days were occupied in tireless activities—

visiting the stations, establishing new ones, constructing forts, settling disputes, pacifying the inhabitants, training his troops, supervising the negotiation of river obstructions, and even helping with the *nuggars* himself—these were some of the more important items of his daily work. Since there was scarcely anyone he could rely on but himself, he felt obliged to be here, there, and every-where. As he said, he had to think of the veriest trifle, even to knocking off the white ants from the stores. At night he slept in a tent, going to bed at eight or nine o'clock to escape from the tor-ments of mosquitoes, and getting up again at dawn. As to his diet, " most extraordinary I can assure you; no vegetables, dry biscuits, a few bits of broiled meat and some boiled macaroni." Not exactly an enviable existence, most people would say, but he preferred it to stiff shirts and dinner parties.

On the last day of July, Gordon left Kerri southward bound. After travelling about two miles, he came upon the Googi rapids—a serious obstruction to his progress. To each *nuggar* there were between sixty and eighty natives hauling on the ropes, which often broke under the tremendous strain, allowing the boat to be whirled away in a six-knot current. One *nuggar* narrowly escaped sinking, while a smaller craft broke loose and was carried nearly four miles downstream before being secured. Altogether, it was an exhaust-ing, trying experience, but, with the assistance of many natives, and above all Gordon's inspiring leadership, the stupendous difficulties were eventually overcome, and, little more than a week after leaving Kerri, the flotilla was able to proceed once more on a stretch of open river. Gordon declared he had never had a more anxious time.

He said there were four main impediments to his progress, namely " the natural difficulties of the river: the march through shy and unknown tribes who have never seen a foreigner: a use-less, untrustworthy set of soldiers and officers encumbered with women—there are a hundred and twenty women and children to a hundred and eighty soldiers: want of good ropes to haul the *nuggars.*"

Notwithstanding the help given him by the natives, Gordon found them distinctly uncertain in their attitude. They appeared to resent the move up river as an intrusion, but those who assisted in the operations presumably found the remuneration more than they could resist. On August 12th, some of them looked like giving trouble, and cautiously approached Gordon's camp, " but our long-range rifles made them think differently. They were evidently people of moods, since one day they would show every sign of hostility, and the next they would visit the camp in the most friendly manner."

Two days later, Gordon scored a notable success in his efforts to pacify the inhabitants when three chiefs, who had been hostile, came in and submitted, expressing regret for their conduct.

As to the weapons used by tribesmen in the Equatorial Provinces, besides their long-headed spears, they carried bows and arrows, the latter having curiously barbed heads. At first, they were much afraid of firearms, but familiarity, combined with the poor shooting of the Egyptian soldiers, tended, as time went on, to lessen their fear and make them more venturesome. When on mischief bent, they seldom came out into the open, preferring to keep to the long grass which, in that part of the country, grew to six, and even eight, feet in height.

Alluding to the Linant disaster, Gordon wrote—" The natives are brave fellows, they know that our soldiers cannot hit them in most cases when they fire, and so in they rush and it is over. The wretched black soldier is not a match for a native with spear and bow; the soldier cannot shoot and is at the native's mercy, if the native knew it." But he was now training his men to shoot, and enrolling a number of natives so as to strengthen his force against aggression. Yet, in his fairness of mind, he could not help sympathising with the inhabitants in their anxiety to keep their own country to themselves, and their tendency to resent the incursion of outsiders. "You will say I am most inconsistent," he wrote in one of his home letters, "and so I am, and so are you. We are dead against our words when it comes to action. We will at morning prayers say forgive as we forgive, and then hurry over breakfast to carry on the squabble of the day before." His acute sense of justice and his generous readiness to recognise the other man's point of view, even when it operated to his own disadvantage, can best be illustrated by the instance of a chief being brought before him accused of misleading a party sent out to seize cattle from an offending tribe. "If he did mislead them," wrote Gordon, "he was a brave, patriotic man, and I shall let him go." And then, with characteristic pity for victims of cruelty in any shape or form—" Poor fellow," he continued, "they had tied his hands so tight that they were quite swollen. How I hate the country and all the work!"

Imagine the horror of the average commander, or the Whitehall wiselings, at such unorthodox, such revolutionary methods. But

Gordon knew what he was doing, and, in doing what he did, probably earned the undying gratitude, loyalty, and respect of this leader of a wild tribe of savages. The exploded notion of those whose position requires them to be good disciplinarians, but who, unfortunately, are not, that only by harsh methods and severe punishment can a proper standard of orderliness be attained, found no place in the mind of Charles Gordon, who knew full well that severity can do no good unless judiciously blended with forbearance; and that situations, from time to time, arise when the exercise of moderation will be in the interests of all concerned. " Truly a different stamp of soldier this from the usual type of which history is so full," wrote Sir William Butler. " What a contrast to any among the long list of later heroes is this man, who, with all his humanity and all his tenderness of heart, is still by far the most successful conqueror of savage races, and the wisest ruler of them, too, that this modern England of ours has seen."

Generally speaking, Gordon gained quite a good impression of these equatorial tribes who, if utterly uncivilised, seemed " singularly free from vice, and managed to get on well without any regular laws." Unilke those of more northerly latitudes, the natives of this unexplored southern region, through which Gordon was now passing, had not suffered from Egyptian ill-treatment, and, consequently, had no reason for fear or hatred of the newcomers. But, when they saw the new stations being established, and realised that the invaders had come to stay, they did show unmistakable signs—not unnaturally, to Gordon's way of thinking—of indignation. " They say," he wrote—" ' We do not want your cloth and beads; you go your way and we will go ours. We do not want to see your chief. This land is ours, and you will not have it, neither its bread nor its flocks.' "

Yet, he continued to explain to them the reasons for his coming; that, far from wishing them harm, one of his foremost aims was to promote their welfare and improve their lot. Only in cases where they paid no attention to his assurances and showed open hostility, did Gordon resort to punitive measures, when the confiscation of some cattle, or the burning of a few huts, would usually bring the offenders to heel. " If they (the natives) are to be put down," he wrote, " it is better I should do it than an exterminating pasha who would have no mercy. . . . I do not want to hurt these people, but we must defend ourselves. . . . People laugh at bows and arrows, but at night they are very disagreeable; for you have no idea whence they come."

By September, Gordon had, for administrative and economic purposes, entirely separated his territory from that of the Governor-General at Khartoum. This proved far more satisfactory, seeing that when dependent on Ismail Yakoob for reinforcements, supplies, and so on, he had the greatest difficulty in getting what he wanted, and was constantly obliged to complain to the Khedive of neglect to comply with his demands. Now, he had become independent of Khartoum, and raised his own revenue, which, after deducting expenditure incurred in his provinces, was remitted direct to Cairo.

New stations were formed at Laboré and still farther south at Duffli, the expedition, now, penetrating deep into the heart of Central Africa, where Gordon appears to have been impressed, above all, by the overwhelming stillness, the loneliness, the solitude. It seemed to him as though he had reached " the end of the world." Unlike the tribes they had left behind, who lived in scattered huts, the natives of these southern regions dwelt, for purposes of better security, inside *seribas;* consequently, neither huts nor inhabitants were to be seen unless one of these concentrations came into view.

The last remnants of his entourage were fading away, leaving him a lone figure in this fever-stricken wilderness of desolation far from the civilised world. As lesser men fell by the wayside, the invincible Gordon went on, undeterred by the perplexities and frustrations encountered at every turn. Still, he had no illusions as to the inevitable effect on his system of this baneful, wearing existence among mosquito infested swamps, exposed to the grilling tropical sun by day and the chill, malarious damp by night, ill-nourished by the coarsest food, exhausted by the daily toil and wrestling with innumerable problems such as the river obstructions, native hostility, and the organisation of his widely scattered forces.

In one of his less optimistic moods, he wrote in a home letter dated October 4th, 1875—" I shall never be fit for anything again, and shall try to retire if I live to the end of the work. . . . I am not fastidious, but cockroach nests in your sugar, rice, etc., do not tempt one to eat. . . . I can talk to no one, so I write a great deal. There are none here to talk to except about their pay, or how they can be made more comfortable."

A fortnight later, Gordon found himself faced with the most serious obstruction yet encountered during his long journey from Khartoum. About five miles up river from Duffli, the newest of his stations lying within three degrees of the equator, he experienced something of a shock on coming to a spot where, for a distance of two miles, the river became unnavigable owing to a succession of cataracts and rapids known as the Fola falls. Gordon must have been momentarily in despair, for he wrote—" It is all over! " But that was, no doubt, due to the initial shock of suddenly coming upon what, at first glance, seemed an insurmountable barrier so near the end of the long, long trail. It was indeed a cruel blow, but he took pains to hide his feelings of bitter disappointment. " I bore it well," he wrote, " and for all you could see it might have been a picnic party to the Fola falls; but it is rather sad, and will give me a mint of trouble and delay." Already, he had brushed aside any question of impossibility, and was beginning to look ahead, thinking only of the additional delay and labour involved through the unwelcome discovery, while banishing from his mind the possibility of defeat.

He decided that the only course open to him was to carry or drag everything overland to the far side of the falls, a distance of two miles. At the end of October, he transferred his headquarters from Duffli to a place called Fashelie, some nine miles up river, where he found the climate less trying. Then, in preparation for the arduous work of moving everything to a point above the falls, he sent for fifty camels, hoping with their help to expedite the inevitably prolonged, wearisome task. In this part of the country, vast tracts of land were covered with long grass which, besides being monotonous to a degree, was awkward from a security point of view, as it enabled hostile natives to approach the camp unseen. Soon it would be possible to destroy it by fire, but as yet the grass was too wet owing to the rainy season.

" You can imagine," wrote Gordon, " what it is—this grass. Here, on level ground, it is as if you were in a pit six feet deep, and within a radius of fifty yards, you can see nothing but the tops of distant hills. . . . Imagine to yourself a sea for fifties of miles of grass six feet high, through which the very narrow paths are with difficulty discernible."

In December, Gordon returned down river to punish the Moogie tribe for their continued hostility. After seizing fifteen hundred of their cows, he left them sadder, if not wiser, to meditate on the folly of their unfriendliness. On getting back to his headquarters, he was greatly cheered by the arrival of the steamer sections carried by porters. After recording this highly encouraging news, however, he repeated his determination not to go upon the lakes himself. " I am not," he wrote, " after nine months of worry, in a fit state to explore anything but my way out of the province."

So ended the year 1875—a year that Gordon could look back on with pride and satisfaction. His achievements had been prodigious, and it is probably safe to say that, in the history of the world, no parallel could be found to his phenomenal success in face of difficulties, dangers, impediments, opposition, and adversities that were beyond description. He had crippled the slave trade; promoted friendliness among tribes that had formerly been hostile to the Government; substituted law and order for corruption and chaos; infused some measure of discipline into his mediocre troops; established a chain of stations stretching from Khartoum almost to the lakes, thereby keeping the Nile open and safe for transport; and, by his wise administration, had converted the southern Sudan from being a serious liability to the Egyptian Government into a going concern that paid its way. Assuredly, the Khedive had much to be thankful for, and could congratulate himself on having found so trusty a collaborator.

CHAPTER XI

The Great Lakes

THE opening of the new year (1876) saw Gordon within measurable distance of his goal, and, but for the unfortunate impediment of the Fola falls, he would soon have reached the lakes. But several months were to elapse before this could be accomplished—months of laborious toil in conveying, over two miles of rough country, the river craft, equipment, and supplies of the expedition.

While this tremendously arduous transport of material was going on, aided by a number of camels that had arrived on the scene, Gordon hurried to and fro along his line of stations, which now reached almost to the lakes, settling disputes here, arranging for supplies there, stimulating the garrisons by his galvanizing presence, his ubiquity, his tireless energy. When travelling by land, he seldom walked less than fourteen miles a day in the broiling equatorial sun, often covering considerably more.

As to his plans for the final stage of the journey, he proposed that his Italian assistant, Gessi—about the only remaining member of his original staff—should undertake the navigation of the Albert Nyanza from a place called Magungo, while he, himself, went overland to Foweira on a bend of the Nile to the east of Magungo, and, establishing stations as he went, continued his advance to the far more extensive Victoria lake.

For three months, the carrying and dragging ceaselessly went on, until, at last, two lifeboats were launched above the falls—a tremendous triumph for Gordon, whose determination to overcome this seemingly impervious obstruction had never, for one moment, faltered. Finally, in mid-April, it was possible for Gessi to take the boats out on to the Albert Nyanza, and to begin the task of exploring this lesser of the two great lakes. His adventures

included a violent storm that brought the terrified Arab sailors to
their knees in prayer, and carried the boats against an island occupied by tribesmen, whose approach had to be stopped by rifle fire.
On his return, about a fortnight later, he reported to Gordon that
the lake covered an area of fifty miles from east to west, and a
hundred and forty miles from north to south. Natives encountered on the surrounding shore, who belonged to the tribes of
Kaba Rega, the hostile satellite of Mtesa, were none too friendly,
being particularly suspicious of Gessi, probably the first white man
they had ever seen.

Meanwhile, Gordon proceeded with his line of posts, now
nearing completion. Returning to Duffli on July 9th, he was
gratified to find that the lake steamer had been assembled and
launched above the falls ready to move. Impatient as always of
delay, he started off for Magungo, intending to explore the route
and map the river to the Victoria Nyanza, lying roughly a hundred
and fifty miles south-east of the smaller lake. The river to
Magungo varied from one to five miles in width, navigation being
hampered by countless islands of papyrus[1], which also fringed the
banks to a width of ten or twelve yards.

On reaching the Albert Nyanza, or first of his two objectives,
Gordon was much struck by the desolate, forbidding atmosphere
pervading this part of the country. " The entrance (to the lake),"
he wrote, " is marked by a mass of papyrus isles. There is no current at all, and it is a most miserable-looking place. . . . What
a wilderness this is up here—not a sound to be heard, and so life-
less and apparently miserable." And again, soon after leaving
Magungo—" The river has dense forests on each side. . . .
It is not more than two hundred yards wide here. . . . A dead,
mournful spot this is, with a heavy damp dew penetrating everywhere. It is as if the Angel Azrael[2] had spread his wings over this
land. You have little idea of the silence and solitude. I am sure
no one whom God did not support could bear up. It is simply
killing. Thank God, I am in good health, and very rarely low,
and then only for a short time."

From Magungo to Foweira and, thence, south-eastward towards
the Victoria lake, Gordon travelled mainly by land, often marching
through dense jungle escorted by a hundred soldiers and many
native carriers. They had to more or less grope their way along,

---

[1] Sedge, from the inner pith of which the ancients made their paper.
[2] In Mohammedan mythology, the angel of death.

for no one knew the country, and on at least one occasion they were lost in the forest without a path to guide them. " It has been terrible work," wrote Gordon, " for, what with wild vines and convolvuli and other creepers, you sometimes get bound hand and foot."

He had now reached Uganda, the country ruled over by King Mtesa, described by Sir William Butler as " the usual mixture of buffoonery, cruelty, and suspicion, which seem to constitute the chief ingredients in the composition of monarchial character in Central Africa." Mtesa clearly wished to appear friendly towards Gordon, whose arrival at Magungo had greatly perturbed him. But he was untrustworthy and vacillating. He even found difficulty in making up his mind whether to be a Mohammedan or a Christian, receiving instruction now in one religion, now in the other. On learning of Gordon's arrival, however, he promptly dropped them both and fell back on his magicians, shutting himself up with them for five hours, so great was his panic at the coming of this astonishing Englishman, who swept all obstacles from his path, and advanced fearlessly into a country hitherto unknown to the white man.

He sent affectionate messages to Gordon, taking pains to assure him that he (Mtesa) was the greatest king in Africa. At his capital, Dubaga, he seems to have been fond of display, and to have surrounded himself with the colourful grandeur so dear to the hearts of savage potentates. From one of his officers who had visited the king, Gordon learned that " Mtesa sits on a chair placed on a leopard's skin; on each hind claw he places a foot, and the tail is in front. In front of him is a large tusk and a heap of charms; on his left sits the Grand Vizier. Mtesa is always arranging the creases in his clothes; the Grand Vizier will stroke down one crease on one leg of his trousers, and —— will do the same to the other." His informant also told him that ten or a dozen executions were carried out each day.

From another account, he recorded—" The Viziers were ranged, ten in number, and all seated; at the end, in a sort of alcove, having an exit (for Mtesa to escape by, I expect), sat on a dais Mtesa, with a huge white turban, dressed in gold-embroidered clothes, holding in one hand a silver-mounted sword, and in the other a sort of carved sceptre." But Gordon adds—"As Bismarck said of Arnim, you cannot believe a word he says "!

In August, Gordon offered to make a treaty with Mtesa, acknowledging the independence of Uganda, and expressing his willingness to guarantee safe conduct to Cairo for the king's representatives. Subsequent communications from Mtesa, however, made no mention of the proposed covenant, so that Gordon allowed the matter to drop, intending to bother himself no longer with the supine King of Uganda, and to turn his attention to the far more troublesome Kaba Rega, who held sway over the Unyoro, or north western province of the country. This truculent chieftain had a considerable following, besides being in league with many of the old slave hunters who would naturally be only too glad of the chance to oppose the author of all their troubles. But Gordon, who had long since decided that Kaba Rega was much too treacherous to allow of peaceful conditions in Uganda, now determined to support his rival, Rionga, with a view to making him supreme in the territory.

By the middle of September, he had reached the neighbourhood of Nyamyongo, about one degree north of the equator and close to the northern shores of the great lake Victoria Nyanza, having surveyed the immense length of the Nile from Berber to its source—a truly remarkable achievement. And now, since he had, from the beginning, made up his mind to forego the honour and glory of being the first to explore the waters of the great lakes, he turned back northward with the intention of reconnoitring Kaba Rega's country. He had left Mrooli, seventy-three miles due south of Foweira, on September 11th, and, in five days, had marched close on eighty miles in tropical heat through the dense forests of an unknown land inhabited by hostile savages.

After describing an attack on his porters following a few yards behind him, when natives, approaching unseen, had thrown their spears, but bolted as soon as they were fired on, Gordon wrote—" This sort of work is much more dangerous for me, humanly speaking, than regular war would be. These blacks can throw their lances fifty yards with a sure aim; and, as the path is very narrow and the bush very dense, one is not comfortable. Besides which I have not overmuch confidence in the troops or officers with me." Yet, though professing to feel uncomfortable, he appears to have been more concerned about the destruction of his butter-tin by a spear than anything else, for in his letter, he ruefully makes allusion to the tragedy!

In the course of his wanderings through these pestilential regions of Central Africa, he may be said to have experienced something akin to the plagues of Egypt, for he had suffered, at one time or another, from the dangerous stings of scorpions and hornets; the ambuscades of savages; the incursions of elephants and hippopotamuses; the visitations of snakes and vipers; the annoyance of rats which made off with his soap, shaving brush, and towel; the torment of all species of insect; the shakings and shiverings of ague; and the fierce onslaughts of mosquitoes. Furthermore, he was struck by lightning; his clothes were reduced to rags in tearing his way through thorn bush; he was, at times, badly shaken by falls in the entangled undergrowth of the jungle; more often than not he had no one to talk to; while he never had anything to read except the Bible, which, however, he studied assiduously.

But, through all these dangers and adversities, these discomforts and deprivations, the solitude and desolation, he passed with apparent unconcern, firm in his belief that everything happened by the will of God, and steadfast in his faith that He would pull him through.

Despite his incomparable spirit, however, his tough fibre, and the remarkable strength of his constitution, not even Gordon could endure so prolonged a spell of arduous service in the enervating, fever-ridden climate of the Equatorial Provinces without at least some detriment to health. And, while he habitually made light of his ailments, there could be no doubt that, at this stage of his mission, the strain and rigours of his daily life were beginning to tell on him. Even he had been forced to admit in one of his letters that it was time he went home.

As to whether he would ever return to the Sudan, he intended to reserve his decision until he had seen the Khedive, for he still felt uncertain of Ismail's support. If he could be convinced that his further services were needed, and if he were assured of better support than the Egyptian Government had given him during the past three years, then he believed it would be his duty to resume the work to which he had set his hand.

Having made up his mind, Gordon became almost schoolboyish in his delight at the prospect of going home. He wrote asking for a winter coat to be sent to Cairo to meet him, and in his letter displayed all the enthusiasm of a youth on the near approach of holidays. By all who have served long periods in far distant parts of the world, thousands of miles from the land of their birth, Gordon's feelings can easily be understood. For, though the keen seeker after adventure finds happiness in unfrequented, more or less uncivilised places, where the unconventional life of freedom appeals to him, there usually comes a time when his thoughts turn towards home, and he pines for a spell on his own native soil. Gordon badly needed a rest from the constant strain and the unbelievably arduous life; and, if reluctant to delay the complete accomplishment of his task, he wisely decided to call a halt until he had talked matters over with the Khedive and visited his relatives in England.

Travelling back by river from Nyamyongo to Mrooli, Gordon's party were obliged to open fire on tribesmen who threatened an attack on the boats. "It was very dangerous work," he wrote, " threading the narrow passages, for the natives could conceal themselves in the rushes, and hurl their spears into the boats without your being able to perceive them."

Before starting on his long homeward journey, he arranged for the establishment of two forts in Kaba Rega's territory, so that the activities of this persistently recalcitrant chieftain could be checked, while, a little later on, when the long grass had become dry enough for burning and the country could be cleared, the punishment Kaba Rega had long been inviting could be duly inflicted. He, therefore, moved northward by land to Masindi, and thence westward by way of Keroto to Magungo, reconnoitring the country with a view to future operations. It was a somewhat hazardous march as he had no more than a hundred soldiers, thirty of them mere boys, while the dense long grass, so encouraging to the tribesmen, encompassed him on every side. "We have been followed," he wrote, " and once the natives seemed inclined to close on us. . . . It is not comfortable work, for the grass is so dense. . . . Kaba Rega went off to the lake (Albert Nyanza) from Masindi as we approached. Thank God we have lost nothing and have brought on our sick."

Finally, he paid a visit to Chibero on the eastern shore of Lake Albert, where he intended to form a station. And then, having made all necessary arrangements, completed his chain of posts, and done everything possible, at the moment, for the security and welfare of this strange land, he, at last, turned his face to the north and, on October 6th, started for Khartoum, Cairo, and England.

On the passage down river, natives concealed in the reeds assailed his steamer with a shower of ebony-pointed arrows, two of which fell on board; but, apart from this solitary display of hostility, the journey to Khartoum proved uneventful, much of Gordon's time being spent in meditating on the line he would adopt with the Khedive. Many points for and against his return to the Sudan were turned over in his mind, but he seems, ultimately, to have decided that his course would depend on the Khedive's attitude. If he appeared particularly anxious for Gordon to resume his work, then he would stay. But, should Ismail show the smallest sign of being lukewarm about it, he would go for good.

It seems curious that he should, long since, have gained an impression that the Khedive was not altogether favourably disposed towards him. For, in reality, the ruler of Egypt could hardly have been more enthusiastic about this astonishing Englishman who was so infinitely superior to every other he had met. Probably the answer is to be found in the inherent dilatoriness of Egyptian methods, and that, when Gordon's letters on matters of urgency remained unanswered for months at a time, he not unnaturally assumed the Khedive to be offended at his outspokenness, or displeased by his demands for supplies needed in the pursuance of his mission. But no such construction would, at any time, have been an accurate one, for, in truth, the Khedive would have done almost anything to avoid being deprived of Gordon's services.

In Khartoum, he learned from nuns at the convent "harrowing tales of the sufferings of the poor natives in Kordofan." "It is dreadful," he wrote. "Thank God, He will in His own time remedy these miseries. Now, to-day, Reason says strongly, ' Do not stay and aid such a Government.' But I do not like to be beaten, which I am if I retire; and by retiring I do not remedy anything. By staying I keep my province safe from injustice and cruelty in some degree. . . . Things have come to such a pass in these Mussulman countries, that a crisis must come about soon."

Before leaving for Cairo on November 12th, he appointed a Colonel Prout of the American army to act for him as Governor of the Equatorial Provinces. Three weeks later, he was in the Egyptian capital seeing the Khedive and his ministers. But, when he left for England in mid-December, nothing had been settled as to his return, Gordon refusing to do more than promise to give the matter further consideraiton.

He reached London on Christmas Eve (1876). Writing to his friend Mrs. F. on Boxing Day from 7 Cecil Street, Strand, he declared—" I am not certain as to my future movements. . . . I feel very inclined to say ' Nunc Dimittis,' for I am tired! " It would seem that he purposely stayed a day or two in London on his arrival so as to avoid the Christmas festivities at his home, and all the fuss and gorging that he detested. But, before the end of the year, we find him down at Southampton visiting his devoted family.

There can be no doubt that, throughout the greater part of the five and a half weeks he spent in England, a battle royal raged

within him as to which was the right path for him to follow—
should he go or stay? In his own words, written before leaving
Khartoum for home, the conflicting forces were thus described—
" Mr. Reason says, ' What is the use of opening more country to
such a Government? There is more now under their power than
they can manage. Retire now and avoid troubles with Mtesa.' But
Mr. Something (I do not know what) says, ' Shut your eyes to what
may happen in future; leave that to God, and do what you think
will open the country thoroughly to both Lakes. Do this, not for
H.H. (the Khedive), or his Government, but do it blindly and in
faith.' "

Eventually, he listened to " Mr. Reason," and, on January
13th, 1877, wrote to Mrs. F. informing her of his decision. " I
saw Lord Derby[1] the day before yesterday," ran his letter, " and in
consequence wrote to his Highness (the Khedive) to say I would
not return—so that is over. I am tired, tired, and no earthly rest
will give me quiet."

In answer to his decision, he received an urgent letter from the
Khedive, begging him to reconsider it. So many similar appeals
for his help in times of crisis were made to Gordon during his
career, that he became not unlike a specialist in a disease for which
he alone knew the cure. Besides being invited to suppress the
Taiping rebellion in China and the slave trade in the Sudan, he
undertook to mediate between Egypt and Abyssinia; he again went
to the help of China when war with Russia seemed imminent; he
complied with a request by the Cape Government to help them in
settling the Basuto question; he was invited by King Leopold of
Belgium to go to the Congo, and tackle the slave traders; and
finally, by way of a change, he was called upon by *his own Government* to go to Khartoum and get them out of their difficulties. In
truth, Gordon came to be known the world over as an expert in
settling disputes and coping with disorder.

In this particular instance, he thought he had done enough,
and had come away with a very poor opinion of the Egyptian Government and their administration. Yet, the Khedive's letter impressed him so strongly with its friendliness and sincerity, that he
was no longer in any doubt as to the Egyptian ruler's genuine
anxiety for him to return to the Sudan. Moreover, he felt it would
be churlish to resist an appeal couched in such cordial, flattering
terms; but he would not commit himself to any promise beyond
consenting to go to Cairo for discussion, and, although as yet he

---

[1]   15th Earl of Derby, Secretary of State for Foreign Affairs 1874-1878.

gave no hint of his intention to make any such demand, he was firmly resolved to confront the Egyptian authorities with an ultimatum to the effect that he would resume his work in the Sudan only if given control of the whole country as Governor-General. He would play second fiddle to no more incompetents such as the lethargic Yakoob. He would tolerate no interference, nor be answerable to anyone other than the Khedive himself. In these conditions, and these alone, would he be prepared to carry on the work already initiated. He did not believe, however, that the Khedive would agree to give him the whole of the Sudan. In a letter dated January 31st, 1877, the day of his departure from London for Cairo, he wrote—" I do not think he will give it, and I think you will see me back in six weeks. . . . I hope to start to-night. I will make a stand at Cairo; and if I see it is no use I will give it up."

During his short rest of five weeks in England, besides spending some time with his family at Southampton, Gordon had visited Gravesend where he met many old acquaintances, and had also found time to look in on his friends, Mr. and Mrs. F., now living at Chislehurst. " He came down, of course, to see us at Chislehurst," wrote Mrs. F., " and spent a delightful evening, interspersing all his conversation with anecdotes for the special benefit of my boys, who were at home for the holidays. He told them how he had seen an elephant kill a man, first kneeling on him and breaking every bone in his body, and then taking the carcase up with his trunk and flinging it over his head, precisely as a dog does a dead rat."

Reaching Cairo early in February, Gordon entered into preliminary discussions with Cherif Pasha, Nubar's successor as the Khedive's chief minister. At the end of a week, his patience—never one of his strongest qualities—had worn a trifle thin, and, becoming tired of the eternal jabber, he rapped out his last word—" Give me the Sudan, or I will not go."

All this time, the Khedive had been unaware of the root cause of the prolonged discussions between Gordon and his minister, who, together with his colleagues in the Government, would not hear of a European, especially a Christian, being appointed Governor-General of the Sudan. It was, moreover, clear that Cherif would be averse to even mentioning so revolutionary a suggestion to His Highness. But now, the Khedive, too, became tired of the delay, and, on enquiring from the British Consul-General as to its cause, he at last learned the truth. Without a moment's hesitation, he consented to give Gordon the Sudan, thus emphasising the high value he placed on his services.

"I went to see H.H.," wrote Gordon on February 13th. "He looked at me reproachfully, and my conscience smote me. He led me in, and Cherif Pasha came in. Then I began, and told him all; and then he gave me the Sudan and I leave on Saturday morning. I have to see him to-morrow. I am so very glad to get away; for I am very weary. I go up alone with an infinite Almighty God to direct and guide me, and am glad to so trust Him as to fear nothing, and, indeed, to feel sure of success."

In a letter, written four days later, beginning "My dear Gordon Pasha," and ending "Your affectionate Ismail," the Khedive told Gordon he had decided to "unite in one great Governor-Generalship the whole of the Sudan, Darfour, and the Equatorial Provinces," and to entrust him with the administration of this immense area. Under him there would be three *vakeels* or deputies, one for the Sudan region of the Nile, including the Equatorial Provinces, one for Darfour, and one for the Red Sea coast and the Eastern Sudan. He also directed Gordon's immediate attention to three main tasks —namely, the suppression of slavery, improving the means of communication throughout his territory, and the settlement of outstanding differences between Egypt and Abyssinia. It was, moreover, decided that Gordon should go to Khartoum by way of the Abyssinian border with the object of opening negotiations with King Johannes, successor to Theodore, as a first measure.

It should here be explained that quite recently Khedive Ismail had turned covetous eyes on Abyssinia. If he could but conquer the warlike people of this age-old Christian kingdom, what an immense addition would be made to his already immeasurable realm. A payment of four million pounds by the British Government for shares in the Suez Canal provided him with the financial resources he needed for the campaign. But, at the very outset, his troops suffered ignominious defeat at the hands of Abyssinia's warriors, with the result that the Khedive's acquisitive aspirations were not persisted in. Nevertheless, there remained an atmosphere of hostility between the two nations, and it was to this that Gordon turned his immediate attention, in the hope of being able to solve the problem and establish peaceful, friendly relations before proceeding to his headquarters at Khartoum.

CHAPTER XII

Governor-General of the Sudan

TRAVELLING by rail from Cairo to Suez on February 18th, Gordon embarked in the frigate *Lateef* for Massawa on the Red Sea. There he stayed for nearly three weeks before moving to Karen, the capital of Bugos, a province formerly belonging to Abyssinia, but now included among the Khedive's possessions. Since Karen lay close to the frontier, he was able to watch the turn of events in Abyssinia, and hoped to gain personal contact with Johannes. But, unfortunately, the king had gone off to the south to oppose an aggressive move by Menelik, the King of Shoa, who had attacked Gondar in central Abyssinia.

"Abyssinia is a cock-pit," wrote Gordon. " Everyone is a brigand or soldier (terms which are synonymous), deeply fanatical against all rites except their own. The ignorant priests rule the country." And in another letter—" The Abyssinian priests would, if they could, and they do sometimes, cut off the hands of any who will not conform to their rites. From what I have seen of these Abyssinians I do not like them at all; they are a set of deceitful brigands according to all accounts, and they look a furtive, pole-cat race."

During his stay at Massawa, Gordon was created a field marshal in the Turkish army, the Khedive sending him an imposing uniform smothered in gold lace. " So,' he wrote in a home letter, " I and the Duke[1] are equals! " In the same letter, he spoke of his command extending along the Red Sea coast as far as Berbera, opposite Aden. The Khedive had indeed entrusted him with a territory of prodigious dimensions, embracing the region of the Nile as far south as the great lakes; the eastern Sudan, extending along the Abyssinian frontier and including the province of Sen-

---

[1] H.R.H. the Duke of Cambridge, Commander-in-Chief of the British Army.

THE   GOVERNOR-GENERAL'S   PALACE
AT   KHARTOUM
as it stands to-day on the site of General Gordon's palace,
of which part of the original staircase still remains.

*(Reproduced by permission of the Sudan Government Agency in
London)*

naar and the Red Sea coast from Massawa to Suakin; and, lastly,
the western Sudan, comprising the vast desert lands of Kordofan
and Darfour. But, for the moment, Gordon's attention and energies were concentrated on the problem of Abyssinia. Little time
elapsed before he realised that the main cause of trouble between
Egypt and Abyssinia was to be found in the activities of one Walad
el Michael, a deposed hereditary chief of Bugos, who had fallen
foul of King Johannes, and, with a force of three thousand men,
had gone over to the Khedive.

A typical soldier of fortune, Michael was always spoiling for
a fight, and he certainly proved a serious embarrassment to Gordon
in his efforts to bring about a friendly understanding between
Egypt and Ethiopia. The deposed chieftain was constantly raiding
across the border, infuriating Johannes, and arousing in his mind
suspicions as to the sincerity of Egypt's desire for peace—feelings
by no means unnatural seeing that Michael and his followers were
subsisting on pay and food provided by the Khedive, and were,
moreover, quartered on Egyptian territory.

Ultimately, Gordon was obliged to move them further away
from the frontier, at the same time making it clear that, unless
they stopped their forays into Abyssinia, the Egyptian Government would cease to furnish them with money and supplies.

At the end of March, realising that Johannes would be engaged for some months with his war against Menelik, Gordon
decided to waste no more time, but to hurry on to Khartoum,
where an ever increasing accumulation of problems arising in various parts of his gigantic command would be awaiting his attention.
Before starting from Karen, however, he sent a message to the
Ethiopian monarch saying he presumed Johannes had agreed to
the terms of peace with Egypt already conveyed to him, but that,
if there were any points he wished to discuss, he (Gordon) would
return in a couple of months.

With his innate modesty and rooted distaste for ostentation
in any shape or form, the new Governor-General took anything but
kindly to all the fuss and ceremony surrounding him. So hemmed
in was he by guards and sentries that he could scarcely call his soul
his own. When about to dismount from his camel, as many as
eight or ten attendants would rush forward to assist him. At the
conclusion of his interview with Walad el Michael, the Abyssinian
knelt to kiss his feet. The magnitude of his position—virtual
dictator over a land stretching far and wide across the African
continent—was such that, in the eyes of the people, Gordon came

to be looked upon as a demi-god. When nearing Karen, he had been met by two hundred cavalry and infantry " with musician and people who danced before me; three horsemen with kettle drums rode before them, beating their little drums."

" I can say truly," he wrote, " no man has ever been so forced into a high position as I have. How many I know to whom the income would be the breath of their nostrils. To me, it is irksome beyond measure. Eight or ten men to help me off my camel as if I were an invalid. If I walk, everyone gets off and walks; so, furious, I get on again." His influence over the people he governed was infinite, his power to control them truly remarkable.

In was early in April that Gordon mounted his fast moving camel and started for Khartoum. Travelling never less than thirty miles a day, and often considerably more, his energy in the terrific heat of the desert was quite astonishing. At every station along his route, he not only enquired into matters of administration, but also gave audience to any of the people, from the highest to the lowest who wished to petition him. This was something new to the unfortunate Sudanese, who had become accustomed to being bullied and whipped, and had never contemplated the possibility of any one in authority listening to their grievances. But Gordon heard them all, doing what he could to improve their unhappy condition, as he moved like an avenging angel through the desert wastes of his vast dominions, putting down abuses, succouring the oppressed and punishing offenders.

" I will (D.V.) do my duty," he declared in one of his home letters," " troublesome and even dangerous as it may be; there is no use being gentle over it—the disease is too grave for gentle remedies." And again, about a fortnight later—" I have to contend with many vested interests, with fanaticism, with the abolition of hundreds of Arnauts,[1] Turks, etc., now acting as Bashi-Bazouks, with inefficient governors, with wild independent tribes of Bedouins, and with a large semi-independent province, lately under Sebehr Pasha[3], at Bahr el Ghazal." What a gigantic task was his! What infinite patience would be required, what gruelling labour entailed, in grappling with the manifold problems confronting him at the outset of his new task.

---

[1]   Greek Mohammedans from Arabia.
[2]   Turkish and Arab frontier guards.
[3]   A prominent slave trader detained at Cairo by the Egyptian Government

When approaching Khartoum, Gordon spent an uncomfortable night at Sennaar on the Blue Nile. " The biting beetles are awful here," he wrote. ". . . There were at least eighty large beetles on my night shirt when I lit the candle." At last, in the early days of May, he reached his headquarters, where he at once set about promoting the welfare of the wretched people, who, for so long, had been ground down under the heel of tyranny, enslaved and ill-treated by their masters, the brutal Pashas, until death came to be regarded as a merciful release from abject misery. He straightway decided to disband the six thousand Bashi-Bazouks, who were, in reality, an unscrupulous band of merciless brigands, undisciplined, inefficient, and intent, for the most part, on plundering the luckless inhabitants, besides helping to advance the interests of the slave dealers. Clearly, so long as these ruffians were retained as frontier guards, or in any other capacity, Gordon's efforts to cleanse the Augean stables of the Sudan could be of no avail. Yet, the disbanding of so large a body of men, scattered about in small, outlying stations, could only be carried out gradually and methodically if disorganisation and trouble were to be avoided.

Recruiting for the force was stopped, and the existing Bashi-Bazouks were systematically replaced by dependable Sudanese troops, until, ultimately, the whole six thousand had been dispersed. In taking this courageous step, Gordon struck a severe blow at the slave traders, who had formerly been able to count on the help of these scoundrels, and, at the same time, released the poor natives from the oppression they had suffered at their cruel hands.

Other immediate steps taken by Gordon included abolition of the *kurbash* (whip), remission of outstanding taxes, and a scheme for providing Khartoum with an adequate water supply. Furthermore, whereas hitherto the shamefully down-trodden people had been denied opportunities for airing their grievances, Gordon was anxious to hear them, facilities being provided at the gates of his palace so that petitions for his consideration could be collected even from the very humblest of his people, the alleviation of whose sufferings he looked upon as his primary responsibility. Yet another important measure was the restoration to the Ulema[1] of " all their ancient privileges which had been taken away from them " by Gordon's predecessor, Ismail Yakoob.

---

[1] The body of professional theologians in any Mohammedan country.

Assuredly, the whole populace of the Sudan—at any rate o
those areas where news of Gordon's sensational activities had, a
yet, penetrated—must have rejoiced at this coming of a liberator
who had lost no time in taking action to deliver them out of th
hands of their oppressors. And so, as the glad tidings spread fa
and wide across the vast spaces of this grievously mismanage
country, the name of Gordon Pasha became synonymous with
justice and mercy.

A fortnight after his arrival at Khartoum, Gordon wrote of hi
first impressions and his work of reformation—" I think the peopl
like me, and it is an immense comfort that, while in the old *regim*
ten or fifteen people were flogged daily, now none get flogged
. . . It is all nonsense for the Turks to say that the people woul
oppose the nomination of a Christian Governor. The people wan
justice. . . . I am breaking up, to the great joy of the people
the Bashi-Bazouks, who, of course, do not love me. A great sorrov
has been taken off the land. The reign of the *kurbash* has ceased
and I do believe the people rejoice at my being here."

Gordon's official installation as Governor-General of the Suda
took place on May 5th at the palace[1], which stood on the banks o
the Nile. In his inaugural address, he won the hearts and confi
dence of the people when he declared—" With the help of God
will hold the balance level."

Having done all that was possible, at the moment, toward
improving conditions in Khartoum, Gordon turned his attentio
to Darfour, whose widespread tracts of desert country stretched fa
away to the westward. This vast province had for some consider
able time been suffering acutely from the depredations of ruthles
slave hunters, and from a general state of unrest attributable almos
entirely to that cause. Chief among the trouble makers wer
Haroun, who claimed to be the rightful Sultan of Darfour, an
Suleiman, son of Sebehr, the notorious slave dealer wh
had been summoned to Cairo by the Government and there de
tained. Both insurrectionists were said to be supported by man
followers, but Suleiman was, undoubtedly, the more formidabl
with a force of desperadoes numbering several thousand.

This was one of the private armies recruited by the slav
dealers to enable them to carry on their nefarious trade. So lon

---

[1] So incensed was the sister of Gordon's predecessor at the supercession o
Ismail Yakoob that she smashed every window in the palace and cut th
divans to ribbons !

as they existed there could be no hope of abolishing slavery. During the previous three years, Gordon's efforts, as we have seen, had been restricted to tackling the scourge in the southern or Equatorial Provinces of the Sudan. But, in the western territories of Darfour and Kordofan, slave hunting and trading had as yet been pursued unchecked. Indeed, the evil business had not only been winked at by the authorities, but, in many cases, it had actually been encouraged by officials of the Egyptian Government. Gordon was, therefore, resolved to break up Suleiman's band of rogues as a first step towards putting down this monstrous slavery and bring-ing peace, together with some measure of happiness, to the perse-cuted people of Darfour. As to Haroun, the would-be sultan, his revolt, though troublesome, was of minor importance compared with the state of anarchy and utter misery brought about by Suleiman and his gang of pillaging cut-throats.

And so it was that, in accordance with his custom of appearing in person wherever trouble arose, Gordon mounted his camel and started for the west with a party of five hundred nondescript soldiers. After nearly three weeks of hard riding across the wide expanse of Kordofan, he reached the borders of Darfour on June 7th. Except for Arabs and natives he was quite alone. Fortun-ately, however, solitude never affected him to any serious extent. More often than not, indeed, he preferred to be alone. " During my long, long, hot, weary rides," he wrote, " I think my thoughts better and clearer than I should with a companion. Any European would be a disadvantage at present."

In one of his home letters, written soon after reaching Darfour, Gordon made the following brief, though striking, reference to his position—" The immense difficulty there is in causing this slave traffic to cease has now come home to me. . . . I have complete power—civil and military. No one would say a word if I put one or ten men to death; and therefore I must be considered entirely responsible if the slave trade goes on; but here is my position. Darfour and Kordofan are peopled by huge Bedouin tribes under their own sheikhs, who are rather more than semi-independent. The country, for the most part, is a vast desert, with wells few and far between, some of which are only known to these tribes. Some of these tribes can put from 2,000 to 6,000 horse or camel men in the field; and a revolt, as I know to my cost, is no small thing in such a country."

Considering the indolence, inefficiency, and abuse of authority that had characterised the regime prior to Gordon's appointment as Governor-General, it is not surprising that he found himself obliged to be ruthless in uprooting the chief offenders. He threw them out right and left, without the smallest compunction, if they failed to toe the line and abandon the evil practices that formerly had been rife. His second-in-command, one Halid Pasha, who roused Gordon's fiery temper by his bumptious, impudent attitude, was summarily dismissed after no more than three weeks in office. And so, even as the joyful news of his benevolence towards the oppressed inhabitants became known throughout the land, grim tidings of his wrath struck terror into the hearts of idle, merciless, perfidious officials, besides spreading alarm and despondency among the slave traders and all manner of wrong-doers. "The wrecks left on my passage are numerous," he wrote from Fogia on the Darfour frontier. "I have set my face as a flint; and regardless of consequences have been hard right and left. I do not wish to be so; I should like to praise, not blame; but seeing what I know of the suffering of the people, I cannot force myself to let things slide."

Haroun, himself, seems to have got wind of Gordon's reputation, for, taking no chances, he retired to the mountain fastnesses of Toura, ancient burial place of the sultans of Darfour, thus leaving Gordon free and unfettered, for the moment, to deal with the less timorous Suleiman, whose headquarters were at a place called Shaka, hub of the slave trade in the western Sudan. His plan of campaign was to withdraw the garrisons that had been hemmed in for months by the tribes, and with a force, strengthened by reinforcements acquired at each station, to subdue, in turn, the two leaders of revolt. He, moreover, hoped to pacify the tribes who had rebelled against their persecutors, without recourse to arms, and even to persuade them to join him in his expedition against Suleiman, the slave hunter.

It will be seen, therefore, that Gordon had two distinct problems to deal with—namely, the suppression of the revolts led by Suleiman and Haroun, and the establishing of friendly relations with the tribes, whose sufferings had brought them to the pitch of turning on their persecutors and besieging them in their stations. In reality, the situation confronting him was very similar to that of the Equatorial Provinces, the chief objects being abolition of slavery and alleviation of the people's misery.

Gordon rode an exceptionally fast camel, so that he often left his escort and retinue far behind. At the frontier station of Fogia, he arrived almost alone, to the great astonishment of the garrison. "I came flying into this station," ran a letter dated June 7th, "in

142

arshal's uniform; and before the men had time to unpile their
rms I had arrived with only one man with me. . . . The escort
id not come in for an hour and a half afterwards. . . . The
ordons and the camels are the same race—let them take an idea
ito their heads, and nothing will take it out. If my camel feels
iclined to go in any particular direction, there he will go, pull as
iuch as you like. . . . It is fearful to see the Governor-General
rrayed in gold clothes flying along like a madman, with only a
uide as if he was pursued." Here, at Fogia, he received the
isignia of the Grand Cordon of the Order of the Medjidie, sent
o him by the Khedive, who had awarded him the decoration for
is services in the Equatorial Provinces.

On his way westward, he passed through a desolate, uninviting
ountry which impressed him with its utter uselessness. " The
ountry is most miserable," he wrote, " a sandy, bush-covered
esert, quite useless for any good purpose, with no water for dis-
ances of forty or fifty miles. . . . It appears that the only pro-
uce of these countries is ostrich feathers. . . . One Syrian
ierchant is buying up all the black feathers, because he says they
vill be wanted for mourning by those who lose friends in the war
Russo-Turkish)."

Gordon's plan to vacate many of the stations would serve two
urposes, for not only would the garrisons be available to swell the
trength of his force, but, by removing the isolated troops whose
ersecution had brought about the enmity of the natives, he hoped
o gain the confidence and support of these ill-used tribes. At
Coashia, one of the stations to be vacated, Gordon found that the
arrison had received no pay for three years! At Dara, where he
rrived in mid-July, eighteen hundred men had been shut up for
ix months without a word of news from the outside world. A
iundred and fifty miles to the south east of Dara lay the rebellious
iuleiman's camp at Shaka. This was Gordon's main objective,
vhere he hoped to strike a decisive blow at the iniquitous traders.

But, before undertaking this vital operation, it was necessary
or him to relieve other isolated stations, notably at El Fascher,
ibout a hundred miles due north of Dara, and to strengthen his
orce as much as possible, for, in the event of Suleiman deciding to
ippose him by force of arms, the son of Sebehr seemed likely to
irove a hard nut to crack. Some idea of the tyranny being suffered
iy the natives at the hands of this merciless brigand may be
;athered from the unhappy condition of one of the most powerful
ribes in Darfour, whose chief fled to Gordon from the neighbour-

hood of Shaka with a tale of misery so grievous that he and his followers could endure it no longer. Though glad of their support and anxious to help them in their desperate plight, the question of supplies was acute, and he foresaw great difficulty in feeding so large an addition to the garrison of Dara. "The whole tribe of Razagat threatens to come to me," he wrote towards the end of July. "How am I to feed them? It is like a white elephant as a present! This is the second tribe which has left Shaka, and they say two more are under way for this place (Dara). These tribes move without any trouble it appears—they never have baggage They ride without stirrups."

Two days later, going out to see a crowd of over two hundred slaves recently taken by the human vultures, Gordon revealed the depths of his sympathy for these luckless natives. Describing the pitiful scene in one of his home letters, he wrote—"It is a sad sight to see the poor little starved creatures looking so wistfully at one. . . . What could I do? Poor souls, I cannot feed or look after them. I must leave it to God Who will arrange all in kindness. . . . Some of them are so miserably thin. I have sent them some *dhoora*.[1] I declare solemnly that I would give my life willingly to save the sufferings of these people. . . . You would have felt sick had you seen them. Poor creatures! Thirty-six hours without food. . . . There were some poor little wretches only stomachs and heads, with *antennae* for legs and arms."

The horrors of this arid, inhospitable land were almost inconceivable. Famine was rife in Darfour, and, the wells being forty and even fifty miles apart, mortality from hunger and thirst presented Gordon with an insoluble problem. "I feel my own weakness," he wrote, "and look to Him Who is Almighty, and I leave the issue without inordinate care to Him."

As if he were not already overwhelmed with troubles and perplexities that would have daunted almost any other man, the Press now began to criticise his methods, and, without knowledge of the appalling conditions surrounding him, or the deadly effect on the country of the heinous slave trade that only drastic measures could cure, denounced his alleged purchase of slaves for the purpose of converting them into soldiers. Is it not strange, this love of fault-finding, even with those least deserving of censure? Assuredly, the archangel Gabriel, himself, if employed on an earthly task, would not escape the lash of ignorant, mean-spirited meddlers.

---

[1] A species of grass closely allied to sugar-cane and beard-grass.

Fortunately, neither praise nor blame had the smallest effect on Gordon, who continued on the lines dictated by his conscience, defying, and completely indifferent to, the consequences. His traducers were apparently incapable of understanding that, by purchasing slaves, he rescued them from slavery; that, by making soldiers of them, he merely introduced a system similar to conscription adopted in all European countries; that, in order to prevent slave raiding, he needed more troops to oppose the traders with their formidable bands of freebooters; and that this was the only means of procuring them. To criticise a man engaged in this noble work, beset on every side by difficulties and crises of which his detractors could have had no conception, would have been sufficiently shabby if their aspersions had been based on a sound foundation; but, when it is considered that the methods complained of were devised by Gordon solely for the benefit of the slaves themselves, and to enable him the more easily to cope with their oppressors, then it becomes difficult to find words adequately expressive of one's contempt for these self-appointed, ill-informed cavillers.

A little later, when shut up in Khartoum and nearing the end of his life, he wrote this criticism of the Press in his diary—" I would never muzzle the press or its correspondents; they are most useful, and one cannot be too grateful to them (I own this more than anyone), but I certainly think that their province does not extend to praising or blaming a man, for by praising, or blaming, an assumption is made of superiority, for the *greater* can only do that to the *inferior;* and no newspaper can arrogate that its correspondent is superior to the General (though I declare I think, sometimes, it may be the case)."

And of generals his diary continues—" The men I should like to see cross-questioned on the country they are in are our Generals, whose whole time is taken up in their offices with courts-martial, etc., etc., an occasional day being devoted to moving men about in formations which are never put into execution in the Field. The *métier* of a General is the Field, not the office."

Whilst at Dara, Gordon learned that one of the tribes, known as the Leopard tribe, had broken out into open rebellion on the road between Dara and Toashia. With a force comprising some of his own troops and a considerable number of loyal tribesmen, he set out to punish the rebels. Coming upon them at a place called Wadar, Gordon's auxiliaries, who were well in advance of the Government soldiers, attacked without delay, utterly destroying their adversaries, one hundred and sixty in number. Later in the day,

Gordon's camp was attacked by seven hundred of the same tribe, who, however, were repulsed, and soon laid down their arms in token of submission. For this success Gordon was indebted to his faithful native allies; but, as usual, the Egyptian soldiers gave him little cause for confidence. " The effect of crushing it (the Leopard tribe) will be great," he wrote. " Never before have they been so disastrously situated."

Continuing his tour of Darfour, he reached El Fascher in mid-August. Here was another garrison that had been reduced to a state of complete inactivity by the natives, who would no longer tamely submit to their oppression, and who had turned against them. Though as many as eight thousand men were quartered at the station, nothing whatever had been done to open up the roads to Oomchanga and Dara, the troops being content to remain indolently within the town.

During his stay at El Fascher, Gordon received a contrite letter from Suleiman, but he paid no attention to it, being unwilling to trust a son of the notorious Sebehr, and requiring substantial evidence of his good intentions before treating him as anything but an enemy. Meanwhile, the breaking up of Suleiman's slave dealing business at Shaka, and the dispersal of his private army of bandits, still constituted the main purpose of Gordon's operations, with the crushing of Haroun's insurrection next on the list.

At El Fascher, he had further reason to be alarmed at the appalling death rate from starvation. " The whole country," he wrote, " is suffering terribly from famine, and it will get worse, I fear. The smell of the putrefying dead (men and animals) is fearful."

Towards the end of August, he received information that Suleiman, at the head of a large force, had moved from Shaka to the neighbourhood of Dara, where he was now encamped. Deciding that he would at once settle accounts with this ring-leader of the slave trade, the Governor-General mounted his flying camel and, followed by his escort, made off across the desert towards Dara. Covering a distance of eighty-five miles in a day and a half, he reached his destination accompanied only by a guide, the rest of his party being hopelessly outstripped and left far behind. Moreover, he completely surprised the garrison, who were flabbergasted on seeing this amazing Englishman dashing through the gate into the town almost unattended. " I came on my people like a thunderbolt," wrote Gordon. "As soon as they had recovered, the salute was fired. My poor escort! Where is it? . , . The people were paralyzed, and could not believe their eyes."

At dawn next day, dressed in the spectacular uniform of a Turkish field marshal, and wearing the glittering star of the Medjidie, Gordon rode over to Suleiman's camp three miles from the town. In a life as packed with hazards as a pod with peas, there was, perhaps, nothing to surpass, either in its incredible audacity or its deadly peril, this striking example of his sublime indifference to personal danger. With a mere handful of Bashi-Bazouks, retained as his bodyguard, he rode straight into the camp of his enemies, three thousand strong, and the very suddenness, the colossal daring of his action, so petrified this band of lawless adventurers that, in their speechless bewilderment, they became docile, even subservient.

As Gordon rode calmly through their lines, saluting to right and left, he might have been paying an early morning visit to one of his own camps, so deferentially, and with every mark of respect, was he received. Much has already been recorded of the quite extraordinary power his personality could exercise over the unruly, the hostile, the rebellious. But never, perhaps, was this almost uncanny domination more conspicuously illustrated than when, with devil-may-care fearlessness, he rode into the very jaws of his most treacherous adversary.

Suleiman, described by Gordon as "a nice-looking lad of twenty-two years," seemed, like the rest of them, thoroughly subdued by this unexpected appearance of the Governor-General in their midst. A belated salute was fired, and, after ordering the arch-slave dealer to report at his headquarters, Gordon rode back to the station. It must have been touch and go despite the show of obsequiousness; and, being well aware of the treachery habitually practised by these creatures, he can have entertained no doubt that, whilst in the camp of Suleiman, his life hung by a flimsy thread. Had this son of a blackguardly father, and his followers, been able to overcome their spellbound embarrassment in Gordon's presence, they might either have killed him, or held him as a hostage for Sebehr, detained in Cairo. But, once again, the majestic power of his unique personality pulled him through and carried the day. "The whole body of Chiefs were dumbfounded at my coming among them," he wrote on September 2nd, the day of his astonishing exploit.

Suleiman and his entourage duly presented themselves before the Governor-General, who promptly spoke his mind, telling them of his intentions in plain, blunt language. He would " disarm them and break them up." After returning to his camp to consider Gordon's ultimatum, Suleiman sent in his submission. Yet, for three days, it was by no means certain that he would not resort to treachery and attack the station. Both fort and garrison were weak, so that the result of a conflict might well have proved disastrous. Afterwards, Gordon learned that Suleiman and his chiefs had sat up all night considering what they would do, and that, although the leader had been in favour of an immediate attack on Dara, his subordinates, for the most part, would not support him, the upshot being that his force became split asunder, compelling him to adhere to his submission and obey the Governor-General's order to return, forthwith, to Shaka.

Thus ended satisfactorily a situation that, but for Gordon's uncompromising attitude of fearless insistence, his manifestation of a mighty power that would tolerate not so much as a hint of opposition, a power that seemed almost supernatural in its overmastering influence, might conceivably have developed into a serious set-back to his plans for quelling the slave trade. As it was, however, his brilliant, bloodless victory proved a most heartening advance towards the complete fulfilment of his task.

Of Suleiman, Gordon wrote—" Sebehr's son looks a spoilt child that a good shaking would do good to. I have tried to be kind to him, but he looks daggers at me. Poor little chap! He has a bitter time of it before him and before he realises the nothingness of the world; brought up in the midst of the most obsequious people and slaves, accustomed to do just what he liked, to think nothing of killing people, or of their misery, and now to be *nothing*! "

" He has no sense of propriety—lolls about, yawns, fondles his naked feet, and speaks as if he were a street boy. . . . He does not seem in the least put out at any hard words I may say. He would have suffered nicely if he had fallen into the hands of an Arab Pasha."

Gordon started for Shaka on September 9th to arrange for the disbanding of Suleiman's army and the final break up of this prominent slave market. On arriving six days later, he found the young Arab leader and his followers much subdued. They received him well, providing him with accommodation in Suleiman's house. " I am in the son's house," he wrote. " He never used to let any-one sit in his presence, and must be shocked at the familiarity with which everyone was treated by me. He is sitting out in the veran-dah—I expect to excite my pity. However, a short diet of humble pie will not be bad for him. What an amount of trouble he has given me and everyone! "

He stayed at Shaka only long enough to give his orders for the disposal of the band. Suleiman was to be sent to the province of Bahr el Ghazal in the equatorial zone, there to be under the surveillance of the Government representative in those parts; while the other slave dealers and their adherents were to be dispersed to various districts of the Sudan. "An enormous country," wrote Gordon, " comes under His Highness by the fall of Shaka. . . . I shall now conclude my letters on Darfour and Shaka etc., with sincere thanks to God for so ruling events that many lives have not been lost in either affair." Nearly two years later, he learned from a man who had been Suleiman's servant that at Shaka they had contemplated seizing him. But doubtless, once more, their courage had failed them when it came to laying hands on the redoubtable Governor-General.

It was now mid September, and, since the slave ring at Shaka had been finally broken up, and, furthermore, Haroun, in his mountain retreat, had, at any rate for the time being, ceased to be a serious menace in Darfour, Gordon turned back towards Khartoum, where, according to letters that had reached him, his presence was urgently required. Famine, so it appeared, was decimating the Equatorial Provinces; there were rows in the capital itself; the Abyssinian question still hung fire; but what upset him most of all was a report that his native secretary—" a man whom I trusted as myself "—had been taking bribes amounting to three thousand pounds. "Is there an honest man in the world?" he wrote disgustedly. " I declare with all my miseries I am sick at heart, and did not my kind God give me strength, I should faint under it." And, in another letter about the same time—"I fear he (the secretary) will be very hardly dealt with. He has deceived me too grossly to be forgiven." Few things roused his anger more easily than dishonesty or greed for personal gain, and, although by nature compassionate, he could not bring himself to extend leniency to a trusted servant who had so flagrantly taken advantage of his absence.

Before leaving Shaka for El Obeid in Kordofan, Gordon settled a dispute, that had threatened endless trouble, with habitual decisiveness and a sagacity reminiscent of the wisdom of Solomon. Two large tribes were divided as to the popularity of their chiefs, some upholding them, others clamouring for their deposition and replacement. Gordon promptly put an end to the disturbance by declaring that " those who wished for A could go with A, and those who wished for B could go with B." He said he would force no one.

As time went on, he became less sanguine as to the possibility of entirely stamping out slavery in the Sudan. It had become so much a part of the life of the country, so fixed and established a business, that there seemed to him only one way of bringing about its total abolition—namely, by tackling the source and preventing raids into the territories of the negro tribes. But, in order to do this effectively, far greater resources than those available to the Egyptian Government would be needed, for untold expenditure and the employment of immense forces would necessarily be entailed. Nevertheless, he was determined to break up the slave markets wherever they existed, and to use the utmost of his powers to check, as far as possible, this wicked, inhuman traffic. It went to his kindly heart to contemplate the misery and wretchedness of the luckless slaves chained together as they struggled along in the fierce heat of the desert, often without food or water, driven onward by their brutal persecutors, many of them dropping in their tracks and dying of starvation, thirst, or exhaustion.

Gordon was told that hundreds died on the road, and that, when they became too weak to go on, the slave traders shot them. " In all previous emancipations," he wrote, " either there has been a strong government to enforce obedience, or the majority of the nation wished it. Here in this country there is not one who wishes it, or who would aid it even by advice. . . . The tenure of slaves is the A.B.C. of life here to rich and poor: *no one* is uninterested in the matter." And again—" No person under fifteen years of age is safe in Darfour or Kordofan. The people are bent on slave traffic. They look on the capture of a slave in the same way as people would look on appropriating an article found on the road." But it was not so much the matter of these individual cases of slave snatching that provided him with food for thought, as the organised raids, the markets, and the chained slave gangs. There, the horrors of slavery were laid bare in all their hideousness, inoffensive men, women, and children being dragged from their homes and subjected to incredible sufferings until death came to them as a happy release.

It took Gordon just about a month's camel riding from Shaka to Khartoum, where he arrived on October 14th, 1877. In little more than a week, he was off again, this time to Berber, Dongola, Wadi Halfa, Assuan, and the borders of Abyssinia. But there had been no rest for him in the capital. ".You can have little idea of the amount of work I have to do," he wrote on leaving Khartoum, " and I never have a Sunday or a day of rest. . . . My huge palace is again desolate. It is a dreary place. I cannot go out of it without having people howling after me with petitions that I will let their sons out of prison, or such-like things; and they follow me wherever I go, yelling all the time. I will not let them be beaten away, as is usually the case, but I take no notice; for how can I release every prisoner? "

During the few days spent at his headquarters, Gordon hanged a notorious murderer at eighteen hours' notice—a salutary example that he said would " tend to keep the town quiet for some months." He knew, full well, that the deterrent effect of the punishment would be much reduced, by delay, and, in his fearless way, he re-solved to ignore red tape, " usual channels," and such-like impedi-ments to efficiency, and to follow the line of reason that his con-science directed.

Alluding to the execution in a letter from Berber dated October 25th, he declared—" I do not care. Had I left the process to go through the usual routine, it would have taken six months, and at any rate the robbers are now afraid, and the man has been hanged." This was typical of Gordon's common sense reasoning. Justice had been done, and the desired object of deterring others had been achieved; that was what mattered. Had he submitted to all the delay and eye-wash of dilatory Government departments, his object would have been defeated, and the state of Khartoum worse than before. Resenting interference himself, and realising the evils it is always liable to bring about, Gordon would not interfere with the governors under him " if they are in any way respectable; for it injures their influence, and my interference can do no good."

By this time, he had ridden something like three thousand miles on camels since leaving Massawa in March, and was begin-ning to feel the strain of these long, tiring rides. On the way to Dongola, he wrote—" I was very tired last night, and felt as if I should fall off my camel: you have but little idea how fatiguing it is." And, four days later—" From not having worn a bandage across the chest, I have shaken my heart or lungs out of their places. In camel-riding you ought to wear a sash round the waist, and another close up under the arm-pits; otherwise all the internal machinery gets disturbed."

At Karen, where he made further attempts to get in touch with King Johannes of Abyssinia, he paid another visit to the freebooter, Walad el Michael, whose not inconsiderable following was at the disposal of the highest bidder. Recording his impressions after the visit, Gordon wrote on December 20th:—"How I hate these Abyssinians—Walad el Michael, etc. I see nothing attractive about them. Their Christianity is only in form, for they seem very little more civilized than the Equatorial tribes. On the other hand, my Bedouin Arabs of Darfour and hereabouts are fine handsome fellows and quite gentlemen. Some of the young ones have a style and carriage which I envy. I never was dignified or grand, and could not be, but these young Ishmaels are every bit the Prince. They do not loll about, or smell like these Abyssinians, though I expect neither wash at any time."

Unable to get any satisfaction as to the whereabouts of Johannes, whose evasive dawdling became exasperating, Gordon returned to Khartoum by way of Suakin and Berber. So ended the year 1877—for Gordon a year of increasing toil in circumstances of the utmost difficulty, and in conditions that few men could have weathered. Despite the discouraging, heartbreaking nature of his work, he could look back on his achievements with pride and no little satisfaction, for had he not freed many of the tribes from persecution, thereby gaining their friendliness and support? Had he not ameliorated the lot of the people, generally, by reforming abuses and abolishing the tyranny of his predecessors? That, in the space of a few months, all this could have been accomplished by a solitary Englishman—perhaps it would be safer to say Scotsman—indifferently supported by local material, and hindered rather than aided by the Egyptian Government, seems almost inconceivable. Gordon had set himself a high standard when he aimed at complete abolition of slavery in the Sudan, and it saddened him to find as time went on that, with Egypt's comparatively meagre resources and the lack of enthusiasm for emancipation, the task could not be fulfilled in its entirety. Nevertheless, much could be done to curb the activities of the slave hunters, and to alleviate human suffering. To this end, Gordon had striven with all the force of his dynamic spirit, and it is not too much to say that, in the short time elapsing since his appointment as Governor-General, he had already revolutionised life in the Sudan. The brutalities of the former régime had disgusted him beyond measure, and he had, long since, resolved to make short work of anyone venturing to resort to such barbarism.

As instances of the atrocities committed by these tyrants, Gordon tells of a Governor of Khartoum—dismissed by him from

his position—who " had prepared razors to shave the beards of
some twenty sheikhs[1] who had not pleased him. This scoundrel,
just before I came up, gave a Captain 1200 *courbatch*[2] (whip)
blows, which cut the flesh from the poor devil's feet and he is still
lame."

---

[1] To shave a sheikh's beard is to inflict on him severe degradation.
[2] Alternative spelling—*kurbash*.

CHAPTER XIII

Downfall of the Khedive

THE new year opened inauspiciously for Egypt, whose foreign creditors now began to put on pressure to such an extent that Khedive Ismail became desperately anxious as to the outcome of his country's precarious financial position. In his extremity, he turned to Gordon as the one man who could help him out of his difficulties. " Come at once to my assistance," ran his urgent telegram, " I know no one who can help me so faithfully in the difficult time that is impending."

This frantic appeal reached Gordon at a place called Shendy, on the Nile, during his return journey from the Abyssinian frontier, and, much as he disliked the idea of going to Cairo with its boring dinners and functions, his loyalty to the Khedive had never for a moment waned, and he felt bound to do what he could for him, if only in return for his unfailing kindness throughout Gordon's service in the Sudan. Towards the end of his long journey to the capital, he wrote—" I do not like at all going to Cairo, but there was no help for it. I have now been one year Governor-General and I have lived a very rough sort of life, so much so that I have lost all my civilised tastes, and have an aversion to my meals that I can scarcely express. The idea of dinners at Cairo makes me quail. I do not exaggerate when I say ten minutes *per diem* is sufficient for all my meals, and there is no greater happiness to me than when they are finished."

Typical of Gordon was his own immediate personal response to the urgent call for economy, most generously insisting on his pay of six thousand a year being reduced by half. Reaching Cairo on March 7th by a train very much overdue, he hurried to the Khedive's palace, where he was expected to dinner, to find they had been waiting for an hour and a half. Ismail welcomed him

154

warmly and sat him down on his right, dirty and travel-stained as he was.

Almost at once, Gordon learned that the Khedive wanted him to accept the presidency of an enquiry into the financial state of the country — a somewhat startling pronouncement seeing that, apart from a generous allowance of common sense, he could boast of no qualification whatever for a position that seemed essentially the province of an expert in political economy. It may well be that the Khedive had been so much impressed by Gordon's skilful administration of the Equatorial Provinces, converting them in three years from a liability to a going concern, that he looked upon him as a kind of wizard who could work miracles, for, to be sure, little short of a miracle could deliver him from the hands of the money-lenders.

To Gordon the prospect was distasteful in the extreme, yet he felt that, in the circumstances, he could hardly refuse, especially as the Khedive had gone out of his way to do him honour and show him every consideration. And so it was arranged, Gordon accepting with some diffidence a position that must surely have made him feel like a square peg in a round hole.

For some days, Cairo had been filling up with foreigners, interested in one way or another in this momentous crisis. Diplomats were there to watch events on behalf of their acquisitive governments, rather like vultures hovering over an exhausted horse in the hope that it will soon die and provide them with some tasty morsels. Creditors, whose frantic anxiety to ensure the safety of their money likened them to ravenous dogs fighting over a bone, crowded into the city to exact their pound of flesh. How cordially did Gordon detest it all, with its functions, its humbug, its intrigues. How he longed for his camel and the desert, far away from the sordid scheming of diplomacy, the avaricious scramble for gain.

Nothing could have exceeded the lavishness of his reception, though this too proved a source of consternation, for, as he said with characteristic humility, he had never been "dignified or grand." "I was taken off to the Palace," he wrote to his sister, "where the Prince of Wales lodged when here! ! I am now writing from this place, and you may imagine my feelings at the splendour. . . . Certainly the honours are overwhelming. Fancy a palace full of lights, mirrors, gentlemen to wait on you, and the building itself one of the finest in Cairo." While, a week later—" I am much bothered, but I get to bed at 8 p.m., which is a comfort, for I do

not dine out, and consequently do not drink wine. Everyone laughs
at me, and I do not care." As Sir William Butler wrote of those
unworthy people who derided Gordon and opposed his every effort
to find a solution of the financial problem—" It is difficult to re-
press a feeling of animosity against the men on whose shoulders
must most justly rest the responsibility of having destroyed, and
deliberately destroyed, the sole chance which the pressure of an
incorruptibly honest and far-seeing man at the head of the Committee on Egyptian Finance would at that time have given to
Egypt."

From the very outset of the enquiry, Gordon was a lone wolf,
fighting single-handed in the council chamber as he had done in
the wilds of Central Africa, in the interests of his employer, the
Khedive. Every hand was against him, for they feared he might
succeed in saving Ismail Pasha from the financial difficulties
threatening to overwhelm his country, thus robbing them of their
spoil. Aware of his remarkable reputation, they might well have
been apprehensive as to his ability to overawe them, even as he had
subdued the savage tribes in the Sudan. They aimed, therefore, to
get rid of him as quickly as possible, for, in the words of Sir William
Butler—" Honest men were not wanted either by the bond-holders
of Egypt or by the rival powers who were hankering after her
flesh pots."

But it need hardly be said that, as long as the Khedive considered his presence would serve a useful purpose, he would not be
got rid of, and in the end, despite his inexperience of high finance,
he put forward a proposal that might have saved the situation.
Unfortunately, however, Ismail lacked the strength of character
required to give his support to Gordon's scheme, with the result
that he lost the confidence of his faithful associate, who straightway
returned to his mission in the Sudan, thankful to be done with the
duplicity and intrigues that had surrounded him for upwards of
three weeks. Before leaving Cairo, he wrote—" H.H. threw me
over completely at the last moment; but far from being angry, I was
very glad, for it relieved me of a deal of trouble. . . . I laugh
at all this farce. . . . I failed in the finance scheme through the
weakness of H.H. I think I could have satisfactorily settled the
question. . . . I do not know how matters will end with me for
I was too outspoken to have strengthened my position."

And so he returned to the work he understood, the lonely
life he preferred to the hustle and gaiety of great cities, where he
felt uncomfortable and ill-at-ease. Back to the desert and the long,

dusty marches, back to all the worries and perplexities, the dangers
and the hardships, yet to a life he would not have exchanged for
any other, a life that perhaps no other man could have lived so
happily and few could have endured.

Travelling back to Khartoum by way of Suez, Aden, and Berbera, Gordon discovered that, from the Red Sea ports, slaves were
being transported across to the Arabian coast. This traffic in human
beings he determined to stop, or at any rate reduce, but, as he
pointed out, " the vastness of these lands is against any hope of
ever doing much in them." His visit to Cairo had done nothing to
alter his poor opinion of the Egyptian administration. On the
contrary, it had tended to increase his misgivings as to the future
of the Sudan under Egyptian sway. In a letter dated April 17th,
1878, from Zeila, on his way back through the eastern Sudan, he
wrote—" I feel quite different to what I did before. I have no
hope whatever in any change for the better in headquarters:
another Khedive would be just the same. Our Government
(English) lives on a hand-to-mouth policy. They are very ignorant
of these lands, yet, some day or other, they or some other government will have to know them, for things at Cairo cannot stay as
they are." These were prophetic words, for that " some day or
other " was a good deal nearer than even Gordon, himself, would
probably have believed.

At the town of Harrar, where he arrived after " a really terrible
journey " of eight days, he met Raouf Pasha, the man he had
removed from Gondokoro some years earlier. The unfortunate
Raouf seemed fated to come up against the fury of an outraged
Gordon, who again dismissed this " regular tyrant " on account
of his unpardonable conduct in a position of authority for which
he was in no way fitted. But one ceases to be surprised at the
futility of Egypt's administration of the Sudan, before and after
Gordon's régime, on learning that, when he finally relinquished his
appointment, the tyrant Raouf Pasha, twice dismissed by him for
gross abuse of his powers, actually succeeded him as Governor-
General! Gordon had always anticipated that, as soon as he
turned his back on the Sudan, there would be a relapse to the
tyranny of the Pashas. And so it turned out. But nothing could
have been more conducive to so disastrous a state of affairs than
the selection of Raouf as Governor-General.

In cases of incompetence, corruption, or brutality, Gordon relentlessly threw out the offenders right and left. " In one month,"
he wrote during his return journey to Khartoum, " I have turned

out three Generals of Division, one General of Brigade, and four Lieutenant-Colonels. It is no use mincing matters." But no doubt most of these were reinstated as soon as Gordon left. At first he had been in the habit of sending delinquents to Cairo to be dealt with there. But, finding that they not only got off scot-free, but were to be seen taking part in court festivities as though nothing had happened, he resolved that, henceforth, they would be punished first and sent to Cairo afterwards. From Harrar, he went on to Massawa, where he learned of more raiding by the treacherous Walad el Michael, who had attacked the Abyssinians on the frontier and killed their commander, Ras[1] Bariou, thus straining relations still further between King Johannes and the Khedive, especially as Michael had been supplied with ammunition for his attack by an Egyptian official, one Osman Pasha. "It is inconceivable," commented Gordon, with justifiable exasperation, in a letter dated May 21st, " what owls these Egyptians are."

At last, he was able to settle down at Khartoum to the mass of work necessarily involved in the administration of so vast a territory, and there he remained for some months deliberating over endless problems ranging from the most trivial appeals by individuals to widespread insurrection. " I can say truly," he wrote from his palace in mid-July, " that my life is one long series of flesh-vexing telegrams, of rows, of disputes, etc. A regular Ishmaelite existence. I am at war with nearly everyone at Cairo, and my crest is a thistle. I could justify my rows; for they arise from dishonest officials, undue interference of Consuls, etc."

That Gordon was very fully employed during this long spell at Khartoum may be gathered from the recurring outbreaks that seemed inseparable from this lawless, tumultuous country. Despite the fact that, wherever he showed himself, he almost invariably transformed anarchy into orderliness by means of a judicious mixture of severity and forbearance, no sooner was his back turned than the trouble-makers would regain their courage and renew their rebellious activities. Suleiman, banished to the distant province of the Bahr el Ghazal, had again collected a numerous following, and, notwithstanding his assurances to Gordon at Shaka, had started a fresh revolt in support of the slave trade. Haroun, encouraged by Gordon's absence in other parts of the Sudan, had emerged from his retreat in the mountains and, once more, was on the warpath in Darfour. While, in Kordofan, a third insurrection

---

[1] Abyssinian title.

had broken out, under the leadership of a man named Sabahi, who had been prominent in Sebehr's rebel army, and who, besides plundering and slave dealing, had murdered one of Gordon's governors at a place called Edowa. The Governor-General could not be everywhere at once, so, for the time being, he remained at his command post, disposing his forces as best he might to meet these three revolts in widely separated parts of his immense territory.

In addition to his responsibility for crushing the rebellions, Gordon was harassed by financial difficulties in the Sudan. He was, moreover, continually hammering away at the slave trade, giving the merciless dealers no rest. "I am striking daily deadly blows against the slave-trade," he wrote, "and am establishing a sort of Government of Terror about it. I have hanged a man for mutilating a little boy, and would not ask leave to do so. I do not care if H.H. likes it or not." This was another instance of his fearlessness in acting on his own responsibility when he considered it in the public interest so to do. He could never rely on being supported by the Cairo ministers; consequently, he was obliged to take the law into his own hands. Only in this way, by swift, stern justice, could he hope to put a stop to these brutal atrocities and maintain, unimpaired, his own authority.

By the end of 1878, poor Gordon, a lonely figure in his huge palace at Khartoum, was beset by widespread troubles, for, in addition to the insurrections alluded to, the Abyssinian question began to assume a more menacing aspect, in no way improved by the treacherous activities of Walad el Michael. His first inclination was to go, himself, to the Bahr el Ghazal and direct the campaign against Suleiman. But, since this sphere of operations was in the hands of the Italian, Romulus Gessi, his capable and trusted lieutenant who had served him so well in the Equatorial Provinces, he decided to turn his personal attention to the other two revolts, namely those in Kordofan and Darfour, where his confidence in vigorous action by his commanders was by no means so pronounced. Moreover, in going to Darfour, he would be able to assist Gessi by checking the flow of Suleiman's old adherents who were now anxious to rejoin him in the Bahr el Ghazal. Furthermore, Darfour being the very core of the slave traffic, Gordon's presence in the province, through which all slaves must pass on their way to Egyptian bondage, would cast a disturbing influence over the rascally traders' operations.

Before starting on this expedition, however, he seized an opportunity of communicating with the elusive Johannes, for which purpose he went up the Blue Nile to Abu Harraz, and thence by camel to Kedaref, where he was met by the king's envoy from Kassala on the Abyssinian frontier. The envoy brought a letter from Johannes, addressed to the " Sultan of Sudan," declaring he would be prepared to make peace with Gordon but not with the Khedive. " Johannes," said the envoy, after drinking half a bottle of cognac at the house of one of Gordon's officers, " will never make a treaty with the Khedive, by which he signs away any of the original territory of Abyssinia, but he will not fight Gordon." As a result of this statement, Gordon telegraphed to the Khedive—" There is no fear of the King's fighting us, so you can do what you like about the treaty."

Meanwhile, Walad el Michael had submitted to Johannes, and was on his way to Gondar to lay down his arms. So that, on retracing his steps to Khartoum, Gordon could congratulate himself on a relaxation of the tension over Abyssinia, at any rate for the moment. But what a life of turmoil was his, turning from one source of trouble to another without respite, using indulgent persuasion where possible, and only resorting to severe measures when no other course could avail.

On leaving Kedaref, Gordon presented the Ethiopian envoy with gifts for the king to the value of a hundred and seventy-five pounds. In a subsequent acknowledgment of the presents, Johannes addressed his benefactor as " *Garden* Pasha my beloved friend! " The measure of trust that could be placed in this vaunted friendship will be revealed before the end of the story. Nevertheless, it served to tide over a difficult period of Gordon's career in the Sudan, when a lull here or there enabled him to devote more individual attention to other spheres of action. His energy was truly remarkable, and when the ravages of an unhealthy climate are taken into account, it seems quite miraculous that he was able to go on day after day, continually faced with situations and problems of unbelievable diversity and complication.

Nor were his difficulties confined to the Sudan, for ever since his straight speaking in Cairo during the financial enquiry, the attitude of the Egyptian Government towards him had been gradually deteriorating. While, throughout his service under the Khedive, he had never been able to count on a full measure of support or co-operation from the Government, he was now subjected to downright opposition. Their iniquitous indulgence of the arch-scoundrel

Sebehr in Cairo; their refusal to punish wrong-doers sent down by Gordon to be dealt with; their shabby treatment of the Sudan in matters of finance; their indifference to the slave-trade, if indeed they did not actually encourage it; the personal hostility of the ministers towards Egypt's most faithful servant—all this deplorable behaviour was directed against a man who was wearing himself out and giving the best years of his life, in appalling conditions, in the interests of their own country.

The trouble lay in their fear of Gordon's unswerving honesty. Dishonest and corrupt themselves, not only did they realise the futility of trying to persuade him to go their way, and eat out of their hands in the obsequious manner of their own officials, but they also saw the danger to themselves of the presence in their midst of a man so essentially honourable, so severely censorious of evil practices. He learned that the Nubar ministry " could not bear " his name. " I was the Mordecai who would not bow to them," he wrote. " Even the Europeans were all against me. Why? Because I will not strip the Sudan to give them money."

And here is an extract from another letter, showing that in no circumstances would Gordon be a party to the Government's dubious methods : — " The only notice from Cairo on the question of these slave brigands was an offer from Nubar to send Sebehr up here — Sebehr having promised to Nubar to pay a revenue of £25,000 a year. Now how could Sebehr pay this revenue? Only by sending down slaves. I declined Nubar's offer, and said I wanted no help from Cairo in that way."

Gordon left Khartoum for Shaka, by way of El Obeid, in March—the hottest time of the year. In day time, the heat was terrific, but the nights were bitterly cold. Describing the march through Kordofan, he wrote—" Imagine yourself journeying on some twenty-six to thirty miles a day, starting at half-past three in the morning, and halting at nine or ten; and then starting again at three in the afternoon, and going on till seven, day after day through a sandy plain covered with dried-up yellow grass and scrub-trees. . . . The country is dried up, and my shortest march with no water is three days. . . . What a country—with districts as much as two hundred miles long and broad without water! "

A day or two before reaching the frontier of Darfour, the route led through jungle, where the heat became stifling in the airless forest. At the frontier, the wells were nearly dry. " I have never," wrote Gordon, " in China or elsewhere, felt such heat."

After suffering intensely from heat and exhaustion, he and his small escort arrived at Shaka, described by him as "this den of iniquity," on April 7th, 1879. Meanwhile, heartening news had reached him from the Bahr el Ghazal, where the excellent Gessi had inflicted several defeats on Suleiman, and had got him on the run. No more crushing blow could be struck at the slave trade than by the final destruction of this formidable band of brigands. Yet, though hard pressed, Suleiman continued to elude his pursuers for some time.

At Shaka, Gordon's sudden appearance created something of a panic among the slave dealers, who, in his absence, had again gathered together for the purposes of their nefarious trade, and whose fear of the Governor-General's vengeance was such that they quickly took to their heels and fled. "The slave dealers," he wrote, "have departed from Shaka, and this place is clean of them, I hope, for ever."

Though the task seemed well nigh hopeless, so vast was the area to be covered, he persisted with dogged tenacity in releasing slaves wherever he found them, and punishing the brutal dealers. In one week, he freed no fewer than five hundred of these wretched creatures, torn from their homes and about to be carried off in conditions of frightful hardship to places as far distant as Marseilles or Rome.

In the midst of his incessant labours, hurrying from one point of trouble to another over wide stretches of desert waste, directing operations against the rebels, Suleiman, Haroun, and Sabahi, and striking hard blows in every direction against the slave trade—in the midst of this whirlwind of trials and anxieties, of intricate problems that he alone could tackle, Gordon was constantly pestered by the Egyptian Government for money. "The Sudan," he wrote feelingly, "always cost Cairo money—never gave any. It is only since I have been Governor that nothing has been given on either side." And again, "They worry me for money, knowing by my budgets I cannot make my expenses meet my revenue by ninety-thousand pounds a year." Such was the state of bankruptcy brought about by an inept Egyptian Government, supported, or rather unsupported, by a host of incompetent officials, that many of the troops in the Sudan were in rags and had received no pay for nearly two years. In answer to yet another demand from Cairo for money, Gordon bluntly replied—"When the nakedness of my troops is partially covered I may talk to you; in the meantime, send me up at once the £12,000 you unfairly took in customs on goods in transit to the Sudan."

Meanwhile, this man of amazing energy, who seems never to rest, is here, there, and everywhere, hunting the rebels, rescuing the slaves, pacifying the populace, scattering the dealers in human merchandise.

Whilst at Shaka, Gordon read in the papers of a British reverse in Afghanistan. His typically outspoken comments, conveyed in one of his home letters, are full of interest. " It is just as well," he wrote, " we have these lessons taught us *en petit*. We are a great deal too confident in ourselves, and despise ordinary precautions. The press is greatly answerable for this over-confidence. Men now risk dangers in the hope of paper distinction. However savage or despicable your enemy may be, you never should despise precautions which you would take against a European foe. . . . I like Nelson's sign—' England expects DUTY.' Now the race is for honours not honour, and newspaper praise. I hate all the boasting of our papers."

Curiously enough, in that same year, 1879, the year of wars in Afghanistan and Zululand, Gordon received a letter from an old friend, expressing very similar views. After declaring that Gordon's name " is already—and will ever continue to be—a proverb throughout that benighted and unhappy land (the Sudan)," he went on—" If you receive and read the newspapers at present, I am sure they must make you sick. We are overflowing with heroes. Such speechifying, such puffing of each other, such presentations of swords, such eating and drinking—from the generals to the drummers—we are all demi-gods: and some of us have actually *done our duty* by fighting for our lives! What a fickle creature is John Bull! A neighbour and old friend of mine tells me of his landing at Dover with his regiment (the 14th) fresh from Waterloo. Immediately he and the other officers were marched to the Custom House and most minutely searched; then along with the men to a naked room without bed, table, or chair—nothing but the bare boards to pass the night upon, besides being well hissed in the streets, accompanied by shouts of ' Down with the Army! Why should we have to pay you fellows? ' and other words of welcome."

At Shaka, Gordon seized four of Suleiman's men, sent to him with assurances that the brigand chief had " never wavered in his allegiance " to the Khedive! They were tried by court martial and shot twelve days later, Gordon declaring that, but for Suleiman's cold-blooded massacres of Government soldiers in the Bahr el Ghazal, he would have reprieved them.

After finally clearing out the slave-dealers' nest at Shaka, he pushed on westward to Kalaka, another slave den. "We have got to the heart of them this time," he wrote, "but for how many years has this been going on?" Continuing his journey over the sandy plains, he reached Dara, the scene of his triumph over Suleiman, on May 4th, subsequently advancing by way of E Fascher, Kobbe, and Kakabieh to Kolkol in the far west of Dar four. Always venturesome and daring, in this march with only sixty men Gordon penetrated into the very heart of the country occupied by the insurgent Haroun.

At Kolkol, he seemed to have reached the "back of beyond," the most distant, lonely, isolated spot imaginable. "The state of the soldiers is deplorable," ran a letter written by him at this dismal outpost. "No one had passed along this road for over two years—in fact Kolkol was a prison. Nothing could describe the misery of these utterly useless lands." On the outward march, the column had been harassed by parties of marauders, who, however were driven off without difficulty. But, before leaving Kolkol for the return journey, information reached Gordon that Haroun had planned to intercept him on the road to El Fascher. He therefore strengthened his small force by taking three hundred men from the garrison to see him "through the worst of the road." "It is," he declared, "the least this garrison can do, after my running such risk, and being at so much trouble to come here to see after them." He evidently felt sure that he would have to fight his way back to El Fascher, for, on the day before his departure, he wrote—"For some years I have been more or less peacefully disposed. I no longer delight in war or fights like this one now before me. I look on the accounts one reads of wars as so much romance writing, and somewhat like the Chinese people I have rather a contempt for the warrior. I do not believe in his prowess as he relates affairs: out of very little indeed you can make such a great deal. Eminent services, etc., are eminent nonsense. 'They loved the praise of men more than the praise of God.'"

But as things turned out, Gordon reached El Fascher without seeing a sign of the rebels, and, in consequence of an urgent request from the Khedive, he left for Khartoum, *en route* for Cairo, satisfied that Suleiman's revolt was virtually at an end, and that the news of his overwhelming defeat would have a salutary effect throughout the Sudan.

At Toashia, he was joined by Gessi—"looking much older"—who gave him an account of the campaign in the Bahr el Ghazal

The fugitive Suleiman, with a much reduced following and very little powder, had now retreated so far into the interior that he found himself menaced by the fierce tribes inhabiting that part of the country. Gessi said that, " whenever the natives got a chance, they killed the slave dealers. Sometimes they would fall on an isolated party; and, on one occasion, they fell on 700 and killed them all." This was their revenge on the slave dealers for robbing them of their children. They even killed the women so as to prevent propagation of the hated species. For his meritorious services, Gessi was made a Pasha, awarded the Order of Osmanhie, and given a grant of two thousand pounds by the Governor-General, one thousand of this sum coming out of Gordon's own pocket.

While Gordon continued his journey to Khartoum, his much gratified lieutenant returned to the Bahr el Ghazal, to complete his task about a month later with the capture of Suleiman, who, together with most of his chiefs, was shot out of hand. Thus ended Gessi's victorious campaign.

Horrified by the quantities of skulls lying beside the track, Gordon gave orders for a number of them to be collected in a pile as an everlasting reminder to the natives of the brutality of the slave dealers. He estimated that, in the three months since leaving Khartoum, he had released nearly seventeen hundred slaves. " Some of these poor slaves," he wrote, " are mere skeletons. No female child, however young, passes unscathed by these scoundrels! The only thing I can do to these slave dealers is to flog them and strip them, and send them like Adams into the desert."

All along the route, Gordon was constantly engaged liberating slaves and punishing their masters. He found that some districts had become almost completely depopulated owing to the depredations of these inhuman monsters. But his was a lone voice crying in the wilderness, and although, wherever he appeared, slave dealing operations were swiftly broken up, the full weight of his avenging hand falling heavily upon the malefactors, he could not be in more than one place at a time, and the spreading of information as to his movements enabled these infamous activities to be pursued in areas which, for the moment, were not dominated by the presence of the Governor-General. The slave traders cared little for such efforts as might be made by Gordon's Egyptian subordinates to interfere with them. It was he they feared, with his steely, penetrating eye, his devastating anger, his supremely masterful personality, and, at his approach, they scattered like chaff before the wind. Nevertheless, he often succeeded in surprising them, when they would be made to pay dearly for their sins. In the circumstances, total abolition of slavery throughout the immense regions of the Sudan seemed pretty hopeless. But at least, Gordon could crush the traders piecemeal, and so go far towards maintaining a stranglehold over the whole sordid business. This he did with a vigour and persistence that earned him the admiration of the world, raising him in public esteem to even greater heights than after his suppression of the *Taiping* Rebellion.

His summons to Cairo was due to another crisis, this time one that seriously threatened the rule of Ismail Pasha, who once again appealed to Gordon in his extremity. But his cry for help had come too late. Reaching Fogia on July 1st, Gordon found awaiting him a telegram announcing the deposition of Ismail and the Sultan's decree nominating his son Tewfik Pasha to succeed him as Khedive. This somewhat startling intelligence, however, in no way affected Gordon, for, despite his sympathy for the deposed Ismail, his feelings towards him had undergone a marked change since the outcome of the financial enquiry, when he was so badly let down by His Highness. Three weeks later, he arrived at Khartoum. " I am a wreck," he wrote on July 21st, " like the portions of the *Victory* towed into Gibraltar after Trafalgar; but God has enabled me, or rather has used me, to do what I wished to do—that is to break down the slave-trade." No wonder he felt a wreck after all he had been through, the long, hot, dusty marches; the constant anxiety; the lack of proper food; the mental strain; the unhealthy climate; the isolation and loneliness; the endless wrestling with seemingly insoluble problems; the crushing burden of responsibility—all these had combined to bring about the first serious failure of his health.

Strong as he was, and endowed with powers of resistance given to few, no mortal man could have emerged unscathed from so tremendously severe a test of human endurance. For upwards of six years, he had lived for the most part either among fever-ridden swamps or in arid desert wastes. In conditions that only a man of exceptionally robust constitution could have withstood, this remarkable product of a famous Scottish clan had made light of hardships and trials that others failed to surmount, until, finally, he was left almost alone to carry on his great work. Yet even he, at last, began to feel the effects of his strenuous life, and to realise it was time he went home. " Thank God, I am pretty well now," he wrote, " but I passed the grave lately, and never thought to see Khartoum."

On reaching the capital, Gordon received the most heartening reports. First, that the rebel Suleiman had been caught and executed by Gessi. And then, that Haroun, the would-be Sultan of Darfour, had been killed and his followers dispersed. In view of the greatly improved situation brought about by these two successes, Gordon felt he would now be justified in laying down his burden for others to take up. He therefore left for Cairo resolved to tender his resignation to the new Khedive.

Arriving on August 23rd, he was received with honours befitting his colossal services to the country. He, however, declined the offer of a special train, because, as he wrote, "in all probability they would have charged me for it!" How well he knew the crafty qualities of the Khedive's ministers, who would descend to almost any roguery for their own discreditable ends. Still, not wishing to administer too obvious a snub to the Egyptian Government, Gordon did agree, against his inclinations, to stay at the palace where he had lodged during his previous visit. But he would have preferred an hotel, for, in his heart, he felt disinclined to place himself under any obligation to these unprincipled Egyptians whom he cordially despised.

In his talks with Tewfik Pasha, he learned that the Abyssinian question was causing him grave concern, and, although Gordon had intended going straight home from Cairo, he generously agreed, at the urgent entreaty of the Khedive, to delay his departure until he had made yet another effort to bring about friendly relations with King Johannes, whose military leaders, Ras Aloula and Wahad el Michael, were believed to be contemplating an attack on the Egyptian territory of Bugos. "I told the Khedive," wrote Gordon, "I would not stay any longer, but would go to Massawa, settle with Johannes, and go home."

CHAPTER XIV

A Daring Enterprise

THERE seems no doubt that Gordon fully expected to find himself involved in a war with the Abyssinians, seeing that, before leaving Cairo, he took carefully considered measures in preparation for eventualities on the Abyssinian border. As always, when the need for action arose, his energy and whirlwind activity were remarkable. He thought of everything, leaving nothing to chance, and, with the initiative of a born leader who believes in direct action and refuses to be hampered by red tape, he made known his requirements and his intentions, in no uncertain terms, alike to ministers, consuls, finance commissioners, military commanders, and tribal chieftains, caring not a rap if, in so doing, he offended the petty dignity of some intervening authority, as long as he got what he wanted without delay.

He wrote to the Consuls-General of England and France telling them, in his customary blunt way, that " they had interfered to get sweet things, and now they must interfere to avoid bitter things." He telegraphed to Aden and Jeddah demanding gun-boats, and summoned the Consul at Jeddah to meet him at Massawa. He sent orders to the frontier tribes to move their families and their cattle back from the Abyssinian border, and to hold their warriors in readiness for action. He arranged for the strength of the frontier garrisons to be doubled, and privately notified the commissioners of debt that he would need three hundred thousand pounds " for the war which is pending." Finally, being fully aware of the enmity and hatred of the Pashas, he fired his parting shot at the Egyptian Foreign Office—" If, on my return, I hear any of the Council of Ministers have said anything against me, I will beg the Khedive to make the evil speaker Governor-General of the Sudan." This, he said, in the case of a Cairo Pasha, would be equivalent to a sentence of death.

KING JOHANNES OF
ABYSSINIA
(EMPEROR OF ETHIOPIA)

(Hulton Library)

From the Red Sea, bound for Massawa, he wrote on September 2nd—"I would sooner have come home straight, but I had it not in my heart to forsake Tewfik till this affair is finished . . . . I have begun to be very tired of the continual wear and tear of my last six years. However, I cannot think of leaving Egypt exposed to her enemies."

Reaching Massawa on September 6th, he discovered that the Abyssinians had already taken possession of the bone of contention, Bugos, so that, if the Khedive decided to persist in his claim to the territory in dispute, he would be obliged to take it by force. However, it became evident to Gordon that nothing could be done towards a solution of the Abyssinian problem and coming to terms with the king unless he actually entered the country and tackled Johannes in his lair. Bearing in mind the Ethiopian monarch's evil reputation for treachery and barbarism, this was a good deal more than an ordinarily venturesome project. He knew full well he would be taking his life in his hands, and that, in view of the king's mercurial temperament, his delight in fiendish cruelty, and his hatred of Egypt, the chances of his safe return were by no means certain. The reader will long since have gathered, however, that the spice of danger invariably proved an incentive to Gordon, and the more perilous its menace, the more eager would he be to accept its challenge. But, before seeking an interview with Johannes, he decided, as a preliminary step, to see Ras Aloula, the Abyssinian commander, to find out, if possible, how the land lay.

On the day of his departure from Massawa (September 11th), he received a telegram from the Khedive directing him " to cede nothing, though he wished to avoid a war "—a most difficult position for Gordon, going almost alone into the heart of a savage, if professed Christian, country, ruled over by an inhuman tyrant who thought as little of condemning a man to mutilation as the average civilised person would think of swatting a tiresome fly. It was not to be expected that the truculent Johannes would meekly consent to the Khedive's demands without concessions of any kind on the part of Egypt. After all, considerable tracts of Abyssinia, including the province of Bugos, had in the past been appropriated by the Egyptians, so that there was at any rate something to be said for the king's hostile attitude, and Gordon's mission became all the more difficult with this proviso that be might concede nothing.

As to going alone, he preferred as a rule to rely entirely on his own unaided resources, to be free to concentrate his thoughts on the work ahead, and to formulate his plans unimpeded by the ideas or suggestions of others. So remarkable was his self-reliance that he felt happier and more confident if left to his own devices.

On September 13th, another telegram reached him to much the same effect as the first—"Give up nothing, but do not fight."

" As if," ran Gordon's derisive comment, " it were in our option to avoid it!" Two days later, a message from Aloula directed him to a place called Gura, scene of the Egyptian army's heavy defeat three years earlier, where the Abyssinian general would await him. After a wearisome mule ride over the roughest country imaginable, the Khedive's envoy arrived at his destination on the afternoon of the 16th. In order to reach Aloula's headquarters, Gordon was obliged to climb to the summit of an " almost insurmountable " hill.

Dressed in the impressive uniform of a Turkish field marshal, he passed through the ranks of Ethiopian warriors to the general's hut. There sat Ras Aloula, attended by an array of priests and others. He received Gordon with cold indifference, accepting the Khedive's letter proclaiming his accession and the mission to King Johannes with little apparent interest. His attitude was sullen, and he left most of the talking to his visitor. Incidentally, Gordon's escort consisted of no more than half a dozen black soldiers, with a secretary, Berzati Bey, who came of an ancient, highly respected Mussulman family, and had been his " most intimate friend for three years."

From the outset of his journey into Abyssinia, Gordon cherished no illusions as to the gravity of his position, for had he not put himself in the power of unscrupulous enemies, who would not hesitate to seize him on the flimsiest pretext ? He felt from the first that he was virtually a prisoner. But, having once decided that only by undertaking an excursion into this wild, unprepossessing country and having a heart to heart talk with the king, could his mission possibly succeed, he had promptly made his plans without a second thought of the serious risk involved—rather, we may be sure, did he revel in the heavy odds against him. In very truth, he had walked into the lion's den, and no one knew better than he how problematical were the chances of ever getting out of it.

But by now, after six years of superhuman effort, he was beginning to tire of the arduous existence, his health had suffered, and a spell of complete rest had become essential. " I confess I am fearfully weary of my life," ran one of his letters written the day after leaving Massawa, "and contemplate with no trouble the chance that Walad el Michael's soldiers may waylay me on the way." Next day, he had complained of "that palpitation of the heart which reduces one to zero." And again, on September 14th, "this prickly heat-rash has turned into boils, so that I am a perfect Job." Obviously, he was thoroughly run down, and the sooner he could get home the better. But there remained much to be done, and, before he could take advantage of the respite he so badly needed, he was destined to undergo more weeks of infinitely exhausting journeying over almost impassable mountain tracks through an unbelievably barren, inhospitable country. Still, his steadfast faith in the power of the Almighty kept him going, and he, of course, had no thought of abandoning his task before everything possible had been done to reach a satisfactory understanding with Johannes.

Whilst at Gura, Gordon learned that Walad el Michael had been taken as a prisoner to *Amba* Gelali, near Adowa. "The Abyssinians," he wrote, "imprison their political prisoners on inaccessible mountains which are called *ambas*. They are of three descriptions. First class, in which the prisoner is hoisted up by means of a basket and pulleys, there being no possible road; second, in which there is one road; third, in which there are two or three roads. There is water and cultivable ground on these *ambas*, and on them the prisoners pass their existence, forgotten and in meditation, till perhaps some new revolution may put them on the throne."

Gordon derived considerable gratification from the news of Michael's captivity, since it meant that at any rate one source of trouble between Egypt and Abyssinia had been removed, and that the difficulty of negotiating with Johannes would, in consequence, be somewhat eased. With scrupulous fairness, he took no umbrage at the cool, not to say insolent, nature of his reception by Ras Aloula, realising the injustice of Egypt's treatment of her neighbour, and feeling that, as the Khedive's envoy, he could hardly expect anything but a frigid welcome. However, towards the end of Gordon's three days' stay at Gura, Aloula became a trifle less sullen and, although unable to come to any terms himself, he directed Gordon to a place called Debra Tabor, near Gondar, where he could see the king and convey to him the Khedive's message.

Before starting on September 18th, Gordon extracted from Aloula a promise that he would not attack Egypt during his absence. But the ruffian sent him by the worst possible route in order to prevent his seeing a good road, with the result that the journey took more than five weeks, and it was not until October 27th that he arrived at the king's abode. In a letter to his friend Mrs. F., dated October 5th, 1879, he wrote—" I have, since September 11th, been wending my way over sheep tracks and endless mountains, towards Debra Tabor, which is near the Tsarra Lake, whence the Blue Nile takes its rise. It is very dull work, and we have yet ten days more before we get to the King's place (Debra Tabor); and then I do not know the result of this voyage. The Abyssinians are a very primitive people, and live as they lived years and years ago, never advancing."

More than once, he was in serious danger of capture by bands of outlaws, but, with an escort of Aloula's men, he eventually reached Debra Tabor in safety, after being maliciously conducted over what King Johannes described as " the worst road in the country." As soon as he arrived, Gordon was ushered into the king's presence. Johannes sat on a raised platform attended by his uncle, Ras Arya, and the chief priest. Guns boomed out a salute, which the king hastened to explain was in honour of his visitor. Now, Johannes was an even greater monster than his predecessor, Theodore, who, himself, took a good deal of beating in the fine art of diabolical cruelty. Probably, there was very little in it, but it would hardly be right to give second place to one who, habitually, cut off the lips of smokers and the noses of those who took snuff, and who dealt with other offenders by cutting off their feet and hands, or by pouring hot tallow into their ears so as to destroy the optic nerve and deprive them of their sight.

" The King," wrote Gordon, " is a man of some forty-five years, a sour, ill-favoured looking being. He never looks you in the face, but when you look away he glares at you like a tiger. He never smiles; his look, always changing, is one of thorough suspicion. Hated and hating all, I can imagine no more unhappy man. Drunk overnight, he is up at dawn reading the Psalms. If he were in England he would never miss a prayer meeting, and would have a Bible as big as a portmanteau."

And again, in his notes on Abyssinia in 1879—" No one can travel without the King's order if he is a foreigner. You can buy nothing without his order; no one will shelter you without his order—in fact no more complete despotism could exist . . . . . . The cruelties the king and his people committed were atrocious. Forty Sudan soldiers were mutilated altogether and sent to Bugos with the message that if His Highness the Khedive wanted eunuchs he could have these."

And here is the impression of one of Gordon's envoys—" The king is a melancholy-looking man, and, I should say, has hardly ever smiled in his life. His life is simplicity itself. His palace consists of two large, round, conical-roofed, thatched houses; one for a reception room, the other his dwelling room—no attempt at the simplest window or door. His horses were in it as well as himself, but this is partly due to tradition."

This, then, was the creature who called himself king and professed to be a Christian, though without the smallest right, except that of conquest, to the throne of Abyssinia, or the possession of a solitary quality consistent with Christianity. Gordon's first interview with Johannes was merely a formal introduction. But, two days later, at the unearthly hour of daybreak, he was again received in audience, when the king enumerated his grievances against the Khedive, and made known to Gordon his demands for restoration of territory forcibly appropriated by Egypt. Then, in reply to the king's enquiry as to why he had come, Gordon referred him to the Khedive's letter. He had neither read it, nor even so much as seen it. Eventually, it was produced and translated by the chief clerk, who received "forty blows" for his negligence!

Gordon asked Johannes to put his demands in writing, and give the Khedive six months for their consideration. To this the king agreed, but said he was about to go to some hot baths, two days away, for his health. " Quite fashionable!" wrote Gordon, in his humorous way, " the baths consist of a hot spring coming up through a bamboo in an old hut." It seems that Johannes realised his demands were excessive, for, on his return to Debra Tabor, where Gordon had awaited him, he wanted to amend them. Finally, on November 7th, he agreed to write a moderated statement of his claims, and consented to a period of six months for the Khedive to consider his reply. This was probably as much as Gordon could have expected, and all might have been well if the king had been a man of his word. But, unfortunately, his moods were as changeable as the winds of heaven, and next day he would do no more than promise to send a letter to Cairo, at the same time peremptorily ordering Gordon to go back to his " master."

There was nothing more to be done. Gordon had been sent on an impossible task, his hands tied by the Khedive's insistence that he should concede nothing to a monarch burning for vengeance against Egypt on account of Abyssinia's lost possessions. With not a morsel to offer in face of the king's demands, some of which at any rate were clearly justified, the mission was doomed to failure from the outset. Moreover, not only was it unfair to subject Gordon to so invidious a position, but, to callously send him on an undertaking involving the gravest danger to himself, with an escort of utterly inadequate strength, was typical of Egyptian ineptitude and lethargic indifference.

Gordon left the same day. When on the point of starting, a letter was delivered to him together with a sum of one thousand dollars. The money he promptly and contemptuously returned. The letter, addressed to the Khedive, he felt justified in opening, since it was essential for him to know whether Johannes meant to honour his promise to allow six months for consideration of his claims. Brief and insolent, the letter ran—" To Mahommed Tewfik. I have received the letters you sent me by that man. I will not make a secret peace with you. If you want peace, ask the Sultans of Europe."

Obviously, it was useless to attempt further argument with a shilly-shallying, indecisive, vacillating creature such as Johannes had shown himself to be. Gordon had even gone so far as to offer his own personal intervention on behalf of Abyssinia in the matter of restoration of certain territories, which he believed should rightly and properly be surrendered by Egypt. But he was, at last, obliged to admit that nothing could be done with such a man, whose obstinacy, hatred, malice, and greed, formed an impassable barrier to the establishment of friendly relations between the two countries.

In the circumstances, Gordon was not sorry to turn his back on Debra Tabor and set out towards the Sudanese border. With an escort of Abyssinians he made for Khartoum, intending to take the route by way of Chelga and Galabat. Bearing in mind the treacherous tendencies of the people of this wild country, there could be no security for Gordon and his small party until they were safely across the frontier, and, so long as they remained in the territory ruled over by Johannes, they could never for one moment relax their vigilance, nor be sure that some devilish act of perfidiousness would not be perpetrated at their expense. Avaricious to a degree, it was fortunate that the Abyssinians could always be " bought," for there seems reason to suppose that, unless Gordon had been able to buy his way along, he never would have succeeded in getting back from this most gallant attempt to bring about a reconciliation between Egypt and Abyssinia.

During the return journey, he was subjected to considerable ill-treatment, being taken across snow-capped mountains without even tents for protection at night. He was, moreover, obliged to endure all kinds of indignities at the hands of these so-called Christians, whose country teemed with churches and monasteries, yet whose way of life was barbaric. The priests glared at him with hatred in their eyes, he was hustled by the insolent soldiery, treated contemptuously by the king, impeded, frustrated, and insulted by everyone—hardly a Christian-like attitude towards a visitor acting as intermediary in the cause of peace between them and their enemies.

Let there be no mistake, Gordon was lucky to get away with his life, or at any rate to avoid finding himself cut off from the world in one of those ghastly *ambas*, to which no access existed save by way of a basket dangling at the end of a rope. There, he might well have been kept as a hostage pending settlement of Abyssinia's differences with Egypt. However, he eventually reached the frontier in safety, but not before he had been outrageously held up by a troop of Abyssinian horsemen who, in the name of the king, rode down upon his party, forcing them to change their direction and make for the Red Sea port of Massawa instead of Galabat on the Sudanese border.

It was on December 8th that Gordon reached Massawa. There he found that the British Government had complied with his request by sending a warship, H.M.S. *Sea Gull*, to his assistance. The Khedive, on the other hand, had done precisely nothing, provoking Gordon's righteous indignation and the followig telegraphic rebuke: "I asked your Highness, when I was taken by King John on November 14th[1], by telegraph, to send a regiment and a steamer with two guns to Massawa. Your Highness has not done so; and had not the English gunboat been here, the place might have been sacked."

Back in Cairo, Gordon faced a storm of vituperation directed against him by Egyptians and foreigners alike. It was not enough that he had spent six of his best years in transforming the vast Sudan from a wild, lawless, chaotic blot on the map, arousing the abhorrence of every civilised country in the world and bringing forth many a protest from European Governments, into a methodically administered land of comparative peace and good order. It was not enough that he had risked his liberty, and even his life, in penetrating almost alone into the very heart of Abyssinia, in a courageous, if abortive, attempt to settle the troublesome question.

---

[1] When virtually a prisoner in the hands of the Abyssinians on the return journey, Gordon managed to send off messages for help.

No, his immense services to Egypt and the countless benefits he had conferred upon the country were not only passed over withou the smallest recognition, but they seem to have been actually re sented by the more unscrupulous members of the Egyptian Govern ment, who saw in Gordon's strong measures of reform the frustrat ion of their evil, avaricious practices. So bitter were his enemie in Cairo that they had the temerity to send to the English Press for publication, one of his *confidential* despatches shamefully mutilated to suit their own wicked designs.

On learning of this disgraceful attempt to discredit him in the eyes of his own countrymen, Gordon went straight to the Khedive and demanded an explanation. But Tewfik put the blame on his ministers, pleading youthfulness as an excuse for his neglect to prevent their highly dishonourable action. After placing Gordon in an impossible position and sending him on a forlorn hope; after cheerfully seeing him embark on an undertaking that might easily have cost him his life; after ignoring his S.O.S. for aid; this young successor to the throne of Egypt, instead of con gratulating him on an almost miraculous escape from the claws of the " Lion of Judah," and expressing admiration for his very gallant efforts on Egypt's behalf, adopted an attitude of annoyance that Gordon, with nothing to offer in the way of concessions, had been unable to induce the Abyssinian king to smile happily over his lost possessions, shake hands, and say no more about it! Tewfik's father and predecessor, Ismail Pasha, had long since made it clear to Gordon that no one could do anything with Johannes; and, if Gordon failed to assuage his hatred of Egypt, we may be sure no *one* could have succeeded.

On the average man, all this hostility, based largely on envy and malice, and so cruelly unjust, must have had a thoroughly de pressing effect. But Gordon, as we have seen, was no ordinary man. All he needed for a contented mind was the satisfaction of knowing he had done his best to carry out the duty assigned to him. For the rest, he cared nothing for the cackle of human geese, nor the snapping and snarling of curs at his heels. That he could conscientiously say, with Lawrence of Lucknow, " I have tried to do my duty," was all that mattered, and, of a truth, no man born of woman can ever have had more cause or justification for such an assertion.

So Gordon handed to the young Khedive his formal resignation as Governor-General of the Sudan, and left Cairo for home. Not a sign of gratitude, not a word of appreciation for his unique services characterised his departure, and, instead of the acclamation, the generous recognition due to Egypt's greatest benefactor, he was allowed by a malicious Government to leave the country, not only unhonoured and unsung, but to the accompaniment of a veritable tornado of vicious opprobrium. After all he had done, what must he have thought of such base ingratitude? For although, as we know, he cared not a scrap for reward or tangible mark of recognition, he would have been less than human had he not felt some modicum of bitterness in face of this shameful treatment. But, his conscience being clear that he had given of his best in the interests of the country he had undertaken to serve, he paid little attention to the yapping of a pack of irresponsible self-seekers that comprised, in addition to members of the Egyptian Government, a number of foreign diplomats—among whom, to their discredit, those of his own country were prominent—journalists, and others.

It was just as well that Gordon went home and refused further service with the Khedive, since not even *his* abnormally robust constitution could resist the ravages of six years' incessant toil in a far from healthy climate with totally inadequate nourishment. According to the opinion of the British Consulate medical officer at Alexandria, who examined him when on his way to England, he was on the verge of a serious breakdown. "I have recommended him," declared the doctor, "to retire for several months for complete rest and quiet—and that he may be able to enjoy fresh and wholesome food, as I consider that much of what he is suffering from is the effect of continued bodily fatigue, anxiety, and indigestible food. I have strongly insisted on his abstaining from all exciting work—especially such as implies business or political excitement."

CHAPTER XV

Call of the East

IT was towards the end of January, 1880, that Gordon, at last, reached England, and, after spending a few days with his family at Southampton, he lost no time in paying a visit to his old friends, Mr. and Mrs. F., at Chislehurst. Recording her impressions of his very welcome reappearance at their home, Mrs. F. wrote—"At about half-past six we heard the well-known voice asking for us, and then the dear face beaming upon us all, delight at meeting again reflected on every feature and reciprocated most heartily. . . . The evening passed all too quickly. He was looking very thin and much older. . . . He said he rejoiced in being free, and intended to take a real holiday and a real rest. He told us he had sent in his resignation to the War Office, but he was not permitted to resign. He gave us an account of how he had presented himself at the Queen's Levée, as in duty bound, and that in passing the Prince of Wales, he had whispered in Gordon's ear, 'Come and see me at lunch-time on Sunday'; and that when he went he found the Duke of Cambridge[1] there with the Prince, and they pressed him very much as to why he wished to resign his commission, and, when he answered, 'Chiefly because he wanted to rest,' the Duke said, 'Take a year's leave, then, or more,' but refused to accept his resignation. . . . Gordon told us much of his African experience. My boys hung upon his words. He told them he had seen strong men on the march cry like little children at the miseries of their position, when, as sometimes happened in marching, there was no place for shelter when darkness came on, and they had had to lie down to sleep just in the road, almost in pools of water, having marched all day in heavy rain—no tents, no

---

[1] Commander-in-Chief, British Army.

fire, and very little food. . . . His last words to me were: ' Will come and see you again soon.' And yet, from a series of mishaps, too long to detail here, he never came again, and though he continued to correspond up to the time of his death, I saw him no more."

At the time of Gordon's unostentatious, unhonoured return to England, the attention of the British public, stimulated, of course, by the Press, had, for some months, been riveted upon Sir Frederick (afterwards Earl) Roberts' campaign in Afghanistan and that of Lord Chelmsford in Zululand. In the former arduous operations, Roberts's famous march from Kabul to Khandahar aroused a storm of patriotic fervour; while Chelmsford's decisive victory at Ulundi over the Zulu tyrant, Cetewayo, filled the newspapers and their readers with unstinted admiration. Swords of honour, decorations, medals, titles were distributed in abundance. Yet, in neither campaign could anything be found comparable to the lone service of Charles Gordon, adventurous pioneer and gallant crusader of the wild, inhospitable, fever-stricken Sudan. But, again, he had accepted service under a foreign flag, and, although performing prodigies by means of his unique gifts for administration, reformation, and the restoration of peace and tranquillity, producing results so remarkable and so far-reaching that probably no other man could have achieved them—in spite of all this, the shameful spirit of antagonism against this heroic rebel—chiefly because he was a rebel—forbade officialdom and the Press to accord him anything but the briefest attention.

How ludicrous that lesser men should have been the recipients of almost hysterical adulation on returning from active service, while, for the second time in his career, our national hero number two was allowed to enter his own country, after the accomplishment of feats that had staggered the world, with but bare recognition of his reappearance! But he could well afford to disdain the shabby treatment of his own land, which stood out in such deplorable contrast to the attitude of the rest of the world. For, by now, he had begun to be credited with something akin to supernatural powers in dealing with difficult situations. Indeed, there arose considerable competition for his services, the aid of this expert in quelling disturbances, putting down abuses, and restoring order, being widely sought in cases that had got out of hand and were beyond the powers of ordinary mortals to cope with. It is, moreover, significant that both the Prince of Wales (later King Edward VII) and the Duke of Cambridge took unprecedented steps to induce Gordon to reconsider his decision to resign his commission, offering him a year's leave or more, so great was their anxiety to retain the services of this outstanding soldier. They had neglected to honour him as he deserved on his return from Egypt, but, nevertheless, fully conscious of his inestimable value to the British Empire, they wanted to make sure of his availability in future emergencies.

Like all rebels, Gordon was never *persona grata* with the powers above him. (As an Irishman who has always been something of a rebel, and in consequence has suffered at times from official displeasure, the writer is in a position to speak on this subject with feeling and not, altogether, without authority.) But, having consistently kept him in the background engaged in mediocre employment, and done little or nothing to acknowledge his stupendous services on behalf of other nations, they almost went down on their knees in their anxiety to prevent Gordon's threatened resignation. His lifetime unpopularity in official circles, followed by a veritable surge of adulation after his death, has been explained by Sir William Butler in these words:—" Men like to think of their hero beloved and honoured during the brief span of his life on earth; they are apt to forget that the very singleness of purpose which made his name appear so wonderful after death, and was the real secret of the success they so much admire, was also the cause of isolation in life and of opposition to fellow-men, which must ever be two of the most potent factors against popularity."

On the last day of February, 1880, Gordon left for Switzerland, where he hoped for a spell of rest and quiet. But it was hardly to be expected that a man of his exceptional capacity would be long in idleness, and, before he had been five weeks at Lausanne, a clamouring for his services began. First came an appeal from South Africa inviting him to accept command of the Cape Colonial Forces. In transmitting the offer to Gordon, the War Office mentioned supposed pay of fifteen hundred a year. Had they known him better, and not habitually given him the cold shoulder, they would have been aware that the matter of remuneration meant nothing to him, and that his acceptance or refusal of the appointment would in no way be influenced by the amount of pay offered. For some time, the Cape Government had been in difficulties over the Basuto problem, and what more natural in their predicament than to turn to the man whose reputation as an alleviator of trouble had become world-wide.

But, to everyone's surprise, Gordon refused the appointment which seemed so eminently suitable for the exercise of his extra-

ordinary talents. It has been suggested as an explanation that, in
a position immediately under the Cape Government, he may have
anticipated being too restricted by official red tape, and interfered
with to an extent precluding freedom of action—a suggestion that,
notwithstanding his subsequent acceptance of the appointment,
seems not unlikely.

Even more curious, however, than his refusal of the Cape
offer, was his decision, soon afterwards, to accompany Lord Ripon,
Governor-General elect, to India as his Private Secretary. Those
who had been astonished at Gordon's rejection of the first job, were
completely flabbergasted by his consent to undertake the second. It
seemed utterly inexplicable, for nothng could have been more uncongenial to a man of his prodigious energy, or more unsuitable
to his superlative capabilities and independent nature. It is difficult to know whether to be the more amazed at anyone venturing
to make such a suggestion or at Gordon's acquiescence. One can
only surmise that, since Lord Ripon had been entrusted with the
carrying out of certain reforms that would, surely, be fraught with
intricate perplexities, he was anxious to have at his side a man of
Gordon's proved ability in handling situations of unusual gravity.

Similarly, it may perhaps be assumed that Gordon, in arriving
at his decision to accept Lord Ripon's offer, felt that India might
provide scope for his boundless enthusiasm as a crusader; and, if
he went in a relatively menial capacity, what did it matter so long
as he could do some good? Furthermore, the "call of the East"
that is said to affect all. once they have tasted the delights of the
Orient, may well have contributed towards his resolve. But, even
before starting, he realised he had made a mistake, for, in a letter
to his old friend Sir Halliday Macartney, he wrote—" You will be
surprised to hear that I have accepted the Private Secretaryship to
Lord Ripon, and that I am just off to Charing Cross. I am afraid
that I have decided in haste, to repent at leisure."

And, in another letter written during the voyage to India, when
off Aden on May 22nd—" I have been an idiot, and took this place
with Lord Ripon, who is a kind and considerate master; but I hate
India, and how I ever could have taken the post is past my com-
prehension. The endless sort of quarrels which seem to be going
on there by all accounts is enough to sicken me. I shall get out of
it as soon as I can."

Gordon arrived at Bombay on May 28th. At once, he found
himself opposed to Lord Ripon over the Afghan question, and it
was this, more than anything else, that decided him to abandon an

undertaking which could only prove distasteful, and which was bound to involve him in conflict with the authorities. His conscience would not permit him to be a party, in any shape or form, to measures that ran counter to his beliefs; nor would he consent to follow accepted methods of bureaucracy which did not conform to his own conception of what was right and proper.

Within three days of his arrival, he discovered what would be expected of him as the Viceroy's Private Secretary, when Lord William Beresford,[1] Military Secretary to His Excellency, asked him to inform a deputation that Lord Ripon had read their address with interest. " You know perfectly well," said he to Lord William, " that Lord Ripon has never read it, and I can't say that sort of thing, so I will resign, and you take in my resignation."

His ill-advised acceptance of the appointment proved an expensive business for Gordon, who, in his scrupulously punctilious way, insisted on refunding to Lord Ripon every penny of the money expended on his behalf. But there was no suspicion of ill-feeling between them, and they parted the best of friends. Of this unaccountable phase of his career, Gordon wrote—"All this Private Secretaryship and its consequent expenses are all due to my not acting on my *own* instinct. However, for the future I will be wiser. . . . It was a living crucifixion. . . . I nearly burst with the trammels. . . . I resigned on June 2, and never unpacked my official dress."

But, no sooner had one door shut than another opened, this time inviting him to a sphere of activity that he understood and that was after his own heart. When almost on the point of leaving India for Zanzibar, where he hoped to resume his war against the slave traders, he received an urgent appeal from China to go once more to her assistance. The telegram, forwarded to him from London, was sent by Sir Robert Hart, Inspector-General of the Chinese Imperial Customs, and ran as follows:—" I am directed to invite you here (Pekin). Please come and see for yourself. The opportunity of doing really useful work on a large scale ought not to be lost. Work, position, conditions, can all be arranged with yourself here to your satisfaction. Do take six months' leave and come."

Believing the appeal to have been instigated by his old friend, Li Hung Chang, Gordon had no hesitation in abandoning his other plans and answering the obviously urgent call for help.

---

[1] 9th Lancers. Awarded the Victoria Cross in Zululand, 1879.

The crisis in China, on account of which his services were invited, had been brought about by the imminence of war with Russia. A strong party of hot-headed warmongers were rattling the sabre and bringing their country to the verge of a conflict that could end only in ignominious defeat, and would, before many weeks had elapsed, see Russia's formidable army at the gates of Pekin. Farseeing, clear-minded statesmen, on the other hand, realised the madness of attempting, with China's meagre resources, to oppose Russia in the field, the celebrated Li Hung Chang risking his life in an ardent bid for peace. It seemed, however, that only by the exercise of exceptionally strong influence could the powerful war party be overcome and induced to think better of their aggressive policy, which, if persisted in, would undoubtedly bring ruination upon the country. With memories of his remarkable exploits still fresh in their minds, the thoughts of those with China's interests at heart turned towards Gordon as the one man who could save her from irreparable disaster.

In his telegraphed reply, Gordon said he would leave for Shanghai as soon as possible, and that as to conditions he was indifferent. He then wired to the War Office for leave, but, in any case, was quite determined to go to China even if it meant resigning his commission. There followed an exchange of telegrams between him and the authorities, in which the latter, true to their tradition of saying " no " on principle, made objections typical of the staff bureaucrat, and eventually refused either to grant him leave or give him permission to go to China. They seemed afraid Gordon might involve them in difficulties; even that he might precipitate the threatened war between China and Russia! This was too much for the hot-tempered Scot, whose anger at so ignoble an inference burst forth in an immediate telegram resigning his commission, and a statement to the Press explaining his action and intentions. " My fixed desire," he wrote, " is to persuade the Chinese not to go to war with Russia, both in their own interests and for the sake of those of the world, especially those of England. In the event of war breaking out I cannot answer how I should act for the present, but I should ardently desire a speedy peace. To me it appears that the question in dispute cannot be of such vital importance that an arrangement could not be come to by concessions upon both sides. Whether I succeed in being heard or not is not in my hands. I protest, however, at being regarded as one who wishes for war in any country, still less in China. Inclined as I am, with only a small degree of admiration for military exploits,

I esteem it a far greater honour to promote peace than to gain any paltry honours in a wretched war."

Surely, those in power should have tumbled to it, by this time, that any attempt to frustrate Gordon in his designs resulted in spurring him on with redoubled determination to fulfil them; while the tone of hostility, that so often characterises official replies to applications, would only have added fuel to the flames, increasing his firm resolve to go through with the project at all costs. His conscience told him that this was right; therefore, as was his custom, he defied the consequences.

Could anything have been more ludicrous—if, indeed, it had not been criminal folly—than the British War Office, whose every effort should have been directed towards evolving a peaceful solution to the Cino-Russian problem, attempting (fortunately without success) to prevent the world's greatest adept at tackling critical situations, subduing war-like tendencies, and promoting peace, from exercising his phenomenal powers to avert a major international catastrophe? Luckily, their efforts to keep Gordon in leading strings proved of no avail, for, on June 13th, he started from Bombay on his way to China, hoping to prevail on the fire-eaters of the Imperial Court of Pekin to abandon their ill-advised policy.

At Colombo, there awaited him a further communication from the War Office, showing once again that, despite their neglect of him, they were ready to make almost any concession when threatened with deprivation of his services. In short, Gordon made them eat humble pie, for, when faced with the resignation of his commission, they wired—" Leave granted on your engaging to take no military service in China." But, having made this concession and so relieved him of the necessity of resigning his commission, they proceeded, as already related, to do their best to tie his hands and render his mission abortive by instructing the British Ambassador, Sir Thomas Wade, so to control his activities that he could do nothing!

They, however, reckoned without their Gordon, as did Sir Thomas Wade, whose high-handed directions, that the liberator of China from the hands of the *Taipings* should remain within the British Legation and " visit no one without his express permission," were very naturally treated with contempt, the Ambassador having, of course, no earthly right to inflict upon Gordon such arrogant restrictions. In truth, he never once set foot inside the legation, and went about his business in unfettered independence!

His first visit was paid to the strong man of China, Li Hung Chang, then in command at Tientsin. Everywhere, intrigue was rife; even some of the foreign diplomats being so ill-advised as to advocate armed rebellion in order to overcome the war party, led by Prince Chun, brother of the Emperor Kuang Hsu. Russia, it is true, was anxious to avoid a conflict, but Li Hung Chang, whose wisdom convinced him of the disastrous consequences of war to China, could not arouse sufficient enthusiasm for the cause of peace to enable him to overawe the powerful, strongly supported fire-eaters, whose mad determination to plunge their country into a hopeless struggle seemed insuperable. This, then, was the situation as it existed when Gordon reached Tientsin in July, 1880—the great specialist called in to apply his superior skill where all other efforts had failed.

He learned, much to his disgust, that attempts had been made to induce Li Hung Chang to rebel against the Government, to lead his army to Pekin, and to seize the person of the Emperor, the instigators of this hare-brained plot—including several foreign ministers—believing that only in this way could war with Russia be averted. Consequently, Gordon found himself confronted not only with the formidable task of preventing an international con-flagration between two vast empires, but, in addition, he must exert his powers to frustrate the fomenters of internal rebellion in China.

It is not easy to believe that the astute Li Hung Chang would, but for Gordon's intervention, have seriously considered acceding to so wild and irresponsible an appeal. But we may be sure that, after listening to the wise counsel of his old associate, for whom he held such profound admiration, any thoughts he might have enter-tained of resorting to revolt, as a means of preventing a flare-up of world-wide significance, would have been decisively abandoned. Still, realising the difficulties of Li's position, Gordon felt he must at all costs stand by him, and, moreover, be entirely free to act in whatever way he considered proper. In these circumstances, he telegraphed to the War Office—"I have seen Li Hung Chang, and he wishes me to stay with him. I cannot desert China in her present crisis, and would be free to act as I think fit. I therefore beg to resign my commission in Her Majesty's service."

In their reply, accusing him of insubordination, the authorities excelled themselves in vindictive malice against this stubborn soldier who, if leading strings were insisted upon, was prepared to throw up his profession rather than submit to them. But once again they over-stepped the mark, allowing their indignation at anyone daring to have a mind of his own, and the courage to express it, to run away with them. For, of course, Gordon was fully entitled to resign his commission in peace time if he wished, and not even the big-wigs of Pall Mall could do anything to stop him. Naturally, he paid no attention to so absurd an accusation, and breathing, no doubt, a deep sigh of relief, as others have done on finding themselves freed from the shackles of officialdom, set about his onerous undertaking with customary vigour and enthusiasm.

After his visit to Li Hung Chang, Gordon made his way to the capital, resolved to do all in his power to avert what threatened to be a world-shattering fracas. In going to Pekin, he knew he was taking grave personal risks, seeing that all his energies, in alliance with Li Hung Chang's minority, were directed against the influential war party. So pronounced was the supremacy of the pro-war element among the Ministers of State in Pekin, that Gordon seemed to be taking his life in his hands. Just as Li Hung Chang was putting his life to the hazard by courageously opposing Prince Chun's war-mongers, so did Gordon, with complete indifference to his own safety, unhesitatingly accept the serious risks in the interests of China and of peace. He must, at all costs, go to the fountain-head, confront the enemies of peace with the unanswerable truths regarding China's present position of military inferiority compared with Russia's resources, and paint a clear picture of the ruination that would be thrust upon their country by those whose folly, self-interest, or aggressive instincts led them to clamour for war.

But, before following Gordon's movements in Pekin, let us for a moment consider the events that led to strained relations between these two great empires, and had brought them to the brink of war. In a former conflict, China had lost the province of Kuldja, and here we find a quite extraordinary similarity between this Cino-Russian situation and that of Egypt and Abyssinia. In each case, one nation suffered from a grievance owing to the other retaining possession of previously captured territory; in each case, the very natural animosity of the aggrieved blossomed into war-like inclinations, bringing matters to the verge of hostilities; in both cases, the retainers of the territories in dispute, though ready to fight if necessary, were anxious to avoid war; in both cases, Gordon was entrusted with the task of pouring oil on troubled waters, and trying to maintain peace. As in the instance of Abyssinia and the province of Bugos, China now demanded the return of Russian occupied Kuldja; and, like the truculent King Johannes, Prince Chun was on the war-path.

Ostensibly, the lost province was the bone of contention, but, of the war party's self-interest in promoting a conflict there can be little doubt. Never before, perhaps, had Gordon been faced with quite so difficult or perplexing a situation, requiring, as it did, a superabundance of qualities seldom to be found in any one man. The questionable directions as to his disposal issued by the home authorities to Sir Thomas Wade, together with the latter's imperious interpretation of them, justified Gordon in ignoring the British Ambassador and giving the legation a wide berth. For, after all, once he had resigned his commission, he was entirely free to go where he liked and do as he thought fit. Moreover, the authorities might have known that Gordon was not the man to be browbeaten by bluff of that sort. And so, in the end, he made them appear exceedingly foolish, pursuing his considered plan of campaign without hindrance as though no attempt had ever been made to restrict his activities. Nevertheless, the farce would have been a tragedy had their efforts succeeded, in which event they would have been responsible for the very catastrophe they were so anxious to prevent.

Despite the ban on his movements imposed by Sir Thomas Wade, Gordon attended several meetings at which leading members of the Grand Council were present. In forceful language, backed by his masterful personality and penetrating, steely grey eye, he treated the assembly of China's highest in the land to a lucid exposition of what they might expect from going to war with Russia. He spoke with vigour and freedom that had little regard for the feelings of his astonished listeners. As Sir William Butler put it—" Sixteen years before he (Gordon) had never hesitated to speak his mind openly to the highest mandarins, and the time that had since passed over him had not changed his habit of truth."

Frankly, almost brutally, he made known to them the pitiful weakness of their fortifications and their ships. When they pointed to the Taku Forts as a bulwark of defence, Gordon derisively exclaimed that these forts, constructed for the protection of Pekin, could be taken in rear. Furthermore, after emphasising the unpreparedness of China's armed services, he is said to have predicted the invasion of Manchuria, and, within a couple of months from the outbreak of war, the arrival of Russian forces at the gates of Pekin. This was straight talking with a vengeance, and must surely have done much to shake the resolution of the war party. Yet, they were obdurate, continuing to espouse their cause even in face of Gordon's solemn declaration that they were in no condition to take the field against so powerful an enemy, and that, in the event of war, he would withhold his help unless they agreed to destroy Pekin's suburbs and gave him a free hand to organise the defence of the capital.

Finally, Gordon's fierce temper, far from improved by six years in the Sudan, could stand no more, and there followed yet another similarity between his Ethiopian and Chinese missions. Blurting out " *idiocy* " as his opinion of the ministers' war policy, he shocked the Chinese interpreter to such an extent that the terrified official would not dare to give his illustrious masters a literal translation of the highly offensive word. It will be remembered that a precisely similar situation arose during Gordon's interview with King Johannes of Abyssinia, when the interpreter refused to give a true rendering of Gordon's strong words for fear of incurring the king's deadly wrath. But, whereas, on that notable occasion, Gordon had insisted on the official doing his duty, this time his method was different and quite devastating in its effect. Angrily seizing an English-Chinese dictionary from the table, he looked up the word " *idiocy,*" and then thrust it under the very noses of the dumbfounded mandarins with his finger pointing accusingly at the Chinese equivalent.

Shocked beyond measure the Grand Councillors undoubtedly were, but they were also, by this time, completely dominated by Gordon's masterful ascendency, and the powerful war party found themselves subjugated by, perhaps, the one man in the world who could have achieved this end. " I said make peace," ran his account of what followed, " and wrote out the terms. They were, in all, five articles; the only one they boggled at was the fifth, about the indemnity. They said this was too hard and unjust. I said that might be, but what was the use of talking about it? If a man demanded your money or your life, you have only three courses open. You must either fight, call for help, or give up your money. Now, as you cannot fight, it is useless to call for help, since neither England nor France would stir a finger to assist you."

The result was a veritable triumph for Gordon, besides being infinitely gratifying to those whose appeal he had so readily answered. Of all the masterly achievements of his wonderful career, this was incontestably one of the greatest, for not only had he arrived in the nick of time to thwart the instigators of rebellion that once more would have plunged the country into civil war, but, with superb assurance, he had performed the incredible feat of standing between two great nations about to fly at each other's throats, and bringing about a peaceful settlement of the dispute. How fortunate that he was able to circumvent the foolish attempts to curb his activities. Had his freedom been restricted in accordance with the ill-advised intentions of the home authorities, the world would have been staggered by the almighty clash of two immense empires.

Before leaving China on completion of this brilliantly conducted mission, Gordon paid a farewell visit to Li Hung Chang at Tientsin; and great, we may be sure, were the rejoicings of these two old friends and collaborators at the happy issue of their joint endeavours.

A memorandum, giving advice as to how best China could be defended against an aggressor, was Gordon's final contribution to the land that owed him yet another debt of gratitude for again steering the ship of state into peaceful waters.

CHAPTER XVI

Ireland, Mauritius, and the Cape

REACHING Shanghai on his return journey to England, Gordon received a telegram from the War Office cancelling the leave already granted him, and refusing to accept his resignation. They were, so it seems, determined to bully and badger him to the end. It was ever thus, and is the same to-day; once the powers that be have, for one reason or another, got their knife in, they delight in keeping it there, occasionally giving it a twist to make sure the victim is kept thoroughly in subjecton. But how exasperating it must have been to find that Gordon seemed quite oblivious either of the original thrust, or the twists so ineptly designed to quell his independent spirit.

As a rule, this unworthy persecution—for it was nothing less— had as much effect on Gordon as water on a duck's back. But, in this particular instance, he felt hurt at being mistrusted. How could he have felt anything but bitterness in his heart when those who should have gone out of their way to encourage his noble efforts in the cause of peace, showed, by their every action, that they feared he might use his influence on the side of war, and, accordingly, did their utmost to tie his hands? "You might have trusted me," he wired from Aden. "My passage from China was taken days before the arrival of your telegram which states 'leave cancelled.' Do you still insist on rescinding the same?"

At this—perhaps for very shame—they relented, telegraphing authority for the leave he wanted. How could they have done otherwise? Here was the empire's most heroic figure on his way home from yet another phenomenal triumph, the fulfilment of which had so nearly been frustrated by their own regrettable interference. Without a shred of justification they had mistrusted his intentions in going to China, and they were now proved to have been utterly mistaken. What could they do but climb down and grant the leave Gordon had so clearly earned?

He arrived in England towards the end of October, 1880. After a visit to his relatives at Southampton and some little time spent in London, he went off on a tour of the south and south-west of Ireland. Solicitous, as always, for oppressed people, Gordon was anxious to investigate the grievances of the peasant tenantry, who were said to be suffering intense hardships at the hands of overbearing landlords. His kind heart rebelled at the thought of the wretched, poverty-stricken smallholders of Ireland being ground down under the heels of oppressive, avaricious, merciless landlords, every bit as much as he had revolted at the unhappy condition of the luckless natives in the Sudan. Yet, he was far too thorough in his methods to accept as true what he heard or read about this seemingly lamentable situation until he had himself tested the accuracy of the allegations. He, therefore, decided to spend part of his leave in a self-appointed mission designed to enquire into the problem and endeavour to find a solution should the reports prove to be correct. Here was work after his own heart, for was not his whole life devoted to the alleviation of suffering? Nor was he ever happier than when engaged in trying to improve the lot of his less fortunate fellow creatures.

Carying a gun, for purposes of camouflage, so as to avoid being suspected of spying on behalf either of landlords or tenants, he quietly toured the countryside, taking careful note of everything that would help him to form a just, unprejudiced opinion. At that time of year, the country was at its dreariest, and he was able to see the life of the peasants at its very worst. Horrified beyond measure at the state of semi-starvation, misery, and wretchedness in which they existed, Gordon resolved to put in writing his views, at the same time advancing certain suggestions of his own for the improvement of conditions generally.

In a letter to a friend, which appeared in the *Times* of December 3rd, 1880, he wrote—" I have lately been over to the south-west of Ireland in the hope of discovering how some settlement could be made of the Irish question, which, like a fretting cancer, eats away our vitals as a nation . . . . . A gulf of antipathy exists between the landlords and tenants . . . . . It is a gulf which is not caused alone by the question of rent; there is a complete lack of sympathy between these two classes . . . . . I call your attention to the pamphlets, letters, and speeches of the landlord class, as a proof of how little sympathy or kindness there exists among them for the tenantry, and I am sure the tenantry feel the same way towards the landlords . . . . . Any half-measures will only place the Government face to face with the people of Ireland as the champions of the landlord interest. The Government would be bound to enforce their decision, and with a result which none can foresee, but which certainly would be disastrous to the common weal."

Then, after detailing a scheme whereby the landlords in the worst areas would be dispossessed and the land be taken over by the Government, he continued—" the state of our fellow-country-men in the parts I have named is worse than that of any people in the world . . . . . I believe that these people are made as we are, that they are patient beyond belief, loyal, but, at the same time, broken-spirited and desperate, living on the verge of starvation in places in which we would not keep our cattle . . . . . The priests alone have any sympathy with their sufferings, and naturally alone have a hold over them."

Gordon thought he had seen the depths of misery and human suffering in China and in Central Africa, but " he tells the people of England that within twelve hours of the capital there exists a deeper misery and a more unnatural injustice." For his pains he was laughed at, and told he knew nothing about it ! All too often that is the fate of reformers, who are seldom popular because the responsible authorities resent an outsider discovering a remedy which they ought to have discovered for themselves, and because they are reluctant to take any steps that would inevitably expose their own culpable negligence. The easiest way out of the difficulty is to pooh-pooh the reformer's suggestions and proclaim them as emanating from an ill-informed meddler. But Gordon was any-thing but ill-informed, for had he not confirmed, with the evidence of his own eyes, all the horrors reported to have resulted from merciless oppression on the part of the Irish landlords? And who could have better judged the situation than the witness of so much human misery in various parts of the world?

In April, 1881, Gordon seems to have reconsidered the Cape Government's proposition asking him to accept the command of the Cape Colonial Forces. But his telegram to the authorities offering his services in the Basuto dispute, inexplicably, brought forth not so much as the courtesy of an acknowledgment. It has been suggested that, round about this period of Gordon's career, becoming exasperated by his unpredictable activities, the authorities contemplated restricting his tireless energy to the limits

f an insignificant home appointment, or, alternatively, compelling
im to retire. At any rate, early in April, 1881, he wrote to a
riend—"For myself (*in re* this forced employment in the
bstructive circle of R.E.) duty was particularly vexatious, for I
hould certainly have come to dire loggerheads with my obstructive
R.E. chiefs. I claim to sympathise with any who try to stem the
ffete administration of our rulers. What we want is a man who
vill steam-hammer all departments to the welfare of our army, and
herefore I do not wish to be shunted out, for I believe that the
ime is near when there will be a cry for such a man, and it is then I
vould like to be active."

From this it would seem that there was, indeed, some intention
n the part of the authorities once more to shelve this tiresome
apper, whose ubiquitous crusading caused them so much anxiety,
et, almost invariably proved triumphantly successful.

It so happened, however, that just when he was wondering
ow and where he could find another outlet for his abundant
nergy, there arose an opportunity, not only of service far away
rom the leading strings of Pall Mall, but, at the same time, of
loing a good turn to an old friend. Sir Howard Elphinstone had
ecently been appointed to the command of Royal Engineers in
he island of Mauritius;[1] but, being anxious to avoid banishment to
o remote a spot, he found himself faced with the choice of offering
considerable sum of money as an inducement to a substitute, or
esigning his commission. In his dilemma, he was lucky to have
s a friend the great Charles Gordon, who readily came forward,
enerously refusing to accept a penny for the exchange. "Oh,
lon't worry yourself," said he, on being told by Elphinstone of his
lifficulty, "I will go for you; Mauritius is as good for me as
nywhere else." This was typical, not merely of Gordon's kindly
ature, but also of his happy-go-lucky, care-free outlook on life.
He would go anywhere in the world at a moment's notice if he
hought he could do good, without a thought of his own welfare
r caring a jot about remuneration. He had been known to start
n an expedition without so much as a sixpence in his pocket,
o utterly indifferent was he to his personal comfort, and so
astonishingly meagre were his needs.

Mauritius did, however, appeal to him in one respect, namely
hat he would be far removed from the toils of red tape, and from
he constant irritations and annoyances of the bureaucrats. Yet,

---

In the Indian Ocean off the East coast of Madagascar.

his first impressions of this not very healthy, rather obscure island were none too happy. In a letter from Port Louis, soon after his arrival, he wrote—" It is not over cheerful to go out to this place nor is it so to find a deadly sleep over all my military friends here. Innately enthusiastic and tremendously energetic himself, in whatever task he undertook, he found it difficult to sympathise with the loafing prevalent among officers of the Mauritius garrison. Indeed there were few human failings he despised more profoundly than laziness. " We are," he wrote, " in a perfect Fool's Paradise about our power. We have plenty of power if we would pay attention to our work, but the fault is, to my mind, the military power of the country is eaten up by selfishness and idleness, and we are trading on the reputation of our forefathers. When one sees by the newspapers the Emperor of Germany sitting, old as he is, for two long hours inspecting his troops, and officers here (Mauritius) grudging two hours a week for their duties, one has reason to fear the future."

Gordon remained in the island for about twelve months, and much as one must admire his unselfish motive in agreeing to the exchange, one cannot but deplore this complete waste of still another year of a life incomparably valuable to the British Empire. Had those precious years of Gordon's career, frittered away on such trivialities as the construction of worthless forts at Gravesend the deliberations of boundary commissions, and the repairing of barracks and drains in the remote island of Mauritius, been used by the authorities in more important spheres of activity, who knows what further glories might not have figured in the record of his phenomenal service?

Nevertheless, dull and uninteresting as his duties in Mauritius undoubtedly were, he entered into them with characteristic zeal and we may be sure that never before had the island barracks been maintained in a better state of repair, nor the drains in a more sanitary condition. But what fantastic employment for the empire's greatest soldier!

Concerning himself, as always, with the welfare of those around him, and ever anxious to do anything towards improving the lot of others, Gordon made it his business to investigate the conditions of life as they existed in this lonely back-water of civilization. As a result of his enquiries, he discovered evidence of dissatisfaction among the colonists, and found, moreover, that their grievances were not without foundation. But, once again, his activities in distant parts of the world would seem to have caused official uneasiness, for, after being promoted to the rank of Major General, and given temporary command of all troops in Mauritius, he was not confirmed in the appointment. As Mr. Boulger has suggested, "Gordon's uncompromising sense of justice was beginning to be known in high official quarters, and the then responsible Government had far too many cares on its shoulders that could not be shirked to invite others from so remote and unimportant a possession as the Mauritius."

To the advice of the Chinese dignitary enjoining young aspirants to fame and fortune to "avoid all vexed questions, be non-committal and invariably humble," to " be plausibly evasive, never criticise adversely and never condemn," might well have been added—" never bring to light abuses, injustices, or hardships that would be likely to prove embarrassing to your superiors!" For those, like Gordon, whose consciences will not permit them to overlook wrongs, and who insist on exposing them no matter whose toes are trodden on or whose dignity suffers, more often than not find a place on the black list and figure as " difficult " or " obstructive." No, those who probe too deeply into matters that may prove awkward for the authorities, and consider it their duty to call attention to them, seldom receive the reward of their honest endeavours. On the contrary, they are usually dubbed a nuisance and side-tracked accordingly. But Gordon cared not a rap for black lists, nor for what people thought of him, being content so long as he acted in the way he believed to be right, leaving his deeds to the judgment of God rather than man.

In his Khartoum journals, he alluded to this stirring up of muddy waters that usually proves so disconcerting to higher authority. " It is a great question of doubt to me if Public Officials ought to so sink their personality as to allow themselves to overlook facts, which must strike them as being not only evil, but also detrimental to our national interests, merely because such facts are likely to be disagreeable to our Government in requiring them to decide on difficult questions."

As the reader will, long since, have gathered, Gordon was a prolific writer. In the course of his career, apart from his voluminous correspondence, he produced, to the infinite benefit of posterity, expositions of his invaluable views on a variety of subjects. During his sojourn in Mauritius, for example, he wrote three papers of deep interest, and doubtless of no inconsiderable worth. These were on Egypt after the fall of Khedive Ismail—a subject on which no one could have written with wider knowledge or more convincing authority; on coaling stations in far eastern waters; and on the value of the Cape sea route as compared with the Mediterranean, Suez Canal, and Red Sea.

In the first paper, his reference to Cherif Pasha, the Prime Minister, shows that, in many respects, he was a man after his own heart. " Cherif," he writes, " is perhaps the only Egyptian Minister whose character for strict integrity is unimpeachable. A thoroughly independent man, caring but little for office or its emoluments, of a good family, with antecedents which would bear any investigation, he was not inclined to be questioned by men whose social position was inferior to his own and whose *parti pris* was against him. In the Council Chamber he was in a minority because he spoke his mind, but this was not so with other Ministers, whose antecedents were dubious. Had his advice been taken, Ismail would have now been Khedive of Egypt."

Included among other interesting points in the Egyptian paper were : —

" It is reiterated over and over again that Egypt is prosperous and contented. I do not think it has altered at all, except in improving its finances for the benefit of the bond holders . . . . . Tewfik is essentially one of the Ameer class. I believe he would be willing to act uprightly, if by so doing he could maintain his absolute power . . . . . He is liberal only in measures which do not interfere with his prerogative . . . . . The present arrangement of Controllers and Consul-Generals is defective. The Consul-Generals are charged with the duty of seeing that the country is quiet and the people well treated. They are responsible to their Foreign Offices. The Controllers are charged with the finances and the welfare of the country, but to whom are they responsible? Not to Tewfik; though he pays them, he cannot remove them; yet they must get on well with him. Not to the Foreign Office, for it is repeatedly said that they are Egyptian officials, yet they have to keep on good terms with these Foreign Offices. Not to the bond holders, though they are bound, considering their power, to be on good terms with them. Not to the inhabitants of Egypt, though these latter are taught to believe that every unpopular act is done by the Controllers' advice. The only remedy is by a Council of Notables, having direct access to Tewfik, and independent of his or of the Ministers' good will, and the subjection of the Controllers to the Consul-Generals responsible to the Foreign Office—in fact, Residents at the Courts."

In the paper dealing with eastern coaling stations, he wrote—
' It is wonderful our people do not take the views of our forefathers. They took up their positions at all the salient points of the routes. We can certainly hold these places, but from the colonial feelings they have almost ceased to be our own. By establishing these coaling stations no diplomatic complications could arise, while by their means we could unite all our colonies with us, for we could give them effective support. The spirit of no colony would bear up for long against the cutting off of its trade, which would happen if we kept watching the Mediterranean and neglected the great ocean routes."

This last reference may well have led Gordon to produce the third of his papers written in Mauritius, recording opinions of particular interest now that the Suez Canal has become a focal-point of universal significance. " I think Malta," he wrote, " has very much lost its importance. The Mediterranean now differs much from what it was in 1815 . . . . . If the entrance to the Mediterranean were blocked at Gibraltar by a heavy fleet, I cannot see any advantage to be gained against us by the fleets blocked up in it—at any rate I would say, let our *first care* be for the Cape route, and secondly for the Mediterranean and Canal. The former route entails no complications, the latter endless ones, coupled with a precarious tenure. Look at the Mediterranean, and see how small is that sea to which we are apparently devoting the greater part of our attention."

Whilst engaged in his duties at Port Louis, and in committing to paper his views on these highly important matters, his future as yet undecided, the Government of Cape Colony made another appeal for Gordon's much sought after services. To Lord Kimberley, Secretary of State for the Colonies, Sir Hercules Robinson, Governor at the Cape, dispatched this telegram:—

" Ministers request me to enquire whether H.M.'s Government would permit them to obtain the services of Colonel Charles Gordon.[1] Ministers desire to invite Colonel Gordon to come to this Colony for the purpose of consultation as to the best measures to be adopted with reference to Basutoland, in the event of Parliament sanctioning their proposals as to that territory, and to engage his services, should he be willing to renew the offer made to their predecessors in April, 1881, to assist in terminating the war and administering Basutoland."

---

[1] He was then a Major General.

It was on April 2nd, 1882, that Gordon received authority to proceed to South Africa. At the same time, a direct invitation reached him to visit the colony as soon as possible to advise them on the important and pressing question of Basutoland.

Realising that the appeal was urgent, Gordon, who never wasted time in personal preparations, left Mauritius two days later in the sailing ship *Scotia*—the only vessel available. Due, however, to adverse winds, he did not arrive at Cape Town till May 3rd.

A rugged, mountainous country, Basutoland lies to the east of the Orange Free State, and is bounded on its eastern border by the famous Drakensberg mountains, which separate it from Natal and the Transkei district of Cape Colony. Out of a population of one hundred and fifty thousand, the Basutos could put into the field a formidable army of good horsemen and good shots, every man animated by intense patriotic fervour. They took pride in their independence, and in the past had resisted stoutly—by force of arms when necessary—any attempt on the part of the Orange Free State or the Cape Government to annexe their country. For years they had been under British protection, and had gladly given their allegiance to the British throne. But they consistently objected to being subservient to any colonial administration.

Then, in 1871, without the consent of the people, Basutoland was handed over by the British Government to the Crown Colony of the Cape of Good Hope. In the following year, the Cape became a colony with responsible Government, "and the Basutos," as Gordon recorded, "were placed virtually under another power. The Basutos asked for representation in the colonial Parliament, which was refused, and to my mind here was the mistake which led to these troubles."

Matters were brought to a head when, in 1880, the Cape authorities proposed to disarm the Basutos—a decision that was met by determined opposition on the part of these independent people, whose way of life was habitually orderly and law abiding provided they were not interfered with. Passive resistance soon developed into a war so embarrassing to the Government that, eventually, they were obliged to appeal to the man whose reputation as a peace-maker had become widespread, begging him to come and help them out of their difficulties.

At the time of Gordon's arrival, Basutoland was split up into four divisions, each under the rule of a native chief. A plentiful supply of arms and ammunition had been acquired through years of labour in the South African diamond fields, the Basuto labourers willingly accepting this mode of payment for their work instead of money, which would not have been so convenient to the mine owners. Oddly enough, the Cape Government approved of this method of payment to the Basutos, resulting, as it did, in a constant stream of rifles, guns, and ammunition into the territory occupied by this freedom-loving race of courageous, hardy African natives. And now, after twelve years of condoning the flow of weapons into Basutoland, they proposed to deprive the natives of the fruits of their industry.

The ensuing war had lasted two years when Gordon reached the Cape, and had proved ruinously costly to the Government. Moreover, so stubborn was the resistance encountered by the colonial troops that they had been able to make but little progress towards fulfilling the edict of disarmament. And so the war went on, draining the colony's coffers to a dangerously low level.

(Many years ago in South Africa, the writer learned from an old and distinguished colonial soldier something of the methods of warfare adopted by the Basutos. They would occupy the summit of a kopjé[1] and arrange a number of heavy boulders along the extreme edge of the crest. When attacked, they would tip them over, sending them crashing down the hillside amongst the ascending troops. They would then jump onto their wiry little ponies, gallop to another kopjé, and precisely the same procedure would be repeated. Facing an avalanche of large, bounding rocks was not, so it seemed, one of the most pleasant experiences of this fine old warrior who had seen a great deal of service.)

With his quick insight, Gordon soon realised that responsibility for the trouble, far from being attributable to the Basuto chiefs, was, in fact, planted firmly on the shoulders, first of the British Government for handing over Basutoland to Cape Colony, without consulting the natives, in defiance of treaties; and, secondly, of the colonial authorities for refusing the Basutos representation in the Cape Parliament and trying to take away their means of defending themselves. Of the four chiefs, three were prepared to come to terms with the colonial Government. But the fourth, Masupha Moshesh, had resolutely refused to recognise the Cape magistrates, to pay hut tax, or to surrender one single weapon, and he it was who had defied the Cape authories for upwards of two years, and withstood all the efforts of their forces to bring him to his knees.

---

[1] Hill.

Gordon's first concern was to collect all possible information as to the causes of the war in Basutoland as a basis for deciding how best the problem might be solved. After careful study of all relevant papers and interrogation of competent witnesses, he drew up, on May 26th, 1882, a most able, comprehensive memorandum, embodying his conclusions as to the origin of the trouble and his considered opinion as to the measures that might, conceivably, bring about a settlement of the quarrel. A few selected points from the memorandum will suffice to show the trend of Gordon's reasoning: —

" The Basuto people, who date back many generations, made treaties with the British Government, which treaties are equally binding, whether between two powerful states, or between a powerful state and a weak one.

" In defiance of the treaties, the Basutos lost land."

" In defiance of the treaties, the Basutos, without being consulted or having their rights safeguarded, were handed over to another power—the Colonial Government.

" That power proceeded to enact their disarmament, a process which could only be carried out with a servile race, like the Hindoos of the plains of India, and which anyone of understanding must see would be resisted to the utmost by any people worth the name; the more so in the case of the Basutos, who realised the constant contraction of their frontiers in defiance of the treaties made with the British Government, and who could not possibly avoid the conclusion that this disarmament was only a prelude to their extinction.

" The inevitable result was that the Basutos resisted, and remain passively resisting to this day.

" I think it would be as well to let bygones be bygones, and to commence afresh by calling together by proclamation a *Pitso*[1] of the whole tribe, in order to discuss the best means of sooner securing the settlement of the country.

" By this *Pitso* we would know the exact position of affairs, and the real point in which the Basutos are injured or consider themselves to be injured.

" This *Pitso* ought to be called at once. All Colonial officials ought to be absent, for what the colony wants is to know what is the matter; and the colony wishes to know it from the Basuto people, irrespective of the political parties of the Government."

---

[1] National Assembly.

CHIEF MASUPHA MOSHESH
OF BASUTOLAND

(Hulton Library)

Gordon's fair, straightforward view of the situation as set out in this memorandum appears to have caused embarrassment, not only to the Colonial ministers, but also to the Secretary of State, Lord Kimberley. Nor is this surprising, seeing that General Gordon, the authority whose help and advice had been sought, had spared neither Government in his assignment of responsibility for the Basuto troubles. Whilst awaiting the outcome of his recommendations, Gordon performed the routine duties of Commandant-General, Cape Colonial Forces, at King William's Town.

Eventually, after the lapse of some weeks, and still without the smallest hint as to whether the Government intended to implement the suggestions contained in his report, he agreed to go into Basutoland and talk to Masupha. If left entirely to himself and not interfered with, or even accompanied, by colonial officials, he believed he would be able to arrange a settlement of the vexed questions; while, as for Masupha, he consented to Gordon's visit provided it was regarded as a private one, and, furthermore, that he went unattended except for his secretary and two servants.

Incredible as it may seem, there appears to be good reason for believing that the Cape authorities, represented by the Secretary for Native Affairs, Mr. Sauer, deliberately led Gordon into a trap, after discovering, as others had done before them, that his keen insight had found them out, and that his strong sense of duty, allied to unswerving honesty and integrity, would not permit him to overlook or conceal their misdeeds. In entering Masupha's stronghold, Gordon, once again, advanced almost alone into the lion's den. Never, perhaps, not even at Dara in Darfour, when with a small escort he rode into the camp of his enemy, Suleiman; at Debra Tabor, when he journeyed into the heart of hostile Abyssinia and confronted the tyrannical Johannes on his own ground; nor at Pekin, when he tackled the fire-eating war party, denouncing their policy as " idiocy "—never, it would seem, had his life been in greater danger than when the Basuto chief, Masupha, suspected him of treachery.

Gordon had undertaken to negotiate with the chief at the urgent request of Mr. Sauer; yet, no sooner had he reached his destination and settled down to discuss the situation, than information was brought to Masupha that hostile forces were advancing to attack him. Instantly, his mind became filled with suspicion, and it was in that critical moment that Gordon's fate hung in the balance. Masupha's first thought was that Gordon had been sent to keep him occupied, and lull him into a feeling of security, while invaders advanced on his territory. An envoy caught in such a predicament would, in any country, find himself in a position of some peril. But, in the hands of a man like Masupha, he could expect no mercy.

In the *Times* of August 20th, 1885, Mr. Arthur Pattison wrote —" Gordon divined his character marvellously, and was the only man Masupha had the slightest regard for. Masupha, if you treat him straightforwardly, is as nice a man as possible, and even kind and thoughtful; but, if you treat him the other way, he is a fiend incarnate."

Such was the man who held Gordon in his power, to deal with after his merciless fashion for what he believed to be a piece of diabolical treachery. In reality, it was poor Gordon who suffered, so it seems, from treachery of the very worst description. In order to test the justification for his not unnatural suspicions, Masupha asked Gordon's advice as to what action he should take. Remembering the violence of his rage at the treachery of the Chinese at Soo Chow, the torrents of wrath that must have convulsed the fiery Gordon on hearing Masupha's information can easily be imagined. His advice was short and very much to the point. " Refuse," he said, " to have any dealings with the Government until the forces are withdrawn." This wise counsel, combined with the obvious sincerity of Gordon's indignation, satisfied Masupha that his visitor had no part in the invasion of his territory. And so the deadly danger that had threatened an abrupt termination to the career of this pre-eminent soldier, passed away, leaving him free to hurry back to Cape Town, vent his just wrath on the real villains of the piece, and cast his resignation at their feet, even as, when a cadet at Woolwich, he had disgustedly flung his epaulettes at the feet of an abusive instructor.

Once more, Gordon had proved himself a champion of oppressed people. Although employed by the Cape Government and acting on their behalf, he would not assist in, nor even stand by and silently witness, what he considered to be their unjust treatmet of the Basutos. As soon as he had made up his mind that the natives were getting a raw deal, he directed the whole force of his overpowering personality to their side, and, while his chief aim lay in finding a solution acceptable to all parties, he would give his aid to no plan that seemed in any way to favour the colony at the expense of Basutoland. It was, indeed, a lucky day for the Basutos when the Cape Government invited Gordon to assist them in settling the dispute. Many a lesser man would have thought of his position, his remuneration, his personal ambition, before deliberately running counter to the ideas of his employers. Not so Gordon, who cared nothing for position, except in so far as it helped him in his task. After five and a half months in South Africa, he left the country considerably worse off than he had been on his arrival; while, as for personal ambition, he had none.

In as much as no immediate settlement of the Basuto question had resulted, Gordon's mission had failed. Yet, the failure was due to no fault of the great crusader, but rather, in the words of an unprejudiced writer, to " Mr. Sauer's intrigues behind his back." Moreover, the failure was only temporary, for, two years later, " practically the very policy " recommended by Gordon was adopted by the British Government, Basutoland being again taken under British protection, and becoming entirely independent of the Cape Government. This was all the Basutos asked, to be left in peace to live their own lives and manage their own affairs, subject only to the terms of their allegiance to the British Sovereign.

Long before Gordon left Cape Town for home, it became clear that he had been invited to South Africa under false pretences, since the request that he would come to advise the Government, and help them out of their difficulties, proved to be merely a disguise for their real intention, namely to coerce the Basutos and force them into subjection. For this purpose, they contemplated using Gordon's genius for leadership first to reorganise the Cape Forces, and then to inflict decisive defeat on the stubborn, stout-hearted natives. Gordon had no objection to the first duty, and, while at King William's Town, threw himself vigorously into the task. He, however, firmly declined to lead a punitive expedition against a people he conscientiously believed to have right on their side. This was, of course, a disagreeable surprise to the authorities, and accounted for their subsequent antagonism towards the man who, had they treated him with fairness and honesty, might well have put an end to their troubles.

Gordon wrote extensively on the Basuto problem, and, in October, 1882, produced an admirable paper on the native question generally. Alluding to this able treatise, Mr. Merriman, a Cape Prime Minister of that era, said—" As a Colony we must try to follow out the ideas sketched by General Gordon." In paragraph five of the paper, Gordon wrote—" Government by coercion is essentially rotten. The Duke of Wellington said that any fool could govern by that means. And it is still more rotten when

Government governs by the rule of coercion without the power of coercion except at great expense."

In a postscript, he declared—"Should Her Majesty's Government manage to arrange with the Basutos in a satisfactory manner, 10,000 splendid cavalry could be counted on as allies in any contingencies in Natal."

He sailed for England on October 14th, with, so it is said, scarcely a penny in his pocket. Far from gaining any financial advantage from his service at the Cape, it is believed to have cost him upwards of five hundred pounds. He had no private income, but had saved a certain amount during his year in Mauritius. Now, this had all disappeared. Even the cost of his passage home he had to bear himself.

CHAPTER   XVII

The Sudan Again

GORDON reached England on November 8th, 1882, with the sands of his great life fast running out. Though still under fifty, his years had been packed with infinitely more arduous tasks, more venturesome exploits, more hazardous missions, more exhausting toil for the benefit of mankind, than, perhaps, any other man of any epoch could lay claim to. His record in *Who's Who* would easily have outstripped in space those of the most illustrious in the land. Yet, again, he stole back to the country of his birth unrecognised by the man in the street, unnoticed, except meagrely, by an undiscerning Press. How strange that only when he had died for England did the authorities of his own country awaken in shame to their shocking neglect to appreciate the immensity of his services. Only then, when too late to do him honour as he deserved, did he become a national hero.

Sir William Butler contrasts the frigid welcome accorded to Gordon by the Colonial and Foreign Secretaries of the day with the enthusiastic appeal of a foreign monarch. " It would be a curious study," he writes, " to compare the receptions given to Gordon on his return by the men at the head of the Foreign and Colonial Offices at this time, with the manner in which a continental king greeted him. ' I now again request you, as you are at liberty, to enter my service,' wrote the King of the Belgians. ' For the moment I have no mission to offer you but I wish much to have you at my disposal, and to take you from this moment as my counsellor. You can name your own terms. You know the consideration that I have for your great qualities.' " Sir William continues— " Nor was neglect on the part of the English official world a thing very much to be wondered at in this case. Few men in our day had greater respect for principles, and less respect for mere per-

sons, than Gordon. . . . The sight of a poor Arab kneeling in
the desert, turned towards Mecca in prayer, was a thing eminently
more worthy of respect in his eyes than the spectacle of an entire
Cabinet of English Ministers eating dinner at the Mansion House."

In making his appeal to Gordon, the task King Leopold had
in mind was a mission to the Congo for the purpose of exercising
his remarkable powers to suppress the slave trade, which flourished
in the Belgian Congo with even more fertility than it had done in
the Sudan before Gordon's ubiquitous vengeance did so much to
free the land from the stigma of this foul traffic in human beings.
The cruelty and misery suffered by the natives of the Congo had
become notorious the world over, and, in his anxiety to put a stop
to the evils that prevailed, the Belgian King could hardly have done
better than choose, as his instrument of suppression, the man who
had revolutionised life in the Sudan, and whose manner of reforming abuses and dealing with troublesome situations in various parts
of the world had borne the stamp of genius.

Readily, Gordon agreed to undertake the mission whenever his
services were required. Meanwhile, to fill in the period of waiting,
he determined to gratify a long-felt wish to visit Palestine and make
a personal study of the historic Holy Land. Leaving England on
Boxing Day, 1882, he went first to Jaffa and thence to Jerusalem.
There, he lived entirely alone, still the lone wolf, happy with his
studying, his research work, and his books, first and foremost of
which was the well-read Bible that never left him wherever he went.

With a sense of satisfaction that the opportunity had, at last,
been vouchsafed to him, he studied the scenes and places that,
during the greater part of his life, he had read about with so much
absorbing interest. He gazed at the spot where the ark first came
to rest on the top of Mount Ararat. He viewed the site of the
Garden of Eden, the altar of burnt-offering, the temple of Jerusalem,
and the gates of the Holy City. But his reactions were not, altogether, what might have been expected, judging from a letter
written to his friend Mrs. F. from Jaffa, where he lodged in the
house of Simon the tanner. " I have done Jerusalem now to my
satisfaction," he wrote. " It never aroused any feelings of reverence. It, however, enabled me to see the types more clearly. To
me this is as any other land, except historically. In that way, as
the scene of great events, it is and ever must be interesting and full
of subjects for contemplation."

From the military point of view, he saw at a glance that " the
Russian Convent commanded the whole city, and was in itself a

strong fortress, capable of holding a formidable garrison, which
Russia could despatch in the guise of priests without anyone being
the wiser."

Gordon remained in Palestine during the whole of the year
1883, and, atlhough occupied in steadily adding to his already
immense store of knowledge, he was not being used in the best
interests of his country. Imagine a man of his age and colossal
attainments being afforded the leisure to spend twelve months on
a sight-seeing tour! He was, to be sure, glad of the opportunity to
visit and explore the Holy Land, but he could hardly have expected,
nor would he have wished, to be ignored by the authorities for so
long. Though deeply interested in the age-old relics around him
and immersed in his studies, his thoughts turned constantly
towards the Sudan, where events were developing to an extent that
even he could scarcely have foreseen.

In their concern to find a solution of the Egyptian problem,
why, in heaven's name, did the British Government neglect to
call upon the one man whose unsurpassed knowledge and experience would have been invaluable? There he was, unemployed and
available at a moment's notice for use in an advisory, or any other,
capacity. The answer is all too clear. Gordon the difficult, whose
plain speaking, independent character, and determination to take
his own line, had caused the authorities so much annoyance, combined, not infrequently, with embarrassment because he turned out
to be right and they wrong—this thorn in their side, whose remarkable ability they were unable to deny, yet, whose valuable
services they were reluctant to employ in any but insignificant
duties, was, for the moment, out of harm's way, absorbed in his
occupation, buried in his books, and in no position to show up the
politicians or cost them precious votes. But for this vindictive
neglect of the country's outstanding soldier, there is no knowing
to what extent the menacing situation in the Sudan might not
have been eased and the course of history altered.

It seems that, in their churlishness, they were averse to using
him if they could help it, but, at the same time, were anxious to
be able to call him to their aid should the situation become
critical.

It was in October, 1883, while engaged in research work near
Mount Carmel, that Gordon received word from King Leopold
asking him to fulfil his undertaking to go to the Congo. His immed-
diate application to the War Office was refused with Molotovian
consistency and a spirit that savoured of the dog-in-the-manger, for,

while, themselves, declining to employ him in a capacity befitting a soldier of his calibre, they were not prepared to let others enjoy the benefit of his talent! That was the position when Gordon hurried to Brussels, arriving in the Belgian capital on January 1st, 1884.

After some deliberation, he came to the conclusion that the only course open to him was to resign his commission, and so be free to accept the Congo invitation. " Retire from the army," said King Leopold, " and I will compensate you." In the words of Mr. Boulger—" In this and every other matter the King behaved towards Gordon in the most generous and cordial manner, furnishing a marked contrast with the grudging and parsimonious spirit of the British Government towards Gordon in China, at the Cape, and now again when destined for the Congo."

So Gordon sent in his papers. This came as something of a shock to the authorities who wanted to have it both ways, namely to keep him on the active list either unemployed or employed in unimportant positions, and to prevent him accepting suitable service under a foreign power. Once more, Gordon had driven them into a corner. What were they to do? The red light of warning continued to blaze in the Sudan with ever increasing menace, making it clear that the time approached when they could no longer afford to ignore the advice and help of the pre-eminent expert on Sudanese affairs. They must, therefore, sink their pride, yet again yielding to their tormentor, whom all the forces of bureaucracy seemed powerless to subdue. So strongly did they feel the need of Gordon's support, in the not far distant future, that they unashamedly reversed their refusal of his application to go to the Congo, and, in addition—so as to make quite sure—authorised him to draw his pay as a general officer while so employed!

By mid-January, however, the British ministers had, at last, come to their senses and decided to invite Gordon to go to the Sudan, there to utilise his great gifts in bringing about a settlement of the country, which, since his departure, had fallen back into a state of anarchy. Afterwards, his services were to be at the disposal of the Belgian King.

On learning the Government's intention, Gordon felt that, before all else, he must go over to Brussels and ask King Leopold to release him from his promise to go to the Congo; for, although he had been careful to stipulate that he could only give his consent " provided the Government of my own country does not require my services," the king had been so extraordinarily magnanimous

FIELD MARSHAL VISCOUNT WOLSELEY
WHEN COMMANDER-IN-CHIEF
OF THE BRITISH ARMY

that he could hardly have withdrawn from the agreement without
His Majesty's assent. In a letter to his brother, Sir Henry Gordon,
dated January 17th, he wrote—" I saw King Leopold to-day; he is
furious." But of course the king had no option but to accept the
situation that had arisen through no fault of the gallant crusader.

On the same date, he wrote to his sister, Augusta—" Do not
mention it, but there is just a chance I may have to go to Sudan for
two months, and then go to Congo." In response to an urgent
telegram from Lord Wolseley[1], he left Brussels that night and was
in London early on the morning of the 18th. Met by Captain
Brocklehurst of the Household Cavalry, he was escorted to Knights-
bridge barracks, and, after removing the stains of travel, went to
see Lord Wolseley, the Adjutant-General, who explained to him the
wishes of the Government. Gordon was to be asked to go to the
Sudan for the purpose of withdrawing the Egyptian garrisons that
were threatened by the overwhelming hosts of the Mahdi.

Later in the day, Wolseley took him to Downing Street, where
he was received by Lords Hartington,[2] Northbrook,[3] and Granville.[4]
and Sir Charles Dilke.[5] In answer to their question as to whether
he understood the position, Gordon replied that he gathered they
wanted him to withdraw the garrisons from the Sudan. " They
were pleased," he wrote in a letter to his sister, " and said ' That
was their idea; would I go? '? I said ' Yes.' They said ' When '?
I said ' To-night,' and it was over. I started at 8 p.m. H.R.H. the
Duke of Cambridge and Lord Wolseley came to see me off." One
can easily picture the scene. The dimly-lit Charing Cross station,
damp and murky on this night of mid-January; the three distinguished soldiers pacing the platform while awaiting departure of
the continental boat train. The portly, heavy build of the Duke
of Cambridge, Commander-in-Chief of the British Army, contrast-
ing with the slim, dapper figure of Lord Wolseley, Adjutant-
General to the Forces; and, between them, the hero of the hour—
though, as yet, time had not allowed of the sensational news being
published to the world—his face set with grim determination, his
eyes glittering with burning ardour which the severity and dangers
of the task before him served but to accentuate.

---

[1] General Lord Wolseley, Adjutant-General to the Forces, Gordon's old
friend of the Crimea (later Field Marshal Viscount Wolseley).
[2] Marquis of Hartington, Secretary of State for War, 1882-1885 (later 8th
Duke of Devonshire).
[3] 1st Earl of Northbrook, First Lord of the Admiralty, 1880-1885.
[4] 2nd Earl Granville, Secretary of State for Foreign Affairs, 1880-1885.
[5] 2nd Baronet, President Local Government Board, 1882-1885.

Kindly as ever, always thinking of others rather than of himself—what a shining example he would have been to-day—he found time, as the train was about to start, for a word of comfort to Colonel Stewart's[1] relatives—"Be sure that he will not go into any danger that I do not share, and I am sure that when I am in danger he will not be far behind."

Knowing that Gordon was almost without money, his old friend, Lord Wolseley, with most praiseworthy forethought and consideration, had collected some two hundred pounds from friends, and this gift, contained in a leather bag, he thrust through the carriage window just as the train began to move. As for Gordon's clothes, they consisted of little more than what he stood up in. And so it was that, simply, quietly, without fuss or display, the great soldier set out on his last crusade of self-sacrifice. With but a solitary companion, the ill-fated Colonel Stewart, he embarked on a mission that seemed fraught with incredible difficulties and grave danger. But he thrived on difficulties, while, as for danger, no one could have been more contemptuous of its menace. "I am not moved a bit," he wrote, "and hope to do the people good."

Many a less generous, less modest man might well have taken umbrage, after years of the cold shoulder, at being called upon, as a last resource, to help the authorities out of their troubles. Not so Gordon. Whatever he may have felt in his heart as to the conduct of men who, having consistently snubbed him, had the temerity to appeal to him for help when in a tight corner, he showed no trace of bitterness, but, in a dignified, soldierly manner, gave quick, decisive answers to the questions put to him, and, knowing it to be his duty, accepted the exacting task without a moment's hesitation.

It has been suggested that responsibility for this delay in sending Gordon to Khartoum rested not so much with the British Government of the day but rather with the British representative in Egypt Sir Evelyn Baring (afterwards Earl of Cromer).[2] This attempt to whitewash the Liberal Cabinet at the expense of a subordinate cannot, however, succeed at the bar of posterity, for the sufficient reason that Sir Evelyn, being subject to the orders of the Foreign Office, was not in a position either to invite Gordon's services, or to refuse to accept them. In fairness to the Government,

---

[1] Colonel Donald Stewart accompanied Gordon to Khartoum.

[2] First Earl of Cromer. As Sir Evelyn Baring he was Her Majesty's Agent and Consul-General in Egypt.

it must be recorded that, when the situation in the Sudan had become serious, the Foreign Secretary, Lord Granville, did repeatedly suggest to Baring the desirability of employing General Gordon at Khartoum. But, once the Government had made up their minds that Gordon was the one man for the job, why, in the name of goodness, did they offer *suggestions* to their representative instead of giving him direct orders with which he would be bound to comply? The whole world knew of Gordon's experience and knowledge of the Sudan. The merest infant, if asked to name the best man to solve the Egyptian problem, would unhesitatingly have produced the only possible answer. Yet, until the eleventh hour had arrived, a timid Government could do no more than offer Gordon's services if the British representative at Cairo thought they would be welcome!

For his repeated advice against calling in the world's outstanding specialist in diseases of the kind then afflicting the Sudan, Sir Evelyn Baring must share, in no small measure, responsibility for the tragedies that followed. The supreme authority, that is to say, Mr. Gladstone's Liberal Government, cannot, however, escape the major share, for they had it in their power to send Gordon to the seat of the trouble long before he actually went—an obvious course which, nevertheless, they neglected to adopt. Had they acted earlier as they were obliged to act eventually, by giving directions rather than offering suggestions, the sad story of the Sudan might well have been different.

When, at the request of Khedive Ismail, Gordon had officiated as president of the finance committee appointed to enquire into Egypt's impoverished condition, he had fallen out with Baring, Britain's representative at the discussions. It would seem that no sooner had they set eyes on each other than a mutual antagonism sprang up between them. Characteristically, Gordon spoke his mind, and we may be sure that, in his wrath, he took little care to choose his words. The result was an enmity that, to the day of Gordon's death, never relaxed.

Unfortunately, when asked whether Gordon's intervention in the Sudan would be welcome, Sir Evelyn allowed personal feelings to influence his judgment. In the end, finding his hand forced by the Government—as it should have been at the beginning—he was obliged to admit that no better man could be found for the job than Gordon.

Now, before accompanying him on his journey, let us consider briefly the situation then existing in the Sudan and the events that led up to it. In an earlier chapter, describing Gordon's expedition up the Nile in 1874, mention has been made of a small island called Abba, some two hundred miles above Khartoum, where, crouching in a cave, an unknown Dervish named Mohammed Ahmed might, perchance, have watched the slowly passing steamer, and wondered what significance was to be attached to its journey. Six years later, this son of a Dongola carpenter began to emerge from obscurity and to make his presence felt. Professing to be actuated by religious fervour, he started on his amazing career by falling foul of a leading religious authority, who countenanced such frivolities as singing and dancing, to both of which Ahmed pretended to object. From this seemingly harmless beginning, the cave-dweller of Abba Island took to preaching sedition under the cloak of a professed desire to uplift the people from their life of self-indulgence, and to eradicate all forms of wickedness and vice.

Inspired by the fiery forcefulness of his utterances, ardent followers soon began to surround him, till, at length, his activities came to the notice of the Egyptian Governor-General at Khartoum —the same Raouf, whom Gordon had twice dismissed, but who, as soon as his back was turned, had stepped into his shoes as ruler of the Sudan. Ahmed's venturesomeness in defying so high a religious dignitary, and upbraiding him for his negligence in failing to enforce the laws of the Prophet as set out in the Koran, besides his commanding personality and determination to resist opposition to his will, aroused the admiration of his fellows and drew to his side a growing band of followers. Official enquiries resulted in the conclusion that the man was mad, further steps to curb his activities being considered unnecessary.

Left to his own devices, the " wretched Dongolawi," as he had contemptuously been called in earlier days, continued with his crusade, having as its ostensible object the strict application of Islamic laws and the relentless denunciation of intemperance, immorality, smoking, swearing, and frivolities of all kinds. But, beneath all this outward show of religious ardour lay a personal ambition no less intense than that of the *Taiping* leader who styled himself the Celestial King, and, as his following increased numerically from day to day, so did the range of his activities extend far beyond the immediate neighbourhood of Abba Island.

Travelling through the extensive province of Kordofan with an armed escort, he appealed to all true Mohammedans to give their service to the cause. The response was encouraging, and, before long, he found himself at the head of a considerable band of fanatical enthusiasts, most of whom were probably actuated more by the chances of material benefits than any genuine feelings of religious zeal.

By the year 1881, Ahmed's influence had become so powerful, and, like the *Taiping* leader, he so played on the gullibility of the ignorant people that, what with all the impressive display of trances, visions, miracles, and prophecies, in fact all the tricks of the trade, he soon became looked upon as superior to ordinary mortals and assumed the title of the Mahdi. In *Eminent Victorians*, Mr. Lytton Strachey tells us—"There is an ancient tradition in the Mohammedan world, telling of a mysterious being, the last in succession of the twelve holy Imams, who, untouched by death and withdrawn into the recesses of a mountain, was destined, at the appointed hour, to come forth again among men. His title was the Mahdi, the guide; some believed that he would be the fore-runner of the Messiah; others that he would be Christ himself." At any rate, from this mystical figure Mohammed Ahmed took his title, and thenceforth proclaimed a holy war.

But, by this time, Raouf Pasha could no longer afford to ignore the mad Dervish of Abba Island, who, on returning from his suc-cessful tour of Kordofan, found awaiting him an order from the Governor-General to go to Khartoum. This he disregarded. Soon afterwards, however, a boat arrived bringing an emissary from Raouf with orders to convey Mohammed Ahmed to the capital "dead or alive." The self-styled Mahdi received his visitor with con-temptuous disdain, and, rising to his great height, his broad shoulders, dark beard, and piercing eyes enhancing the impres-siveness of his general appearance, he addressed the emissary in these words—"By the grace of God and His Prophet I am the master of this country, and never shall I go to Khartoum to justify myself." Attended, as he was, by a strong, heavily armed guard, nothing could be done to carry out the orders of the Governor-General, whose representative was obliged to return to Khartoum with the disquieting news.

In August, 1881, a small Egyptian force of two companies, sent to round up the impostor and his followers, suffered ignominious defeat, being almost annihilated by the greatly strengthened Mahdists, who naturally gained considerable confidence as a result of their easy victory over the Government troops.

Meanwhile, in Egypt there arose another revolt. Dissatisfied with the incompetent administration of Turkish Pashas, who occupied most of the more important positions in the Government at Cairo, the Egyptian army, led by one Arabi Pasha, broke into open mutiny, and, owing to the impotence of the Cairo authorities, the situation became so serious that the British Government intervened. Alexandria was bombarded by the British fleet, while a strong force under Lord Wolseley landed in Egypt. Admirably guided by a naval officer using the stars for direction, they attacked Arabi's mutineers at Tel el Kebir, inflicting upon them a crushing defeat. So ended this brief campaign of 1882, a naval bombardment, followed by a solitary land battle, sufficing to bring hostilities to an abrupt conclusion. This intervention by British troops, and the famous victory of Tel el Kebir, gave England a sure footing in Egypt, and, although it was intended to withdraw the troops as soon as law and order had been restored, a resumption of the old Pasha regime gave so little cause for confidence in the administration that it was deemed wise to retain them in the country.

Returning to the Mahdi's activities, he now decided that the small island of Abba seemed likely to become too hot for him. Consequently, he betook himself with his followers to the far west of Kordofan, setting up his standard, bearing a design with the curious mixture of a cross and the Koran, at a place called Jebel Gedir. More than one attempt was made by local Egyptian garrisons to intercept him, but he had no difficulty in warding off these somewhat spiritless attacks. During his progress through the country, he roused the people to a high pitch of enthusiasm for the new cause, which, as they fondly hoped, would enable them to avenge themselves for the misery suffered under Egyptian rule and the heavy hand of the Pashas. Highly gratifying, from the Mahdi's point of view, was the enrolling under his banner of the notorious Baggara horsemen of Kordofan, the most intrepid, savage fighters in the Sudan.

At Jebel Gedir, the Mahdi set about organising his followers, preparing them for his holy war, and establishing a code to which all must scrupulously adhere under pain of the most drastic penalties. As a uniform representing his new order, he dressed his men in the *jibbeh*—a white smock decorated with patches of various colours. Twice, during this period of organisation and training, the Mahdists heavily defeated Egyptian forces sent from Khartoum to attack them. At last, his preparations complete, the Mahdi opened his revolt against Egyptian authority in the Sudan by laying siege to El Obeid, the capital of Kordofan, at the same time dispatching expeditions under his Khalifas[1] into the provinces of Darfour and the Bahr el Ghazal.

Completely surrounded and cut off though they were, the garrison of El Obeid, commanded by an excellent soldier, one Said Pasha, resisted all the Mahdi's efforts to take the city by assault. After holding out stoutly for six months, however, they were compelled, in January, 1883, to surrender through lack of food. This signal victory gave the Mahdi control of the vast province of Kordofan, besides augmenting his ever growing resources in war material and money, one hundred thousand pounds being swept into his coffers as a result of the surrender. El Obeid now became his headquarters, and there he established himself to plan and organise the conquest of the entire Sudan.

Though posing as a holy man, a messenger from God charged with the task of uplifting the people and cleansing them from unrighteousness, Mohammed Ahmed was, in reality, a tyrant of the very worst description, who ruled his followers with despotic brutality. Firmly acknowledging him as the Mahdi, his fanatical legionaries accepted the cruelties inflicted on them in the belief that God's emissary could do no wrong. Similarly, the debaucheries he was said to practise, in defiance of his own edicts, excited no great concern nor astonishment, since God's chosen servant would be above all rules of conduct prescribed for the ordinary man.

Some idea of the character of this monster may be gained from a glance at his penal code. "The blasphemer was to be instantly hanged, the adulterer was to be scourged with whips of rhinoceros hide, the thief was to have his right hand and left foot hacked off in the market-place. No more were marriages to be celebrated with pomp and feasting, no more was the youthful warrior to swagger with flowing hair: henceforth the believer must banquet on dates and milk, and his head must be kept shaved. Minor transgressions were punished by confiscation of property, or by imprisonment and chains. But the rhinoceros whip was the favourite instrument of chastisement. Men were flogged for drinking a glass of wine, they were flogged for smoking; if they swore, they received eighty lashes for every expletive; and after eighty lashes it was a common thing to die."

His striking appearance was in keeping with the position of supreme authority over a vast army of fanatical tribesmen. Clothed

---

[1] Subordinate commanders.

in turban and white *jibbeh*, anointed with attar of roses, musk, and sandal-wood, his massive figure presented a noble spectacle. Yet, apart from his appearance, there was little about him that could be described as noble. In truth, he could compete, not without reasonable chances of success, with all the notorious tyrants of history, and, although he denied his adherents even the most harmless pleasures, he, himself, indulged unashamedly in excesses and lived in the lap of luxury.

From Gordon's journal, it appears that " the Mahdi puts pepper under his nails, and when he receives visitors then he touches his eyes and weeps copiously; he eats a few grains of *dhoora* openly, but in the interior of the house he has fine feeding and drinks alcoholic drinks. One cannot help being amused at this pepper business. Those who come in for pardon, come in on their knees, with a halter round their necks. The Mahdi rises, having scratched his eyes and obtained a copious flow of tears, and takes off the halter! As the production of tears is generally considered the proof of sincerity, I would recommend the Mahdi's recipe to Cabinet Ministers, justifying some job."

It was on November 4th, 1883, that the Mahdi inflicted his most crushing defeat on the Egyptian forces that vainly tried to overcome him. An army of ten thousand men, mostly of poor quality, commanded by a British officer, the gallant Colonel Hicks, set out from Khartoum to attack the rebels at El Obeid. Exhausted and without water after their long march across the desert, they were surprised by forty thousand of the Mahdi's fiercest fighters and literally cut to pieces.

This disaster to Egyptian arms was soon followed by others. The garrison of Dara in Darfour, commanded by a most able soldier, Slatin Pasha, was obliged to surrender after offering the stoutest resistance, the entire province of Darfour falling into the hands of the rebels. They, moreover, penetrated deeply into the Bahr el Ghazal, while, in the Eastern Sudan, Osman Digna, one of the Mahdi's outstanding commanders, extended the revolt as far as the Red Sea. Through these and other notable successes, the greater part of the Sudan had, by this time, fallen under the heavy heel of the Mahdi, who now began to prepare for his *coup de grace* by closing in on Khartoum.

This, briefly, was the situation when the British and Egyptian Governments decided to withdraw the Egyptian garrisons that yet remained unconquered, and Gordon was invited to undertake the difficult task of giving effect to their decision.

MOHAMMED AHMED
("THE MAHDI")

(Hulton Library)

A few days before leaving England for the last time, Gordon
was visited by Mr. W. T. Stead, celebrated as editor of the *Pall
Mall Gazette*. As a result of this interview, there appeared in the
green-coloured evening paper of those days an authoritative statement by Gordon, from which these passages have been selected : —

"So you would abandon the Sudan ? But the Eastern Sudan
is indispensable to Egypt. It will cost you far more to retain your
hold upon Egypt proper if you abandon your hold of the Eastern
Sudan to the Mahdi or to the Turk than what it would to retain
your hold upon Eastern Sudan by the aid of such material as
exists in the provinces. Darfour and Kordofan must be abandoned.
That I admit; but the provinces lying to the east of the White
Nile should be retained, and north of Sennaar . . . . . "

"Nor is it only England that has to face the danger. The
success of the Mahdi has already excited dangerous fermentation
in Arabia and Syria. Placards have been posted in Damascus
calling upon the population to rise and drive out the Turks. If
the whole of the Eastern Sudan is surrendered to the Mahdi, the
Arab tribes on both sides of the Red Sea will take fire . . . . .

"I see it is proposed to fortify Wady Halfa, and prepare there
to resist the Mahdi's attack. You might as well fortify against a
fever. Contagion of that kind cannot be kept out by fortifications
and garrisons . . . . .

"You must either surrender absolutely to the Mahdi or defend
Khartoum at all hazards. The latter is the only course which
ought to be entertained . . . . .

"The great evil is not at Khartoum, but at Cairo. It is the
weakness of Cairo which produces disaster in the Sudan. It is
because Hicks was not adequately supported at the first, but was
thrust forward upon an impossible enterprise by the men who had
refused him supplies when a decisive blow might have been struck,
that the Western Sudan has been sacrificed. The Eastern Sudan
may, however, be saved if there is a firm hand placed at the helm
in Egypt. Everything depends on that . . . . .

"As regards Abyssinia, the old warning should not be lost
sight of—' Put not your trust in princes ' . . . . .

"It will cost two millions to relieve the Sudan garrisons and
to quell the revolt . . . . . At first, until the country is pacified, the
Sudan will need a subsidy of £200,000 a year from Egypt. That,
however, would be temporary. During the last years of my administration, the Sudan involved no charge upon the Egyptian
Exchequer. The bad provinces were balanced against the good,

and an equilibrium was established. The Sudan will never be a source of revenue for Egypt, but it need not be a source of expense. That deficits have arisen, and that the present disaster has occurred, is entirely attributable to a single cause, and that is the grossest misgovernment . . . . .

"The Turks,[1] the Circassians,[1] and the Bashi-Bazouks[1] have plundered and oppressed the people in the Sudan, as they plundered and oppressed them in the Balkan peninsula. Oppression begat discontent; discontent necessitated an increase of the armed force at the disposal of the authorities; this increase of the army involved an increase of expenditure, which again was attempted to be met by increasing taxation, and that still further increased the discontent. And so things went on in a dismal circle, until they culminated, after repeated deficits, in a disastrous rebellion . . . .

"The movement is not religious, but an outbreak of despair. Three times over I warned the late Khedive that it would be impossible to govern the Sudan on the old system, after my appointment to the Governor-Generalship. During the three years that I wielded full powers in the Sudan, I taught the natives that they had a right to exist. I waged war against the Turks and Circassians, who had harried the population. I had taught them something of the meaning of liberty and justice, and accustomed them to a higher ideal of government than that with which they had previously been acquainted. As soon as I had gone, the Turks and Circassians returned in full force; the old Bashi-Bazouk system was re-established; my old *employées* were persecuted; and a population which had begun to appreciate something like decent government was flung back to suffer the worst excesses of Turkish rule. The inevitable result followed . . . .

"The Sudanese are a very nice people. They deserve the sincere compassion and sympathy of all civilised men. I got on very well with them, and I am sincerely sorry at the prospect of seeing them handed over to be ground down once more by their Turkish and Circassian oppressors . . . . .

"So far from believing it impossible to make an arrangement with the Mahdi, I strongly suspect that he is a mere puppet, put forward by Elias, Sebehr's father-in-law, and the largest slave-owner in Obeid, and that he has assumed a religious title to give colour to his defence of the popular rights . . . . .

"Now, with regard to Egypt, the same principle should be observed that must be acted upon in the Sudan. Let your found-

---

[1] Employed under the Egyptian Government in the Sudan.

ations be broad and firm, and based upon the contentment and welfare of the people. Hitherto, both in the Sudan and in Egypt, instead of constructing the social edifice like a pyramid, upon its base, we have been rearing an obelisk, which a single push may overturn. Our safety in Egypt is to do something for the people; —but, whatever you do, do not break up Sir Evelyn Wood's[1] army, which is destined to do good work."

Gordon took exactly a month to reach Khartoum. He had intended travelling by way of Suakin, thus avoiding Cairo with its tiresome officialdom and the inevitable functions that he detested. But, on arrival at Port Said, he was met by Sir Evelyn Wood and persuaded to stay a day or two in the capital before resuming his journey to the Sudan. His distaste for Cairo can easily be understood. On each of his previous visits, he had found the Egyptian officials difficult to deal with, and on his departure for England in 1879, openly antagonistic. He had been pestered with dinner invitations, which, however, he seldom accepted, dining out being one of his chief anathemas. Official functions, equally productive of pain and grief, had to be endured. But, above all, he would be expected to touch his hat to the British representative, Sir Evelyn Baring, with whom, as we know, he had already crossed swords. That a soldier of Gordon's unique experience and surpassing knowledge of the Sudan should be required to take orders from a civil service official seems fantastic enough. But, when the animosity known to exist between the two men, who had acquired a rooted dislike to each other on sight, is taken into account, the great soldier being obliged to subordinate himself to a *civilian,* on a mission essentially demanding the exercise of Gordon's *military* genius, assumes an even more impossible aspect. Sworn enemies from the word " go," and as different in temperament and outlook as any two men could possibly be, nothing would have made them see alike on any conceivable subject. Consequently, the less they saw of one another, the better it would be for the smooth working of Gordon's plans and the success of his mission. He should, of course, have been given a free hand to utilise his boundless knowledge and his remarkable gifts as he thought fit, and should not have been placed in the ignominious position of taking orders from a civil official fifteen hundred miles away. As Sir William Butler so rightly declared—" The electric wire is a marvellous addition to man's power when it is in powerful hands, but it is a terrible

---

[1] Major General (later Field Marshal) Sir Evelyn Wood, V.C., Sirdar of the Egyptian Army.

engine of national destruction when it induces a Minister, seated in an office-chair, to imagine that he sees the full depth of the horizon which the man of action is beholding at the far end of the telegraph."

The authorities should, long since, have realised that Gordon was at his best and greatest when left alone. Self-reliance being one of his most prominent qualities, he always found it difficult to tolerate the meddlesome interference of bureaucracy, and, having received his instructions from the Cabinet ministers in London, he required no advice or directions from Cairo as to how those instructions should be carried out.

Despite the extreme gravity of the situation, which, but for the British Government's neglect to call upon him sooner, might well have been avoided, Gordon faced his tremendous task with cheerful confidence, undismayed as to the future provided he received the full, unstinted support of both British and Egyptian Governments, and was not subjected to unnecessary interference. No doubt he anticipated attempts at interference should he visit the capital, and wished to avoid a *contretemps* at the outset of his mission. However, a message brought to him from his old friend Sir Gerald Graham,[1] begging him to overcome his personal feelings and go to Cairo for a brief stay, had the effect of inducing him to break his journey. Accompanied by Sir Evelyn Wood, he arrived in Cairo on January 24th. Next day, Khedive Tewfik appointed him Governor-General of the Sudan—a position he now assumed for the second time.

He spent but two days in the capital, and, before leaving for Khartoum, had a talk to the old slave-dealer, Sebehr, still detained in Cairo for reasons of security. Much of Gordon's time during the journey from England had been occupied in earnest deliberation as to the wisest course to pursue in order to achieve his object, his thoughts, not unnaturally, turning towards the man who, at one time, exercised so powerful an influence throughout the Sudan. And, although no one knew better than he did the sinister character of Sebehr, in searching for means of subduing the Mahdi he began to think it might be possible to utilise the old ruffian's undoubted power over the tribes to bring about a solution of the problem. But, when brought face to face with him in Cairo, he saw that Sebehr's bitterness at the fate of his son, Suleiman, had in no way

---

[1] See page 34.

abated, and that negotiations between them would be difficult, if not impossible.

In a memorandum on the slave-dealer, written by Gordon the day before their meeting, he declared—" If Sebehr bears no malice personally against me, I will take him to the Sudan at once." We are told that, during the interview, " Sebehr could scarcely control his feelings," and appeared to have a special grudge against Gordon. Nevertheless, the newly-appointed Governor General " would still have taken him with him, if only on the ground that he would be less dangerous in the Sudan than at Cairo." However, Sir Gerald Graham, who was present during the meeting between the arch-trader in human beings and the man who had done so much towards suppressing this evil traffic, considered that Gordon's life would be in serious danger if he took with him this utterly unscrupulous scoundrel, enraged as he still was at the fate of his son.

Unmoved, as always, by any sort of personal danger, Gordon could not agree with the Cairo authorities, who, however, declined to release Sebehr, thereby causing the project to be dropped for the time being. This abortive attempt to give effect to an idea that might well have proved helpful was the first of repeated recommendations that Sebehr should be sent to Khartoum, where his influence might be usefully employed in support of the Governor-General's efforts to bring the Mahdi to his senses. Who knows what direction the course of events might not have taken had Gordon's request been acceded to? To be sure, his instructions were limited to the evacuation of the Egyptian garrisons, and the establishment of some form of government in the Sudan. But it was not long before he realised the virtual impossibility of withdrawing the garrisons, at this advanced stage of the insurrection, unless the activities of the Mahdi were halted, either as a result of negotiation or by his defeat in the field.

On the night of January 26th, 1884, Gordon left for Khartoum accompanied by Colonel Stewart and four Egyptian officers. Between that date and his arrival at the Sudanese capital, sensational happenings took place in the eastern Sudan, where Osman Digna was besieging the towns of Sinkat and Tokar. Attacked by an Egyptian force four thousand strong under Baker Pasha—a British officer and brother of Sir Samuel Baker, Gordon's predecessor in the Equatorial Provinces—this capable leader of Mahdists not only repulsed the attack, but inflicted on the Egyptians an overwhelming defeat that resulted in both the beleaguered towns falling into his hands, thereby seriously weakening the position of Khartoum.

From Cairo, Gordon proceeded up the Nile to Korosko, where he arrived on the evening of February 1st, starting next morning by camel to cross the two hundred and fifty miles of desert to Abu Hammed. For six days, he pushed on through the " waterless sea," as Arabs describe the Nubian Desert, his mind ever busy with plans for solving the innumerable problems that lay ahead. Though few could have been found to look upon his task as anything but hopeless, Gordon knew not what it was to be dismayed by the severity of any undertaking. Indeed, the more formidable the difficulties appeared to be, the firmer became his determination to overcome them. Consequently, he entered upon what most people regarded as a forlorn hope with the utmost zeal and enthusiasm, confident that, if he failed to gain his ends by peaceful means, he would, in the last resort, have no difficulty in subduing by force of arms " a feeble lot of stinking Dervishes," provided, of course, he received the requisite support from both British and Egyptian Governments. At the same time, he felt that these same Dervishes, in open revolt, were capable of so hampering operations for withdrawing the Egyptian garrisons as to render the task impracticable, and that he must first put a stop to their activities, either by peaceful settlement or force of arms.

Another four days' travel took him to Berber, where he publicly proclaimed the reason for his coming; and thence on to Khartoum, which was reached on February 18th.

CHAPTER XVIII

Khartoum

NEARLY five years had gone by since Gordon left Khartoum, expecting never to see it again. Yet, in the country's hour of desperate need, he had come once more to lend the priceless aid of his unrivalled ability. Again, he became the lonely tenant of Khartoum's spacious palace, every nook and corner of which he knew so well, and where he had spent long hours of arduous toil in the interests of that immense country, at once so fascinating yet so forbidding.

The city of Khartoum, for ever to be associated with the name of Gordon, lies at the junction of the Blue and the White Nile, distant some eighteen hundred miles from the mouth of the great Nile, where the famous river flows into the Mediterranean. About the end of the first quarter of the nineteenth century, on the tongue of land separating the two rivers, an Egyptian settlement was established. This quickly developed into a substantial township, which soon became the capital of the Sudan and the seat of government, its name, Khartoum (elephant's trunk), being adopted owing to the shape of the strip of land on which the town was built. Before long, it became notorious as the heart and core of the shameful slave trade and the assembly place of merchants, whose ivory business was of insignificant value compared with their lucrative traffic in slaves.

Not until the Mahdi started his activities was anything done to fortify the Sudanese capital. Even when Gordon arrived, in February, 1884, the construction of earth-works and forts had by no means been completed, and he it was who first put Khartoum in a proper state of defence.

Gordon's immediate actions bore close resemblance to those following his first installation as Governor-General, for, as he had predicted, no sooner had he turned his back on the Sudan than the old malpractices were resumed, the country sliding back into its former deplorable state of corruption and mismanagement. In truth, he had to start all over again, dispersing the unscrupulous Bashi-Bazouks, clearing the over-populated prisons, abolishing the *kurbash* and the stocks, and ordering the destruction of the records of unpaid taxes. The deliverer from oppression and misery had returned to the scene of his former triumphs to restore to the people conditions of life they had enjoyed under his wise, compassionate rule, but which had been denied them by the harsh Egyptian and Turkish overlords who succeeded him.

His arrival, moreover, put new heart into the garrison and people of Khartoum, whose morale had not been improved by the pessimistic attitude of the commandant, Colonel de Coetlogon, who, as early as January 9th, had " telegraphed to the Khedive, strongly urging immediate withdrawal from Khartoum." He is said to have held a poor opinion of the efficiency of the garrison, which, in turn, had little confidence in its commander. He was anxious to abandon what he regarded as a hopeless task, repeatedly applying for " authority to leave with the garrison." This being the state of mind of Khartoum's leader, it is hardly surprising that the people, lacking inspiration and encouragement, came perilously near to panic. Then, at a moment when anything might have happened, there arrived in the nerve-stricken city a message of good cheer and comfort from the outside world—" General Gordon is coming to Khartoum." These six words had had an immediate effect on the population of the city, who remembered the wonders performed by this amazing Englishman in the past.

But, if the news of his coming produced universal joy, it was as nothing compared to the scenes of frantic delight that attended Gordon's entry into the capital. " The whole population," we are told, " men, women, and children, turned out to welcome him as a conqueror and a deliverer . . . . . The women threw themselves on the ground and struggled to kiss his feet; in the confusion Gordon was several times pushed down; and this remarkable demonstration of popular confidence and affection was continued the whole way from the landing-place to the *hukumdaria*, or palace."

In a proclamation issued to the people on his arrival, the new Governor-General said—" Let it be known to you all that I have been appointed, in concert between the Khedive's Government and the Government of Great Britain, Governor-General of the whole Sudan; and the Sudan has now become an independent State, to

HOUSES IN OLD KHARTOUM

(Reproduced by permission of the Sudan Government Agency in London)

govern itself without the intervention of the Egyptian Government in any way whatever."

One of Gordon's first acts was to send another request to Cairo for the services of Sebehr, whose presence in Khartoum would, he now firmly believed, be helpful to him in his endeavour to find a peaceful issue to the increasingly menacing situation. But, again, his request proved unavailing, no attention being paid by those in power, hundreds of miles away, to the urgent entreaties of the man on the spot, who naturally knew far better than they did what measures were necessary to deal with the grave problems confronting him, and what course of action would be most likely to succeed.

As a result of the disaster to Baker Pasha's force when attempting the relief of Sinkat and Tokar, and the subsequent fall of these two towns to the besieging Mahdists under Osman Digna, the British Government would appear to have suddenly abandoned their hopes of a peaceful settlement and switched over to a war-like policy, for, within a month of Gordon's arrival, a strong force of British troops, commanded by Sir Gerald Graham, landed at Suakin on the Red Sea, and, advancing inland, defeated Osman Digna in two hard-fought engagements at El Teb and Tamai. In both battles, the rebel tribesmen fought with great ferocity and fanatical bravely, but they found the opposition of disciplined British troops a very different matter to that of the mediocre Egyptians, and, in each instance, were driven off with heavy losses.

Oddly enough, however, having inflicted this signal punishment on the Mahdi's henchman, the British Government felt they had done enough, and withdrew the whole of General Graham's force to Suakin. Had they pursued the campaign, the Mahdi would, no doubt, have been overcome, Khartoum could have been saved, and with it the precious life of England's outstanding military figure. But, as it was, the defeats suffered at El Teb and Tamai served but to stir up the smarting tribes, who became eager for revenge; while others who had been undecided as to their loyalties, interpreting the British withdrawal as a sign of weakness, hesitated no longer, and threw in their lot with the Mahdi. British intervention had, therefore, done far more harm than good, the situation at Khartoum proportionately deteriorating and poor Gordon's immense difficulties being correspondingly enhanced. The chances of coming to terms with the Mahdi had been thrown away by the refusal to send Sebehr to Khartoum in response to Gordon's repeated requests, and by the carnage of El Teb and Tamai. As Sir William Butler wrote—" The door of peace had been slammed at Tamai, and the Arab was as certain to take his revenge at Khartoum as the sun of the Sudan was to shine."

When Sir Gerald Graham landed at Suakin, Khartoum had been accessible on all sides. Three weeks later, when the British force was withdrawn, the Mahdi had begun his investment of the city. What could be more indicative of the disastrous effect on the situation produced by the British Government's action? By their ill-advised policy, first to intervene by sending an expeditionary force to Suakin, and then to withdraw before the full strength of the Mahdi had been crushed, they embarrassed their faithful servant at Khartoum, rendered his situation even more precarious than before, and added immeasurably to the already heavy burden of his responsibility.

Comparing the situation in the Sudan when he resigned his position as Governor-General with the existing state of affairs at Khartoum, Gordon wrote in his diary—" *When I left,* I could say ' no man could lift his hand in the Sudan without me ', and now we cannot calculate on our existence over twenty-four hours."

Realising that prospects of a peaceful solution no longer remained, he telegraphed to Cairo—" If Egypt is to be quiet the Mahdi must be smashed up." But his appeal for reinforcements and for demonstrations of British support along the line of communication with Egypt, was ignored, the British Government continuing to refuse consideration of the proposals made by their gallant emissary, to whom they had entrusted this desperate mission. In characteristically blunt terms, Gordon spoke his mind—" You will not let Egypt keep the Sudan, you will not take it yourself, and you will not permit any other country to occupy it."

Early in March, telegraphic communication broke down placing Khartoum in a position of almost total isolation. " I shall be caught in Khartoum," wrote Gordon, " and even if I was mean enough to escape, I have not the power to do so."

The situation on Gordon's arrival called for immediate steps being taken to fortify Khartoum, as well as the position at Omdurman on the opposite or western bank of the White Nile. As a sapper, he was able to set about this task with the advantage of expert knowledge of the most up-to-date methods. In addition to the earthworks and wire entanglements, Gordon made use of land mines electrically wired together. Three lines of these infernal machines were laid before the city walls, and so effective did they prove that, for the best part of a year, not once did the rebel tribesmen succeed in penetrating beyond the third line. He established a network of telegraph lines, so that, from his command post on the palace roof, he could keep in close touch with the various defence works.

At his disposal were nine river steamers, by means of which he brought to Khartoum supplies for a prolonged siege. Furnished with guns, and fitted with bullet-proof iron plates, they were used to great advantage against the besiegers. The population of the city comprised some forty thousand civilians and a garrison of, approximately, eight thousand men, Egyptians for the most part, with a proportion of Sudanese. Owing to Gordon's foresight and energy, five months' supply of food was collected by his steamers and stored in the granaries. With care, it could be made to last considerably longer.

In the middle of March, partly with a view to the destruction of a rebel fortification at Halfiyeh, on the right bank of the Nile some twenty miles north of the capital, and partly for the purpose of testing the metal of his troops, Gordon sent out a force, nearly a thousand strong, under the command of Colonel Stewart. The result proved disconcerting in the extreme, for the expedition was ignominiously put to flight by a comparatively small band of rebel horsemen. The defeat being attributed by the soldiers to treachery on the part of two Pashas, these officers were tried by court martial and shot. But the affair did nothing to strengthen Gordon's confidence in the material he would have to rely on for the defence of Khartoum. Thereafter, he took no more risks of depleting his slender force by embarking on enterprises outside the city, keeping his men within the perimeter, concentrating on their training in defensive warfare, and, above all, encouraging them to hold on by his own inspiring, vitalising leadership.

By the end of the first week in April, he had evidently decided not to count on being aided by either the British or Egyptian Government, and had made up his mind to formulate his own plans for alleviating the situation of intense gravity confronting him. Hemmed in by the Mahdi's legions, and unable to obtain official assent to his urgent proposals, it is hardly surprising that a man of his unusual self-reliance should have fallen back on his own resources and taken the initiative, no matter whether the measures he adopted met with Government approval or not. Always prone to take his own line, to act according to his conscience, defying the consequences, he was the last man to sit down and let matters slide just because a lethargic Government declined to accept his recommendations. That he now intended to ignore red tape and act as he

thought best is instanced by the following message to Sir Evelyn Baring, dated April 8th, after a month of telegraphic breakdown: —
" I have telegraphed to Sir Samuel Baker to make an appeal to British and American millionaires to give me £300,000 to engage 3,000 Turkish troops from the Sultan and, send them here. This would settle the Sudan and Mahdi for ever. For my part—I think you will agree with me—I do not see the fun of being caught here to walk about the streets for years as a dervish with sandalled feet. Not that (D.V.) I will ever be taken alive. It would be the climax of meanness after I had borrowed money from the people here, had called on them to sell their grain at low price, etc., to go and abandon them without using every effort to relieve them, *whether those efforts are diplomatically correct or not*[1]; and I feel sure, whatever you may feel diplomatically, I have your support, and that of every man professing himself a gentleman, in private."

In another telegram to the British representative at Cairo, dated April 16th, Gordon again revealed his determination to take independent action: —"As far as I can understand, the situation is this. You state your intention of not sending any relief up here or to Berber, and you refuse me Sebehr. I consider myself free to act according to circumstances. I shall hold on here as long as I can, and if I can suppress the rebellion I shall do so. If I cannot, I shall retire to the Equator and leave you the indelible disgrace of abandoning the garrisons of Sennaar, Kassala, Berber, and Dongola, with the *certainty* that you will eventually be forced to smash up the Mahdi under greater difficulties if you wish to maintain peace in, and, indeed, to retain Egypt."[2]

Before the end of April, telegraphic communication between Khartoum and Cairo was finally severed, and thence-forward the stricken city became cut off from the outside world save for occasional runners who succeeded in eluding the prowling Dervishes. Every possible subtlety was devised by these brave messengers to conceal their despatches, so that in the event of search they would not be found. One of them, who triumphantly passed through the Mahdi's lines, carried a minute message hidden beneath his thumb nail![3] So faint were the chances of his runners getting through that Gordon is believed to have, purposely, sent out information exaggerating the strength of the garrison and the

---

[1] Author's italics.
[2] This prediction was fulfilled by the battle of Omdurman, in 1898.
[3] See page 85.

resources in food and war material that remained to them, intending, thereby, to convey to the Mahdi a false picture of the situation
inside Khartoum. It may well be, however, that one or more of
such misleading statements did reach the hands of the British
ministers, and that it was from this source they gained an impression that things were not so bad as they had been led to believe.
Yet, be that as it may, the information in their possession pointed
so overwhelmingly to the urgent need for immediate action, bearing in mind the great distances to be covered and the abnormal
difficulties of the country to be overcome, that nothing can excuse
the Government of the day, under the leadership of Mr. Gladstone,
for their unbelievably casual attitude towards the grave position
into which they had thrust their heroic representative.

Not that there was any lack of prompting them to do their
very obvious duty; indeed, they were urged to awaken from their
lethargy in the Press, in the House of Commons, and, above all,
by Queen Victoria, herself, who was ever ready to take up the
cudgels on behalf of her soldiers when she considered they suffered
from undue interference or neglect on the part of her ministers.
"It is alarming," ran a telegram from Her Majesty to Lord
Hartington, Secretary of State for War. "General Gordon is in
danger; you are bound to try to save him . . . . . You have incurred
fearful responsibility."

In May, with the telegraph line cut and Khartoum more
isolated than ever through the fall of Berber, the ominous
silence enveloping the desperately situated city, on which the
eyes of the world were fixed in admiration, roused the spirit
of the British people, while the Government's inactivity inflamed
their passions. Mass meetings of protest were held in London and
Manchester. Subscriptions towards a relief fund were appealed
for in the newspapers. It was suggested that public prayers for
General Gordon should be offered in all the churches of the British
Isles. Even a vote of censure, moved in the House of Commons,
failed to stir the Government into action. In short, all classes and
grades of society had become seriously concerned about Khartoum
and its intrepid commander except the ministers of the Crown, who
continued complacently to ignore the entreaties, nay the demands,
of the British public.

In a telegram, presumably addressed to the British represent-
ative at Cairo, Gordon gave utterance to the bitterness in his heart
—"Is it right," he asked, "that I should have been sent to
Khartoum with only seven followers, after the destruction of Hicks'

army, and no attention paid to me till communications were cut?"

Soon, it became apparent that the Mahdi was content to sit down before Khartoum until starvation compelled its capitulation. He did not, however, remain inactive, his warriors replying vigorously to the fire from town and river craft, the accuracy of their shooting being demonstrated by the armour plating of two steamers which bore the marks of nearly a thousand bullets in each case. Moreover, from time to time, the enemy launched assaults on the defences, only to be pulled up short by the highly effective mine fields. Casualties suffered by the garrison, to the end of July, were estimated at thirty killed and between fifty and sixty wounded; while, during the same period, Gordon's riflemen fired as many as half a million rounds.

Fortunately, Khartoum could boast of a well stocked arsenal, where Gordon found ample supplies of munitions besides workshops and skilled craftsmen capable of maintaining the necessary provision of war material. But not so fortunate was the unreliability of a proportion of the population, whose sympathies were with the Mahdi and his widespread insurrection. Thus were Gordon's difficulties greatly increased, since to the task of defending Khartoum against the besieging tribesmen was added the responsibility for coping with spying and sabotage within his own lines.

Gordon tackled this difficult problem with his usual thoroughness, committing to prison several prominent citizens who were said to be in league with the Mahdi, and thus effectively restraining the disloyal activities of this section of the community. In his journal of October 21st, he wrote—"Today is New Year's Day of the Arabs, 1302 (Moharram).[1] I think the Mahdi speculated on a rising in the town, but that the arrests have put him out in his calculations."

On the other hand, until the end of October when the Mahdi arrived in person, the ranks of the garrison were swelled almost daily by the desertion of rebel tribesmen. Thereafter, however, so great was their awe of this once obscure native of Kordofan who now ruled over most of the Sudan's immense territory, this welcome flow of reinforcements to Gordon's command abruptly ceased; while, through fear of the Mahdi, combined with disappointment at the Government's failure to relieve the city, soldiers of the garrison began to go over to the rebels.

So as to give the reader some idea of the Khartoum defences and Gordon's dispositions, a brief description of the situation as

---

[1] The first month of the Mohammedan year.

it was after the ingenious sapper had completed his arrangements
will not, perhaps, be inappropriate at this stage. Khartoum's
position between the Blue and the White Nile, and close to the
point where the two rivers meet to form the Nile proper, rendered
the city unapproachable by land except from the south. Gordon's
plan, therefore, was to patrol the waterways with his armed steamers,
and to concentrate his main defence measures on the southern
side of the town, which extended almost across the tongue of land
between the converging rivers. A wall forming the city's southern
boundary had, originally, covered nearly the whole width of the
" tongue "; but, unfortunately, its western end had suffered from
inundations and been washed away. The gap, however, was
effectively closed by land mines. In front of this wall were, of
course, the earthworks, wire entanglements, and the three lines of
electrically connected mines.

In adddition to the river steamers, protection on the north-west
side was provided by the fort at Omdurman on the left bank of
the White Nile, and on the north-east side by a small fortification
known as North Fort on the right bank of the Blue Nile. The fort
at Omdurman was held by two hundred and forty specially selected
men under Ferratch Pasha, an excellent black officer promoted by
Gordon and appointed to the command of this key position.

At both ends of the southern wall, heavy barges, on which guns
were mounted, afforded additional protection. Gordon thought
of everything. Nothing was left to chance. Spending much of his
time on the palace roof, whence, by the aid of a telescope, he could
survey the defences, he was always at the helm. Day and night,
with little respite for sleep, this great leader of a forlorn hope kept
a watchful eye on the fluctuations of the siege. Through his
thoughtfully provided system of telegraphic communication, he
was able to keep himself informed of every occurrence, and, at all
times, held his finger firmly on the pulse of the situation. Never,
perhaps, has the gift of self-reliance been more fortunately possessed,
for, as in China, as in the Equatorial Provinces, as in his campaign
against the slave trade, Gordon had to think of everything himself.
Unlike the orthodox commander in the field, he was not surrounded
by a staff of officers to relieve him from much of the toil of mind
and body. Through the worst part of the siege he stood alone,
the only other white man in Khartoum being a foreign diplomat.
Consequently, it fell to his lot, not only to think of everything that
required to be done, but also to perform many tasks that, in the

absence of reliable subordinates, he felt it his duty to undertake. Nothing was too much trouble, nothing was beneath his notice.

Months later, when told of the final tragedy at Khartoum and the death of its commander, one who had been in the city during the siege and had succeeded in escaping to safety, burst into tears, testifying to the esteem and affection of the people for their great leader. He took pains to ensure the fair and proper distribution of food according to the resources in hand; as a substitute for money he introduced notes bearing his seal and signature. He succoured the poor, helped the needy, visited the sick, inspiring everyone by his shining example with encouragement and hope. The people of the hard-pressed city worshipped him as their defender and protector, whose mighty power held in check the ruthless hordes that threatened to overwhelm them.

Telegraphing to the Khedive, the inhabitants of Khartoum revealed their veneration of Gordon in these words—" Weakened and reduced to extremities, God in His mercy sent Gordon Pasha to us in the midst of our calamities of the siege, and we should all have perished of hunger and been destroyed. But we, sustained by his intelligence and great military skill, have been preserved in Khartoum until now."

Yet, the authorities in Cairo and London were asking why Gordon did not make good his escape. That would have been—to repeat his own words telegraphed to Sir Evelyn Baring—" the climax of meanness." Needless to say, Baring took the opposite view, professing to look upon it as Gordon's duty to leave the city and its inhabitants to their fate. Left to their own devices, what chances would the garrison have had of resisting the Mahdi without the driving power, without the invigorating, inspiring presence of their revered commander. Furthermore, would not Gordon's departure have had an inspiriting effect on the Mahdists, enduing them with renewed energy and encouraging them to greater efforts to gain possession of Khartoum?

Like his masters, sitting complacently in Whitehall, Baring wished to avoid the expense of a relief expedition, feeling that, once Gordon had left the city, no further action by the British Government would be necessary, since the people of Khartoum would merely be " taken prisoner by the Mahdi." If Sir Evelyn honestly believed that no more than this would follow the fall of the capital, he must indeed have been afflicted by an abnormally short memory, for had not the fall of Berber at the end of May been attended by a ruthless massacre of the inhabitants, and was

THE WATERFRONT OF KHARTOUM
AS IT WAS IN THE TIME OF
GENERAL GORDON

(Reproduced by permission of the Sudan Government Agency in London)

there any reason to suppose that the Mahdi's fanatical, blood-thirsty tribesmen would be any less savage in dealing with the people of Khartoum? If he really thought that the Mahdi would burden himself with forty thousand prisoners and show them the compassionate treatment normally accorded to prisoners in civilised warfare, he could hardly have appreciated the situation as a whole, or have gained a very clear notion of the utterly inhuman methods habitually adopted by the rebel leader. Yet, he it was under whose instructions Gordon had been told to place himself.

Gordon, of course, knew full well what would happen if he were to accede to pressure and attempt to make his way out of Khartoum. And, in any event, how could he abandon the people who looked upon him as their saviour? What could be more despicable than to let them down in the hour of their greatest need? Nothing would induce him to go, neither the pleadings of Baring, nor directions from home. In his isolated position, he rightly considered himself free to act in accordance with the exceptional circumstances that only he could appreciate, and surely it was nothing short of presumption for anyone in the outside world to venture an opinion as to what the resolute defender of Khartoum should, or should not, do. He alone was capable of sound judgment, since he alone possessed the requisite knowledge.

Before river transport had become no longer possible except by running the gauntlet of the rebels, he had sent out of Khartoum as many as two thousand six hundred refugees; whereas during the same period, the garrison had been reinforced by precisely *seven* men.[1] After Gordon's death, his sister received a letter from the officer who took over the refugees at Assouan and Korosko, telling her of their boundless admiration for the great man who had miraculously delivered them from their perilous position. " I may mention," wrote Colonel Duncan, " that I saw and spoke to every one of the refugees who came down, and to many of the women and children. Their references to your brother were invariably couched in language of affection and gratitude, and the adjective most frequently applied to him was 'just.' . . . It was touching to see the perfect confidence they had that the promises of Gordon Pasha would be fulfilled."

The long siege dragged on from day to day, week to week, month to month, the reserve of food, carefully husbanded though it was, becoming reduced to dangerously low levels. Meanwhile,

---

[1] Gordon's staff.

the authorities at home were engaged in a prolonged argument as to the best method of effecting Gordon's relief. Their failure to appreciate the extreme urgency of the situation seems almost incredible, for, quite apart from their personal obligation to the man who had so readily undertaken a task that ought never to have been asked of him, they should have realised that the fall of Khartoum would be followed by a reign of terror throughout the Sudan, that this must be prevented at all costs, and that not a moment was to be lost in making the necessary arrangements. Yet, not before August did they finally decide on a plan that Lord Wolseley had recommended as early as April and, from time to time, had continued to advocate.

The unconscionable delay in arriving at this decision to send an expeditionary force to Khartoum was succeeded by an equally exasperating dilatoriness both in the preparation and the dispatch of the force. It was hardly surprising, therefore, that Gordon began to wonder whether he and the ill-fated city, with its thousands of unfortunate inhabitants, had been forgotten by the rest of the world. How often each day, standing on the flat roof of his palace, did he direct his telescope to the north and gaze across the countless miles of parched desert, hoping to see the tell-tale dust clouds heralding the approach of long overdue relief? But the relievers had not yet started on their long, arduous journey over immense distances of arid land and treacherous water, and each time the lonely watcher, fully alive to the fact that only the utmost haste could save the rapidly deteriorating situation, turned away, without a morsel of comfort for the half-starved populace, to continue with unabated energy the great work to which he had set his hand.

Long since had he abandoned all thought of evacuating the garrisons and establishing some form of settled government, for the fall of Berber, resulting in Khartoum's complete isolation, conclusively prohibited the carrying out of such measures, if, indeed, the possibility had ever existed. Now, it had become a matter of fighting for their lives against an implacable enemy of great numerical superiority who hemmed them in on every side, and of trusting to the arrival of a relief force before they had exhausted their supplies of food.

At the end of July, in a message that reached London two months later, Gordon wrote these significant words—" In four months (that is end of November) river begins to fall; before that time you *must* settle the Sudan question." Some idea of the inexcusable delay in sending help to Khartoum may be gathered from the plain, unvarnished truth that, although the city's state began to be really serious in May, no decision had been reached by the British Government until August; the commander of the relief expedition, Lord Wolseley, did not arrive in Egypt before September; while only in the middle of November were preparations complete for moving up the Nile from Dongola. Not until then was the full significance of the delay revealed, for when, at long last, all had been made ready for a start, the river had fallen to such an extent that the task of negotiating the rapids presented a most difficult, if not impossible, problem. Here lay the crux of the whole unhappy business, because, if the preliminary arrangements had been less deliberate, and had been attended by a proper appreciation of the paramount need for haste, all would have been ready before the fall of the river introduced this fatal obstacle to the advance of Lord Wolseley's expedition. And, as if this calamity were not enough, it synchronised with the arrival of a message from Gordon telling of Khartoum's critical condition and the urgent need of early relief.

What was to be done? Gordon's old friend of the Crimea, at the head of a picked force of ten thousand men, found himself faced with a situation of the utmost gravity. Lord Wolseley had taken infinite pains in organising the expedition, and, like the fine soldier he was, had been determined to leave nothing to chance. Still, in his conscientious desire to allow for every conceivable eventuality, he appears to have overlooked the all important necessity for speed if he were to succeed in achieving the object of the operations, and, moreover, to have failed to take into account the rise and fall of the Nile. Had Gordon been aware of Wolseley's timetable, he could have told him at once that he might just as well stay at home for all the help his expedition would be to Khartoum. Leaving Cairo on September 27th, Wolseley planned to reach Wadi Halfa on October 8th, Dongola on November 14th, Korti on December 30th, Metemmeh in February, and Khartoum on March 3rd. But the situation had already become desperate before the troops of the expedition assembled at Dongola in the middle of November, when Gordon's message telling of Khartoum's plight came into the hands of Lord Wolseley. And only then did the Commander-in-Chief appear to recognise the extreme urgency of the matter, and that not a day, not an hour, must be wasted if Khartoum were to be saved.

Finding the river route impracticable, Wolseley decided to cross the Bayuda desert from Korti to Metemmeh, where, according to Gordon's information, five steamers, with nine guns, were awaiting his arrival. But, since no provision had been made for an overland advance, a further lamentable delay occurred, several valuable weeks being occupied in procuring camels, training them for the work, and accustoming the men to these strange beasts.

Let us now return to the events in and around Khartoum as the siege progressed and the condition of the beleaguered people grew more and more grievous. Early in September, Gordon determined to take advantage of the river being at its height and to send down one of his steamers with the object of conveying full information on the situation to the authorities. For this purpose, he chose the *Abbas*, a small paddle-boat of light draught which seemed the most likely of his flotilla to overcome the difficulties of the journey to Dongola, in particular the numerous cataracts of Dar Monassir. The *Abbas* was to be escorted by other steamers until clear of the Mahdi's tribesmen, when the escorting craft were to assemble at Metemmeh, there to await arrival of the British expeditionary force. The escorting steamers were those mentioned by Gordon in his message received by Lord Wolseley at Dongola.

Since the beginning of the seige, there had been in Khartoum no more than five Europeans including Gordon himself, the other four being Colonel Stewart; Mr. Power, the *Times* correspondent and acting British Consul; M. Herbin, the French Consul; and Mr. Hensall, the Austrian Consul. On the day before the steamers were due to start, Herbin, Stewart, and Power, each in turn, asked Gordon for permission to go down in the *Abbas*. In all three cases, willing consent was given, despite the fact that this would leave the Governor-General with but a solitary European to face the most critical part of the siege. Here are Gordon's own words bearing on the departure of the *Abbas*, as recorded in his diary:—
"I determined to send the *Abbas* down with an Arab captain. Herbin asked to be allowed to go. I jumped at his offer. Then Stewart said he would go if I would exonerate him from deserting me. I said, 'You do not desert me. I cannot go, but if you go you do great service.' I then wrote him an official; he wanted me to write him an order. I said, 'No; for though I fear not responsibility, I will not put you in any danger in which I am not myself.' I wrote them a letter couched thus:—'*Abbas* is going down; you say you are willing to go in her if I think you can do so in honour. You can go in honour, for you can do nothing here; and if you go you do me service in telegraphing my views?'"

It did not, of course, need three people to convey his views, and there can be no shadow of doubt that Gordon, with his innate kindliness, was anxious to give them this chance of saving their lives, and at the same time, for their peace of mind, wished to make it appear that by going they were doing him a service. This was in keeping with his generous, unselfish nature. He must have known that each of them, especially Colonel Stewart, would have been helpful in relieving him from some of the innumerable duties that would fall to his lot after their departure. Yet, he assured them—"you can do nothing here." Only the Austrian Consul steadfastly refused to leave what he considered to be his place of duty, insisting on standing by Gordon to the end.

It was on September 10th that the *Abbas* and her escort moved off down the river with a number of troops and nine guns, the whole flotilla being under the command of Colonel Stewart. Five days later, Gordon received the cheering information through a spy that the steamers had safely passed Shendy, some two hundred and fifty miles down stream. But this was the last he heard of the unhappy venture till, in November, his hopes were dashed to the ground by news of disaster overtaking the *Abbas*. It would appear that, after bombarding the rebel positions at Berber, the flotilla continued on its way until clear of the hostile tribesmen, when, in accordance with Gordon's orders, the escorting steamers turned back towards Metemmeh, leaving the *Abbas*, now to all appearances out of danger, to pursue her journey to Dongola.

As bad luck would have it, however, she struck a rock and had to be abandoned at a place called Dar Jumna, where Colonel Stewart decided to procure camels and make their way across the desert. Meanwhile, he and his companions were offered hospitality by a local sheikh. Now Gordon, with his usual punctilious regard for detail, had issued specific directions for the security of the expedition, such as—"Do not anchor near the bank—do not collect wood at isolated spots—trust nobody." Had these instructions been implicitly obeyed, disaster might have been avoided. But as it was, failure to pay strict attention to Gordon's words of wisdom cost the lives of everyone who landed from the stranded steamer, for, no sooner had the Europeans accepted the sheikh's offer and been shown into his hut than they were treacherously attacked and done to death, the luckless natives from the *Abbas* suffering similar treatment. The malevolent sheikh was, of course, a supporter of the Mahdi, to whom he promptly dispatched the whole of the documents taken from his victims, laying bare the full facts of Khartoum's desperate state.

When, in October, rumours of the disaster suffered by Colonel Stewart and his party reached Gordon's ears, he was inclined to doubt their truth, for had he not made every provision for their safety? But soon, indisputable confirmation came to him from the Mahdi, himself, who was able to quote from the diaries and other papers seized at Dar Jumna and now in his possession.

" In the name of God the merciful and compassionate," ran the Mahdi's letter to General Gordon, " praise be to God, the bountiful Ruler, and blessing on our Lord Mahomed with peace.

" From the servant who trusts in God—Mahomed the son of Abdallah.

" To Gordon Pasha of Khartoum: may God guide him into the path of virtue, amen!

" Know that your small steamer, named *Abbas*—which you sent with the intention of forwarding your news to Cairo, by the way of Dongola, the persons sent being your representative Stewart Pasha and the two Consuls, French and English, with other persons, has been captured by the will of God.

" Those who believed in us as the Mahdi, and surrendered, have been delivered; and those who did not were destroyed—as your representative afore-named, with the Consuls and the rest—whose souls God has condemned to the fire and to eternal misery.

" That steamer and all that was in it have fallen a prey to the Moslems, and we have taken knowledge of all the letters and telegrams which were in it, and of the maps, which were opened to us (translated) by those on whom God has bestowed His gifts, and has enlightened their hearts with faith, and the benefits of willing submission. . . . All has been seized, and the contents are known. . . . We prefer to send you part of the contents and mention the property therein, so that you may be certified; and in order that the truth may make a lasting impression on thy mind— in the hope that God may guide thee to the faith of Islam, and to surrender; that you and your followers may surrender to Him and to us, that so you and they may obtain everlasting good and happiness."

There follows a long catalogue of the documents claimed by the writer to have fallen into his hands.

" We never miss any of your news," the letter continues, " nor what is in your innermost thoughts, and about the strength and support—not of God—on which you rely. We have now understood it all.

" Tricks in making cyphers, and using so many languages, are of no avail. . . .

"As to your expecting reinforcements, reliance for succour on others than God, that will bring you nothing but destruction, and (cause you to) fall into utmost danger in this world and the next. . . . No doubt you have heard what has happened to your brethren, from whom you expected help, at Suakin and elsewhere, whom God has destroyed, and dispersed and abandoned.

" Notwithstanding all this, as we have now arrived at Mushra el Koweh, at a day's journey from Omdurman, and are coming, please God, to your place, if you return to the Most High God, and become a Moslem, and surrender to His order and that of His Prophet, and believe in us as the Mahdi, send us a message from thee, and from those with thee, after laying down your arms and giving up the thought of fighting, so that I may send you one with safe conduct, by which you will obtain (assurance of) benefit of the blessing in this world and the next. Otherwise, and if you do not act thus, you will have to encounter war from God and His Prophet. And know that the Most High God is mighty (able) for thy destruction, as He has destroyed (others) before thee, who were much stronger than thou, and more numerous.

"And you, and your children and your property, will be for a prey to the Moslems, and you will repent when repentance will not avail. For, after the beginning of the battle were you to surrender, it would be from fear, and not willingly, and that will not be accepted."

After a postscript in which the Mahdi claimed to have brought under his subjection the provinces of the Bahr el Ghazal and the Equator, the letter ended with a large seal inscribed—

" There is no God but Allah.
" Mahomed is the prophet of Allah.
" Mahomed the Mahdi Abd-Allah."

This was indeed a bitter blow, both on account of the losses sustained and because of the documents, which would have impressed Lord Wolseley with the precarious state of affairs, falling into the hands of the Mahdi. As in the case of all eventualities, however, Gordon accepted this calamitous news as the will of God, his faith unshaken by misfortune. " It is very sad," he wrote, " but being ordained, we must not murmur."

Still, he seems to have suffered some heart searchings as to whether he should blame himself for the catastrophe. " If *Abbas* was captured by treachery," he wrote, " then I am not to blame; neither am I to blame if she struck a rock, for she drew under two feet of water; if they were attacked and overpowered, then I am to blame, for I ought to have foreseen the chance and prevented their going." But he believed neglect of proper precautions to have been the cause of the disaster. " I feel somehow convinced," he continued, " they were captured by treachery. Stewart was not a bit suspicious (I am made up of it). I can see, in imagination, the whole scene, the sheikh inviting them to land, then a rush of wild Arabs, and all is over! "

From no standpoint could Gordon be held blameworthy for the *Abbas* tragedy. His decision to send the flotilla down river had been actuated by two urgent necessities, namely (a) the conveyance of information to the outside world of Khartoum's predicament; and (b) the provision of armed transport to assist the British relief expedition. He had made the most carefully considered arrangements and issued the clearest possible orders to safeguard the steamers. In disregard of those orders, so it would seem, Colonel Stewart and his followers had walked into a trap from which there was no escape. All three Europeans had gone of their own accord, leaving Gordon entirely free from reproach.

In sending away these armed river craft, Gordon's action must surely fill the student of history with nothing but admiration, for was he not denuding himself of their valuable support at Khartoum in order to render all possible help to the relievers who, he hoped, would soon be approaching? But, far from being close at hand, it was not until September 10th—the very day Gordon's steamers left Khartoum—that the first transport of the expeditionary force sailed for Egypt, and, as we have seen, another two months were to go by before the troops reached Dongola.

And now, poor Gordon was left more utterly alone than ever, his shoulders being required to bear an even greater burden than before, since he no longer had a second-in-command to help him, and, apart from the Austrian Consul, he remained the only white man in Khartoum, a solitary figure on the palace roof, pensively pacing to and fro and, from time to time, taking up his telescope to search the distant horizon for anxiously awaited signs of help drawing near. When not engaged in any of his multifarious duties in connection with the defence of the city and the welfare of the inhabitants, he would write prolifically in his journals, laying bare

is innermost thoughts. " What a contradiction is life! " he wrote.
" I hate Her Majesty's Government for their leaving the Sudan
fter having caused all its troubles; yet I believe our Lord rules
eaven and earth, so I ought to hate Him, which I sincerely do not."

The measure of his solitude and complete isolation can be
ssessed from his having recourse to making friends with a mouse,
vhich Gordon believed to be a lady " judging from her swelled out
ppearance," and which he permitted to feed from his plate. Never-
heless, he infinitely preferred a lonely existence in primitive sur-
oundings to the conventionalities of civilisation. " I dwell," he
vrote, " on the joy of never seeing Great Britain again, with its
orrid, wearisome *dinner* parties and miseries. How we can put
p with those things passes my imagination! It is a perfect bond-
ge. I would sooner live like a Dervish with the Mahdi than go
ut to dinner every night in London. I hope, if any English
5eneral comes to Khartoum, he will not ask me to dinner. Why
nen cannot be friends without bringing the wretched stomachs in,
s astounding."

In recording his condemnation of the British Government's
amentable attitude towards the Sudan question, Gordon singled
ut Lord Granville, the Foreign Secretary, for special castigation,
epresenting him as " lounging away his morning at Walmer Castle,
pening the *Times* and suddenly discovering, to his horror, that
Khartoum was still holding out." His references to the powers
bove him were, however, characterised more by ridicule than
itterness. He wrote humorously, for instance, of Gladstone's
nania for wood-chopping and the peculiar shape of his collars. Sir
Evelyn Baring was caricatured in the margin uttering words of
" shocked pomposity"; while officials and diplomats generally
eaped their quota of his not unnatural displeasure. He described
nimself as the " victim of hypocrites and humbugs," and likened his
osition to that of Uriah the Hittite. But, although he had
een given an impossible job, having undertaken the task he was
irmly resolved to see it through, come what might, and was deaf to
ll entreaties that he should make good his escape. " I declare
ositively," he wrote with no little indignation, " and *once for all,
hat I will not leave the Sudan until every one who wants to go
own is given the chance to do so, unless* a government is estab-
ished which relieves me of the charge; therefore if any emissary
r letter comes up here ordering me to come down, *I will not obey
t, but will stay here, and fall with town, and run all risks.*" Those
vere the words of the real Gordon who, like Nelson, was prepared

to turn the blind eye to an order that he conscientiously believed to be wrong.

" I must say I hate our diplomatists," he wrote in his journal. " I think with few exceptions they are arrant humbugs, and I expect they know it."

—*From a sketch by General Gordon.*

Sir Evelyn Baring and Mr. Egerton (another Foreign Office official), who are obviously portrayed in the sketch reproduced above, came in for much of Gordon's criticism in his journal.

Of the British Government, he recorded—" Her Majesty's Government refused to help Egypt with respect to the Sudan, refused to let Egypt help herself, and refused to allow any other power to help her: this cannot be disputed or explained away. . . . This tardy succour under pressure and Baring's despatch, establishes the unwillingness to help. . . ."

" . . . It is all very well to say you ought to consider the difficulties of the Government, but it is not easy to get over a feeling that a hope existed of no expedition being necessary, owing to our having fallen. As for myself, personally I feel no particular rancour on the subject, but I own I do not care to show I like men, whoever they may be, who act in such a calculating way, and I do not think one is bound to act the hypocrite's part and pretend to be friendly towards them. . . . I know of no sort of parallel to all this in history, except it be David with Uriah the Hittite. . . . What I judge is the indecision of Government. . . . I own to have been very insubordinate to Her Majesty's Government and its officials, but it is my nature, and I cannot help it. . . . Because I criticise Baring, Egerton, and the Foreign Office, it is not that I think I am superior, but because I would like them to see how others, outside themselves, view things."

These journals, in which, so it seems, he jotted down his thoughts as and when they entered his head without fear or favour, were sent out from time to time, as opportunity offered, until an ominous silence clamped down upon the ill-starred city. As he sat recording his thoughts to the accompaniment of the crackle of musketry and the crashing explosions of gun-fire, he is to be pic-tured plainly dressed, the only mark of his position as Governor-General of the Sudan being the red *fez* or *tarbush*. His uniform and other possessions, including the money collected by Lord Wolseley, had been lost at Berber *en route* from Cairo to Khartoum. The journals revealed a situation to stir the heart of the least emotional, presenting a picture of this righteous man, standing like a rock in the midst of strife and turmoil, spreading the encouraging influence of his calm, impassive demeanour among those around him, who looked up to him and worshipped him as their staunch protector—a picture of the great crusader, bearing a weight of responsibility, anxiety, and worry that few men, if any, could have sustained for half as long, making light of a desperate situa-tion, and cheerfully, often jocularly, going about his diverse duties as though no cause for alarm existed. No more magnificent example could have been set by a commander in a tight corner, for he was here, there, and everywhere, directing and encouraging his troops, who, from a more or less worthless rabble, had been converted into reasonably efficient soldiers by Gordon's superhuman energy and perseverance; while his fatherly interest in, and personal attention to, the civilian population, served to bolster up their morale and, save for a proportion of intriguers and pro-Mahdists, to ensure their loyalty to himself.

We learn how he would turn for a moment from his endless activities to watch with interest the impressive spectacle of a turkey cock " every feather on end and all the colours of the rainbow on his neck " parading the palace yard; how he would derive intense amusement from the obvious surprise of his Sudanese soldiers on suddenly catching sight of their " black pug-faces " reflected in the palace looking-glasses. Such brief interludes, insignificant in them-selves, acted, no doubt, as a safety-valve on the constant pressure and strain of Gordon's daily life.

Alluding, in these diaries, to a typical red tape demand from a far off official for information as to " exactly when he expects to be in difficulties " about provisions, Gordon wrote—" If he (the official) will only turn to the archives—a delicious word—of his office, he will see we have been in difficulties for provisions for some months. It is as if a man on the bank, having seen his friend in a river already bobbed down two or three times, hails, ' I say, old fellow, let us know when we are to throw you the life buoy. I know you have bobbed down two or three times, but it is a pity to throw you the life-buoy until you are *in extremis,* and I want to know exactly.' " He, however, added these words of self-criticism:— " Blessed is the man who does not sit in the seat of the scornful. I own it is not right to scoff at one's superiors, but I do not do it in malice, and I hope those who are remarked upon will not be offended."

The most modest of men, he, nevertheless, could not record in his journals the day to day happenings of the siege without revealing, all unwittingly of course, a picture of unique heroism that thrilled the world of that era, and will remain for all time a source of wonder and admiration. But at last, unhappily, the absorbing pages written by the lonely occupant of Khartoum's palace ceased to flow out from the surrounded city, complete and utter isolation descending upon it with enveloping implacability.

CHAPTER XIX

The Desert Column

THOUGH all concerned with the deplorable delay in sending relief to Khartoum must share responsibility for the
disaster that followed, no one was more culpable than the
great Liberal leader and Prime Minister of the day, Mr.
Gladstone. For he it was who, week after week, month after month,
obstinately refused to listen to the voice of public clamour or to
advice from any quarter whatsoever. Supported, presumably, by
his Cabinet, he firmly declined to budge an inch in spite of intense
feeling throughout the country, turning a deaf ear alike to entreaties, demands, and threats. Nothing could move him to do
what the vast majority of the British people, nay the people of the
whole civilised world, believed to be right. And why? Why did
this great statesman flatly refuse to send aid to his gallant envoy,
cut off from the world and surrounded by a host of savage fanatics?
He can have been in no doubt as to the seriousness of the situation,
and, in any case, the widespread public outcry must have indicated
the urgent need for action. But Gladstone was, above all else, a
politician. A relief expedition would involve the Liberal Government in heavy expenditure, and heavy expenditure might cost the
Liberal party valuable votes—the first and foremost consideration
of most politicians. And so, the first minister of the Crown held
out against world-wide opinion until his faithful, heroic servant,
far away in the besieged city, began to wonder, not without justification, whether he had not been utterly forgotten.

In a speech by Lord Lytton[1] bearing on the situation at Khartoum, these words of irony were uttered—"Ask General Gordon, if
he ever comes safely home to us, what he and his still unrescued

---

[1] First Earl of Lytton, Viceroy of India, 1876-1880.

garrison have learned to think of the high sense of national honour, the chivalrous courage, the unflinching good faith of Mr. Gladstone and his Radical Cabinet." This stirred Lord Lytton's audience to give three cheers for Gordon.

Why, then, did Gladstone eventually give in and, at the eleventh hour, consent to dispatch an expedition? Again, it was political expediency that influenced his decision. Threatened with the resignation of a member of his Cabinet unless he agreed to send help to Khartoum, the wily old man knew full well that refusal would be followed by the downfall of his Government, and, being driven into a corner, decided to abandon his uncompromising attitude as the only course open to him if he were to remain in office. How unfortunate that the minister concerned, Lord Hartington, Secretary of State for War, could not have persuaded himself of the necessity for this noble gesture some weeks earlier. And what must have been his feelings when the belated expedition reached its objective only forty-eight hours too late? Lord Hartington had been largely instrumental in assigning the Sudan mission to General Gordon, and, since the fall of Berber, bringing about Khartoum's complete investment, he had been conscience stricken and embarrassed by the Government's indecision. But, although as early as March 25th he had been urged by Queen Victoria "to try to save" Gordon, it was not until the end of July that he roused himself to the pitch of presenting an ultimatum to his Chief. "A question of personal honour and good faith," he said, "and I don't see how I can yield upon it."

We are told that Lord Hartington was "slow in movement, slow in apprehension, slow in thought and the communication of thought, slow to decide, and slow to act." Hardly a suitable character, one would have thought, for a War Minister. He had, it is true, though without success, tried to persuade the Cabinet to agree to an expedition, and, before confronting Gladstone with his final word, had repeatedly implored him to reconsider his attitude. Yet, the tragedy is to be found in just that sluggishness of thought, decision, and action of which we are told. When days, if not hours, were of importance, he allowed weeks, and even months, to go by whilst literally nothing was done to alleviate the growing tension at Khartoum. Nevertheless, deliberate as he was, Lord Hartington must be given credit for standing out from among his colleagues of the Government, and being the sole member of it to adopt a course of action independent of the calls of party politics. It must have taken no little courage to defy his formidable superior. But, since he was able to accomplish it in the end, how calamitous that he took so long about it.

Once Mr. Gladstone's prejudices had been overcome, an expedition of ten thousand men was sanctioned, Lord Wolseley was appointed to command it, and the required sum of money for its cost voted in Parliament.

Now, we have seen that, although the relief force was sanctioned in August, the middle of November had been reached before the specially selected troops were concentrated at Dongola in readiness to start by the river route. It has also been recorded that, owing to the fall of the river, Lord Wolseley decided to send part of his force across the Bayuda desert from Korti to Metemmeh, where they would be within a hundred miles of Khartoum, and where Gordon's steamers were waiting. But, owing to the time occupied in procuring camels and in training both them and their guides, another month elapsed before troops of the Desert Column began to arrive at Korti from Dongola, and not until December 30th did the march across the desert begin.

The expeditionary force comprised one cavalry regiment (the 19th Hussars), nine battalions of infantry, four camel corps, a naval brigade of bluejackets and marines, a battery of Royal Artillery, and two camel batteries. These were the troops at the disposal of Lord Wolseley, whose orders from the Secretary of State were couched in the following terms:—

" The primary object of your expedition is to bring away General Gordon and Colonel Stewart,[1] and you are not to advance further south than necessary to attain that object, and when it has been secured, no further offensive operations of any kind are to be undertaken."

Rather more than two thousand men took part in the historic march from Korti to Metemmeh, a distance of one hundred and seventy-six miles, water in any great quantity being available only at Jakdul, a little over half way across the Bayuda desert, and Abu Klea, fifty-three miles further on. Lord Wolseley appointed Major General Sir Herbert Stewart to command the Desert Column on this desperate attempt to reach Khartoum before disaster could overtake the city and its dogged defender.

On December 30th, Stewart advanced into the desert with about eleven hundred men and two thousand two hundred camels, his

---

[1] Colonel Stewart's departure from Khartoum was then unknown to the Government.

orders being to establish a post at Jakdul, and, should the supply of water prove inadequate, to use his own discretion as to the desirability of pushing on to Metemmeh. Otherwise, he was to leave part of his force at the wells and return to Korti to collect the rest of his column. Bearing in mind the extreme urgency of the situation, these methods must seem cumbersome and wasteful of the precious time that yet remained in which to accomplish the purpose of the expedition. But an unfortunate shortage of camels precluded the possibility of transporting all the stores required for establishing a depôt at Jakdul in one journey. Consequently, the luckless beasts had to do the ninety-odd miles three times over, involving a delay of about ten days—a delay that enabled the Mahdi to take Khartoum and cost General Gordon his life.

Sir Herbert Stewart's first march to Jakdul was accomplished without opposition, only a few Dervishes being seen in the far distance. These few, however, sufficed to acquaint the Mahdi with what was happening, the halt at Jakdul to await the arrival of the main body giving him ample time to intercept the column. In his conduct of operations in the field, the great " Stonewall " Jackson adhered closely to three main principles, one of which was to pre-serve the utmost secrecy in order to spring a surprise on his oppon-ent, believing the advantages accruing from surprise to be well worth the difficulties inseparable from bringing it about. Now Stewart's first advance to Jakdul was in the nature of a surprise, and had his orders enabled him to push on to Metemmeh instead of turning back to Korti, those ten vital days would have been saved, and, by the time information of the British advance reached the Mahdi, it might well have been too late for him to intercept and delay the column.

But, on his first arrival at Jakdul, on January 2nd, Stewart found plenty of water in the wells, and, although fully conscious of the need for haste, he felt bound by his orders to return to Korti for the remainder of his force. Finally, on January 8th, he again set out for Jakdul, this time at the head of over sixteen hundred men. The only horsemen with the Desert Column were one hundred and thirty-five officers and men of the 19th Hussars under Colonel Percy Barrow,[1] a distinguished soldier who had only recently recovered from a very severe spear wound received during the battle of El Teb. English horses being considered unsuitable for hard

---

[1] A year later, when tent-pegging at Cairo, Colonel Barrow re-opened the wound, his death following after thirty hours of acute suffering.

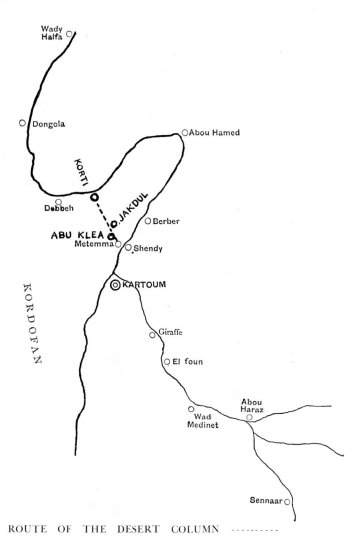

ROUTE OF THE DESERT COLUMN ----------

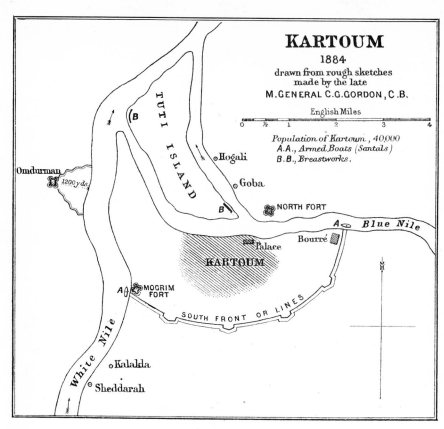

KARTOUM
1884
drawn from rough sketches
made by the late
M.GENERAL C.G.GORDON, C.B.

English Miles

0   ½   1   2   3   4

Population of Kartoum, 40,000
A.A., Armed Boats (Santals)
B.B., Breastworks.

TUTI ISLAND

(B)

Hogali

Goba

Omdurman
1200 yds.

B

NORTH FORT

A   Blue Nile

Palace   Bourré

KARTOUM

A   MOGRIM
FORT

White Nile

SOUTH FRONT OR LINES

Kalakla

Sheddarah

KHARTOUM DEFENSES IN 1884
FROM SKETCHES MADE BY
GENERAL GORDON

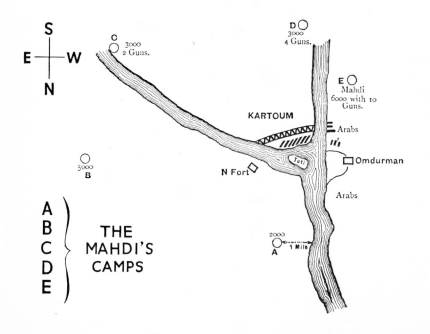

S
E   +   W
N

C 3000
   2 Guns.

D 3000
   4 Guns.

E Mahdi
   6000 with 10
   Guns.

KARTOUM

Arabs

5000
B

Tuti

Omdurman

N Fort

Arabs

A }
B }   THE
C }   MAHDI'S
D }   CAMPS
E }

2000
A   1 Mile

work in the trying climate, the regiment was mounted on wiry little Syrian Arabs as used by the Egyptian cavalry.

On the 14th, leaving a small garrison at Jakdul, the column continued its march towards the Nile.   Two days later, when approaching the wells of Abu Klea, the 19th Hussars, who were far in advance of the main body, came upon a number of hostile tribesmen, a patrol under Major French (afterwards Field Marshal the Earl of Ypres)[1] putting them to flight and driving them back into a gorge.   Soon afterwards, owing to the reappearance of Arab horsemen on both flanks of the hussars, Colonel Barrow dismounted his men and, with carbine fire, kept the enemy at a respectful distance until the arrival of the column, when a *zariba* was formed for the night some three and a half miles from the wells.   There could be no doubt that the Mahdi had already been informed of the British advance, since large numbers of his followers appeared in the distance as the camp was being formed and opened a desultory fire at extreme range, causing a few casualties.   Sniping into the camp continued throughout the night, but, apart from interference with the men's rest and several horses being hit, no serious damage resulted.

With the coming of daylight, however, the enemy's fire became heavier, a number of casualties being suffered.   Then, at nine o'clock, as the column was being formed in square for a resumption of the march, some five hundred of the enemy, mounted and on foot, began to threaten the rear face.   Whereupon, the 19th were ordered out to check the Arabs and enable the column to advance. Progress was inevitably slow owing to the heavily laden camels, carrying ammunition and water, necessitating frequent halts.   Moreover, the undulating nature of the ground demanded careful precautions against surprise.   It was, in fact, from one of these depressions in the desert that a dense mass of white-clothed Arabs, several thousand strong, suddenly arose and swooped down upon the small band of specially selected, highly trained British soldiers, moving slowly in square towards the wells of Abu Klea.

Aided by the unevenness of the ground and the screening of their attack by the retiring cavalry, the enemy rushed forward with tremendous vigour and fanatical fearlessness, the main assault by tribesmen on foot being supported by a charge of horsemen. On their return to the square, Barrow's hussars used their carbines to assist the infantry, and so devastating was the fire of the de-

---

[1]   Author's father.

fenders, who unloosed a veritable hail of shot and shell, that on three sides of the square not a solitary Arab succeeded in approaching within three hundred yards. On the fourth side, however, a great horde of howling savages, displaying complete indifference to the murderous fire poured into them, managed to get to close quarters, and, using their steel weapons with extraordinary dexterity, some of them actually forced their way into the square. There ensued a fierce hand-to-hand struggle, in which the tribesmen showed their deadly prowess in the use of sword and spear.

Though momentarily overwhelmed by weight of numbers, the well-disciplined British troops quickly recovered, and no more than five minutes had elapsed before every Mahdist who broke into the square had been either killed or driven out. By this time, the enemy's initial ardour becoming cooled by the steady, well-directed fire and by the heavy losses they had suffered, the whole mass retired, harassed by the 19th, who, however, were unable to raise a gallop, their horses, after thirty hours without water, being completely done up.

The battle of Abu Klea was short and sharp, British casualties amounting to seventy-four killed and ninety-four wounded, while the enemy left as many as eleven hundred dead around the square out of a total estimated at approximately nine thousand men. It was subsequently revealed that the Mahdi, on learning of the British advance, had sent a force of picked men into the Bayuda desert to frustrate the attempt to relieve Khartoum. Not until late that night did the column reach the wells, from which the Arabs had been dispersed by the ubiquitous cavalry.

Next day, January 18th, after constructing a fort for the defence of the wells and establishing a post for care of the wounded, the column, led by the 19th Hussars, moved off once more into the desert with twenty-five miles yet to be covered before reaching the Nile. Starting late in the afternoon and marching through the night, the gallant little force, on the success of whose mission so much depended, and for the fulfilment of whose task speed was essential, could progress but slowly in the darkness through the trackless wastes, with men and beasts scarcely able to keep going from exhaustion.

Invigorated at daybreak by the welcome sight of the river, not more than six miles away, the wearied soldiers pushed on, Sir Herbert Stewart being anxious to reach the much-needed water before meeting with further opposition. But this was not to be, for, as his troops pressed forward towards the Nile, large numbers of the enemy, conspicuous in their white *jibbehs,* suddenly appeared on the summit of a ridge, and began to advance on the British force.

As quickly as the exhausted condition of the men allowed, a *zariba* composed of brushwood, biscuit boxes, and every available means of obstruction was formed, the Arabs, meanwhile, firing on the position with increasing intensity. Quite early in the engagement, a grievous loss was sustained when Sir Herbert Stewart, a fine soldier, received a wound from the effects of which he soon died, and, before the *zariba* had been completed, many casualties were suffered from the enemy's fire, which, as the morning wore on, became heavy. Finally, the hussars being withdrawn into the *zariba,* a square was formed outside, and, at about two o'clock in the afternoon, under the command of Colonel Sir Charles Wilson, Stewart's successor as leader of the Desert Column, the advance was resumed.

Under a heavy fire from three sides men fell thick and fast, until, all at once, the firing ceased and, with tremendous impetus, an immense host of tribesmen rushed madly at the square. They found, however, the well-trained, severely disciplined British soldiers a very different proposition to their frequently defeated enemies, the Egyptians. Met by a steady fire poured into their massed ranks with relentless precision and accuracy, the Dervishes, despite their fanatical bravery, were soon held up by the deadly stream of bullets that mowed down their foremost warriors and tore great rents in their packed formation. Then, as though staggered by the impenetrable wall of fire and its devastating effect, they turned and fled, resounding cheers from the British square speeding their headlong flight. Not one of them had been able to get to close quarters, so overwhelmingly destructive was the fire of the British infantry.

The Mahdists did not renew their onslaught, leaving the column to continue its advance to the river, which was reached soon after nightfall. So ended the battle of Metemmeh, sometimes known as Abu Krou, the name of the village on the left bank of the Nile, close to which the column halted at the end of the desert march. In the course of this second fight within three days, the British force suffered the loss of nine officers and one hundred and twelve rank and file killed and wounded.

By the evening of January 20th, the whole of the Desert Column, including those left behind to defend the *zariba,* had assembled at Gubat, on the left bank of the river and some three miles to the south of Metemmeh. There they were joined next morning by Gordon's steamers, one of which, the *Bordeen*, sent down on December 14th, brought news of the critical state of affairs at Khartoum. More precious days were occupied in preparation for starting on the final effort to reach the besieged capital in time, but, at last, on the morning of January 24th, Sir Charles Wilson with two hundred men set off up the river in two steamers, the *Bordeen* and the *Talataween*, to cover the ninety-odd miles separating Gubat from Khartoum.

Meanwhile, the main body of the Desert Column remained at Gubat, until, in the middle of February, the whole force under Major General Sir Redvers Buller, V.C., was withdrawn to Korti.

As for the original River Column commanded by Major General Earle, this force was able to start only two days before Khartoum fell, and, as in the case of the Desert Column, it was ultimately recalled to its starting point.

CHAPTER XX

The Doomed City

IT was not until the end of October, 1884, that the Mahdi arrived in person before Khartoum and assumed command of the besiegers. His presence had an inspiriting effect on the tribesmen, who became galvanised into activities that hitherto they had been content to neglect. Now that they were under the eye of " God's messenger " they no longer dared to desert, and it behoved them to look alive in the performance of their duties lest the awful wrath of their despotic leader brought about unthinkable consequences.

No sooner had the Mahdi appeared than he began to tighten his grip on the doomed city—for doomed it assuredly was unless help arrived without delay. News of Lord Wolseley's advance had impressed the rebel commander with the need for haste in his operations for the taking of Khartoum, compelling him to abandon his original plan for starving the garrison into submission, and to prepare a determined assault on the defence works.

In an attack on November 8th, the enemy tried to overcome the difficulty of the minefields by driving cattle before them. But this cunning design was defeated by Gordon with the use of rockets which stampeded the animals, twenty of them falling into the hands of the defenders. Four days later, the garrison suffered two disasters, in the cutting of communications between Omdurman and Khartoum, and the grounding of the steamer *Hussinyeh* whilst engaged in helping to relieve the pressure on the key position at Omdurman. Only one steamer, the *Ismailia,* now remained at Gordon's disposal, and this he utilised almost exclusively in support of the defence of Fort Omdurman, which he calculated should have two hundred and fifty thousand rounds of ammunition, besides enough biscuit and water to last six weeks.

By mid-November, the Mahdi's tribesmen were disposed as shown on the accompanying map sketched by General Gordon.

Now, inasmuch as the hostility and activity of the Mahdi's legions, roused to a high pitch of excitement by the presence of their leader, grew daily more intense, so, proportionately, did Gordon's anxieties and the tremendous strain on him increase as time went on. His temper, never a very certain quantity, became more and more unreliable as the stress and tension of his daily life took inevitable toll of his strength both mental and physical. Yet, like many another whose anger is quick to rise, he would almost immediately repent of his outbursts and often try to make amends. For example, becoming exasperated with an offending clerk, Gordon boxed his ears, " and then, as my conscience pricked me," he wrote, " I gave him $5. He said he did not mind if I had killed him—I was his father."

That he, himself, was not unaware of the awe instilled in those around him by his stern, if eminently just, methods, may be gathered from his reported concern on noticing the ill-concealed alarm and quaking limbs of those brought before him. Ever since the execution of the two Pashas in the early days of the siege, Gordon had blamed himself for undue severity, describing their fate, in the light of mature consideration, as " judicial murder." So convinced did he become of the injustice of his decision that he decided to pay one thousand pounds to each of the families of the dead Pashas. Impetuosity was often the cause of this self-impeachment, his sensitive conscience urging him to atone for impulsive actions induced by his fiery temperament, and to compensate those who had suffered from his hasty outbursts.

It was the Mahdi, himself, who one day roused him to a paroxysm of rage. Obviously in total ignorance of the character of the man he addressed, the rebel leader ventured to send Gordon a letter, together with a mysterious bundle. " In the name of God! " he wrote, " herewith a suit of clothes, consisting of a coat (jibbeh), an overcoat, a turban, a cap, a girdle, and beads. This is the clothing of those who have given up this world and its vanities, and who look for the world to come, for everlasting happiness in Paradise. If you truly desire to come to God and seek to live a godly life, you must at once wear this suit, and come out to accept your everlasting good fortune."

Did the writer, who, incidentally, was no fool, really believe that so preposterous an artifice would be likely to succeed? Enraged at the insolence of the Mahdi's suggestion, Gordon flew into one of his ungovernable passions, and, seizing the offensive garments, trampled them under foot.

Another communication that reached him from the rebel lines came from the captured Slatin Pasha, who, ever since the fall of Dara in December, 1883, had been a prisoner in the Mahdi's camp. Thinking to secure more favourable terms for the people of Dara if he were to embrace the religion of Islam, he had resorted to this expedient before surrendering the town. On this account his life had been spared. But he could expect no sympathy from the devout Gordon, who was so disgusted at Slatin's renunciation of his faith that he indignantly declined to pay any attention to his plea for rescue from the Mahdi's clutches.

In the middle of December, 1884, believing the relief force to be well on the way, Gordon sent off another of his steamers, the *Bordeen*, to Metemmeh with information of the hapless state of Khartoum. He also entrusted the Arab captain, Cassim el Mousse, with the last of his journals to leave the city, together with certain personal messages. The final entry in his diary conveyed to the outer world the parlous condition to which the dilatory methods of the authorities had reduced him. " Now mark this," he wrote from the bitterness of his heart, " if the Expeditionary Force—and I ask for no more than 200 men—does not come in ten days, *the town may fall*, and I have done my best for the honour of our country. Good-bye."

To his friend, Colonel Watson, in Cairo, he wrote—" I think the game is up, and send Mrs. Watson, yourself, and Graham my adieux. We may expect a catastrophe in the town in or after ten days. This would not have happened (if it does happen) if our people had taken better precautions as to informing us of their movements, but this is ' spilt milk.' "

In a message to his old comrade in arms, Lord Wolseley, there appeared the following ominous request:—"As it seems impossible we shall meet again in this world, I would ask you to see that my family do not lose by my death."

In another of these last letters, he told his favourite sister, Augusta—" I decline to agree that the expedition comes for my relief; it comes for the relief of the garrisons, which I failed to accomplish. I expect Her Majesty's Government are in a precious rage with me for holding out and forcing their hand. This may be the last letter you will receive from me, for we are on our last legs, owing to the delay of the expedition. However, God rules all, and, as He will rule to His Glory and our welfare, His will be done. . . . I am quite happy, thank God, and, like Lawrence, I have *tried* to do my duty."

An entry in Gordon's journal reveals his deliberations as to his course of action in the event of Khartoum falling. "I toss up in my mind," he wrote, "whether, if the place is taken, to blow up the palace and all in it, or else to be taken, and, with God's help to maintain the faith, and if necessary to suffer for it (which is most probable). The blowing up of the palace is the simplest, while the other means long and weary suffering and humiliation of all sorts. I think I shall elect for the last, not from fear of death, but because the former has more or less the taint of suicide, as it can do no good to any one, and is, in a way, taking things out of God's hands."

Daily, now, the plight of the besieged became more and more desperate. Food supplies were getting low, and, by the end of December, the effects of famine began to be felt among the luckless inhabitants. "Truly I am worn to a shadow with the food question," wrote Gordon, "it is one continued demand."

The new year dawned to the whistle of shells thrown by rebel guns into the city, and the ever growing rattle of rifle fire. Of the original population of Khartoum only fourteen thousand now remained. Fifteen thousand unreliables had been sent over to the Mahdi, some two thousand six hundred refugees evacuated, and the rest delivered out of their miseries by merciful death. To such straits were the people reduced that improvisations to help out the daily decreasing rations included "rats and mice, the leather of boots, the straps and plaited strips of skin of native bedsteads, gum of mimosa, and the inner fibre of the palm tree."

No wonder poor Gordon felt worn to a shadow, his kind heart rebelling at the suffering of these innocent people, for whom he could no longer provide adequate sustenance.

For the defence of Khartoum much depended on the fort at Omdurman, so gallantly held by Ferratch Pasha after communications with the city had been cut, since it covered the weak part of the southern defences where the wall had been demolished by inundations. But, on January 15th, 1885, following the most stubborn resistance, the garrison was starved into surrender and, from that moment, the fate of Khartoum was sealed. Encouraged by this success, the Mahdi redoubled his efforts to take the city, the fighting becoming more and more severe. Gordon's palace became the favourite target of the rebel gunners, while constant

raids tested the defence and probed for a weak place in the entrenchments.

The situation could hardly have been worse. Yet, without a
sign of dismay, Gordon continued to hold on, refusing to listen to
counsels of despair and the clamourings of leading citizens for surrender. As an instance of the ingenuity he employed in devising
means of strengthening the defences and deceiving the enemy, it
is recorded that after procuring in the bazaar considerable quantities of cloth, and having it dyed brown, he set it up in lines to
represent earthworks, while behind these calico walls his men constructed strong fortifications.

Although, for obvious reasons, no official records of those last
tragic days of the prolonged siege were ever obtainable, a few scraps
of information were collected from survivors of the ultimate
disaster, revealing a condition of hopeless desolation, in which the
incomparable Gordon remained calm and composed, a shining
example of inspiring leadership. In order to bolster up the morale
of the people, he resorted to an artifice whereby rumours of
approaching help were disseminated among them. To these fake
rumours he added his own daily exhortation to the effect that next
day would see the end of their miseries. But the next day came
and went without a sign of the promised succour. " What more
can I say? " exclaimed Gordon to a merchant. " The people will
no longer believe me. I have told them over and over again that
help would be here, but it has never come, and now they must see
I tell them lies. I can do nothing more."

Manifesting the tremendous strain upon him that never for a
moment relaxed, Gordon's hair turned white, and no evidence could
be more conclusive as to the degree of mental turmoil through
which he passed. Still, this was the solitary outward and visible
sign that he had in any way been affected by the immensity of his
responsibilities or the incredible difficulties of his position. Though
endowed with the venerable appearance afforded by white hair, his
activity and tireless energy continued undiminished; but nothing,
not even Gordon's unquenchable spirit, could compensate for the
disastrous lack of food which sapped the vitality of the soldiers,
reducing them to little more than lay-figures.

The nightmare of starvation now held the city in its merciless
grip, the morale of the populace and the effectiveness of the troops
daily deteriorating. But Gordon was determined to hold on to the
end, scorning to haul down his colours for " a feeble lot of stinking
Dervishes." " Stinking " they may well have been, but they cer-

tainly were not "feeble," seeing that the Mahdi had assembled before Khartoum a mighty host of fearless warriors drawn from some of the most warlike tribes in the Sudan.

The dying flicker of hope revived to some extent when, on January 20th, news of the British victory at Abu Klea reached the grievously afflicted Sudanese capital. In the camp of the Mahdi, however, the effect of the news was to impress on the rebel leader the necessity for immediate action that would deliver Khartoum into his hands before the Desert Column could arrive. He was well aware of the weakened state of the defenders, and, moreover, the spectacle of the wounded brought in from Abu Klea had whipped his followers into a condition of fury that nothing could restrain. He, therefore, set about his plans for a decisive assault.

Under cover of darkness, he moved the greater part of his army across to the right bank of the White Nile during the nights of January 24th and 25th, bringing the spear-head of his attack opposite the demolished part of the southern wall. Then, in the darkest hour before dawn of the 26th, his silent company, seething with lust for vengeance against the infidel, and inspirited by a final oration from the Mahdi assuring them of victory, crept forward towards the doomed city. Suddenly, with a swirl of gleaming *jibbehs*, they hurled themselves upon the defences. For a few moments, the echoes were awakened by a thunderous burst of rifle and gun fire, accompanied by mine explosions; but the resistance proved negligible, and, in next to no time, long-suffering Khartoum was over-run by the rebels.

Precise details of what followed will never be known. It seems, however, that when the foremost Mahdists reached the centre of the town they were confronted by General Gordon and a few devoted helpers. The moment for which he had often prayed had at last arrived. His fond hopes that he would be spared the ghastly accompaniments of prolonged illness, terminated by a natural death in his bed, were now to be realised. His prayers had been answered. The savage end he was about to meet he faced with characteristic composure, his attitude of calm disdain momentarily disconcerting the hulking spearmen, specially selected by the Mahdi to account for Gordon's person.

But his tragic fate was not long delayed, and as he stood there amidst the ruination around him, a dignified, soldierly figure, calmly accepting the will of God, two Dervish spears ploughed their way into his body, which then suffered further mutilation at the hands of frenzied swordsmen.

Presently, as the captive, Slatin Pasha, sat in chains among the victorious tribesmen, he saw the dripping head of Gordon being conveyed to the Mahdi's tent in token of the overwhelming success attending the morning's operations. True to his bestial nature, this brigand chief disguised as a man of God, ordered his followers to exhibit the head in a conspicuous place, where it could be stoned by the passers-by and desecrated by the gluttonous vultures of the desert.

How strange that, in his diary of September, Gordon should have written—" Haunting the palace are a lot of splendid hawks. I often wonder whether they are destined to pick my eyes."

Two days later, Sir Charles Wilson, with his two steamers, reached the vicinity of Khartoum, only to find the city in the hands of the Mahdi and to learn of Gordon's death. With these dismal tidings he returned to Metemmeh, conveying to an anxious world news that had long been dreaded. Wilson's desperate effort to fulfil the object of the expedition was dogged by misfortune from the outset. To such an extent had the river fallen that progress was inevitably slow, danger of the steamers running aground presenting a constant source of anxiety. On the afternoon of January 25th, the *Bordeen* struck a rock, and it was not until the following night that she could be cleared. By that time, Khartoum had already been taken and Gordon killed.

Even more eventful was the return journey. Under heavy fire from the rebels the two steamers set off down stream on January 28th. Next day, the *Talataween* sank after hitting a rock, the *Bordeen* being lost in similar circumstances on the 31st. Ultimately, the stranded occupants of both vessels were extricated from their predicament by another steamer brought to their aid by Lord Charles Beresford, a young naval officer destined to attain high rank and distinction in his profession and to become one of the Royal Navy's most popular figures.

Sir Charles Wilson's news of the catastrophe shocked the universe, more especially because of the narrow margin by which the relief force fell short of its objective. Small wonder if horrified spectators of this appalling disaster all over the world turned their thoughts to the obstinacy of Mr. Gladstone, the shilly-shallying of the Cabinet, the delay in preparing and dispatching the expeditionary force, the apparent inability of Lord Wolseley to realise the extreme urgency of the situation and the need for haste, and, finally, the lapse of four precious days before Wilson's steamers started up the Nile in the last gallant attempt to retrieve a lost cause.

Yet, despite all these exasperating delays, relief arrived but two days late. To be sure, the lamentable effect would have been the same no matter whether help arrived two days or two months late. But the limited extent of failure tends to stress the sorry truth that if only decisions, prepartions, and actions had been less deliberate, and had been undertaken with a keener sensibility of Gordon's desperate situation, the disaster could have been prevented, the invaluable life of this predominant soldier could have been saved, and an enduring stigma on British history avoided.

Gordon's almost uncanny accuracy in predicting future events is instanced by an entry in his journal of October 13th, 1884, which ran—" It is, of course, on the cards that Khartoum is taken under the nose of the expeditionary force, which will be *just too late.*"

Only after making the supreme sacrifice was Gordon officially accorded his rightful position among the Empire's foremost sons. In the hearts of the people—not only of England but of foreign countries as well—there had for years been a warm place for the great deliverer of the oppressed, the romantic crusader. Moreover, by nations other than his own, his very remarkable powers had been conspicuously recognised and his services rewarded. Yet, notwithstanding his extraordinary achievements in China, Central Africa, and elsewhere, the British authorities could never forgive or forget the independent spirit that urged him to take his own line and forbade him acting in a manner contrary to the prompting of his conscience. He could, it is true, be not unjustly described as a rebel. But it was against incapacity, incompetence, ignorance, the dilatoriness of red tape, the absurdity of being required to accept directions from authorities hundreds of miles away, who could know little or nothing of the circumstances surrounding him—it was against drawbacks such as these that he rebelled, and thereby earned the displeasure of his superiors. Like Nelson, he had the courage to ignore an order issued by higher authority too remote to understand the situation as clearly as he could, if he conscientiously believed the order to be wrong. And, although action taken on his own initiative proved almost invariably to be right, the powers above him appear to have resented his direct methods, to have labelled him " difficult," and, accordingly, to have kept him as much as possible in the background, while denying him anything but the meanest reward for his stupendous work in Asia and Africa.

General Gordon's martyrdom at Khartoum, however, served to bring about a reaction in official circles, awakening the authorities, albeit belatedly, to an uncomfortable realisation of their niggardly treatment and ungenerous neglect of the man who only now, after laying down his life for Queen and country, attained at last his well-deserved position among the empire's national heroes.

Probably, few events have moved the world so intensely as the tragedy of Khartoum and the lonely death of this great soldier. In all the circumstances surrounding the catastrophe there was to be found abundant food for imagination. The picture of this inveterate leader of forlorn hopes unhesitatingly coming to the rescue of the British Government in their dilemma; his dash across the desert to the threatened capital of the Sudan; his delirious reception by the overjoyed citizens; his solitary life in the great palace of Khartoum, befriended only by a mouse; his dramatic defence of the beseiged city; and, lastly, his valiant unconcern when facing violent death—this sequence of stirring pictures appealed strongly to people of all nations, and ultimately established Gordon as, perhaps, the most universally conspicuous figure of that age.

Queen Victoria revealed her infinite distress at the unhappy outcome in a letter full of gracious, comforting words addressed to Gordon's sister, Augusta.

"*How* shall I write to you," declared the sorrowful Queen, "or how shall I attempt to express *what I feel*. To think of your dear, noble, heroic Brother who served his country so truly, so heroically, with a self-sacrifice so edifying to the World, not having been rescued. That the promises of support were not fulfilled—which I so frequently and constantly pressed on those who asked him to go—is to me *grief* inexpressible! indeed it has made me ill . . . . . Would you express to your other sisters and your elder Brother my true sympathy, and what I do so keenly feel, the *stain* left upon England, for your dear Brother's cruel, though heroic, fate !"

Bearing in mind the Queen's feelings about Gordon, her profound admiration for his unique services, her bitter disappointment at the Government's failure to save his life, and her mortification at " the stain left upon England," how strange it seems that nothing was done, by way of a posthumous honour, towards making amends for the unpardonable official neglect of General Gordon during his lifetime. This would at any rate have been some consolation to his family, the bitterness of whose feelings can well be imagined. To be sure, in the sudden access of official remorse, expenditure was authorised for the erection of a statue in London to Gordon's memory, and the provision of a grant for the benefit of his relatives.

Still, though he himself cared not a jot for reward, ever striving for *honour* rather than *honours,* the whole civilised world would have felt that something like justice had at last been done to a man deserving nothing but the best his country could do for him, had some very special token of universal esteem and gratitude been vouchsafed as a first step towards perpetuating his memory and keeping green for posterity the record of his unparalleled achievements. But as it was, this national hero, whose name had become familiar throughout the world for his adventurous crusades in the cause of freedom and of right, passed into history with scarcely anything to show for his prodigious services other than honours bestowed upon him by foreign states.

The Liberal Government of the day had the opportunity of making a generous gesture that would have done belated honour to their faithful and gallant servant, and, at the same time, have done something to lessen the blow that very naturally descended on their heads at the instance of an outraged public. Yet nothing was done, with the result that the statue erected in honour of one of Britain's most worthy and distinguished soldiers, displays to mystified sight-seers the incomprehensible information that Gordon died with no higher rank than that of a Major General, and that the reward of his own country for years of the most arduous, inestimable work that, perhaps, no other man could have accomplished, amounted to precisely a Companionship of the Order of the Bath!

To the public outcry that followed the tragedy of Khartoum was added an insistent, nation-wide demand for immediate vengeance upon the Mahdi. But, once again, Mr. Gladstone was adamant, obstinately refusing to listen to the public clamour or to accept Lord Wolseley's recommendation that the expeditionary force should be employed to punish the Dervish impostor, disperse his followers, and restore British prestige in the Sudan. This time the old man did not eventually give way, Lord Wolseley being reluctantly obliged to return home with his troops, leaving the Mahdi virtual master of the immense territory stretching from the Egyptian border to the Great Lakes and from Abyssinia and the Red Sea to the western limits of Darfour.

Though Mohammed Ahmed, the self-styled Mahdi, died not long after his triumph at Khartoum, he was succeeded as the rebels' leader by the Khalifa Abdullahi, who maintained despotic sway over the Sudan until, in the year 1898, at Omdurman, the Mahdists were finally defeated and dispersed by the British army

STATUE OF GENERAL GORDON
originally erected in Trafalgar Square, London, but
later moved to the neighbourhood of Whitehall
Gardens where it now stands.

(Hulton Library)

under Major General Sir Herbert Kitchener (afterwards Field Marshal Earl Kitchener of Khartoum). Thus, after an interval of thirteen years, Gordon was at last avenged; the chastened warriors were driven from Khartoum; and peace, for which the great crusader had toiled so indefatigably, and in pursuit of which he had sacrificed his life, enfolded the Sudan in its refreshing embrace.

Lord Tennyson wrote this epitaph for General Gordon: —

> " Warrior of God, man's friend, not here below,
> But somewhere dead far in the waste Sudan,
> Thou livest in all hearts, for all men know
> This earth hath borne no simpler, nobler man."

INDEX